Lincoln's America

Lincoln's America 1809–1865

Edited by Joseph R. Fornieri and
Sara Vaughn Gabbard

SOUTHERN ILLINOIS UNIVERSITY PRESS
Carbondale

11 10 09 08   4 3 2 1

Library of Congress Cataloging-in-Publication Data
Lincoln's America: 1809–1865 / edited by Joseph R.
Fornieri and Sara Vaughn Gabbard.
     p. cm.
 Includes bibliographical references and index.
 ISBN-13: 978-0-8093-2878-9 (alk. paper)
 ISBN-10: 0-8093-2878-X (alk. paper)
1. Lincoln, Abraham, 1809–1865—Political and
social views. 2. United States—Politics and government—1815–1861. 3. United States—Politics and
government—1861–1865. 4. United States—Social
conditions—To 1865. 5. United States—Intellectual
life—19th century. 6. Lincoln, Abraham, 1809–1865.
7. Presidents—United States—Biography. I. Fornieri,
Joseph R. II. Gabbard, Sara Vaughn.
 E457.2.L838 2008
 973.7092—dc22   2008002939

This fiery trial through which we pass, will light us down, in honor or dishonor, to the latest generation.

—Abraham Lincoln to Congress, December 1, 1862

———

This book is dedicated to "the latest generation"
Isabella and Natalie Fornieri
Jessica and Daniel Gabbard
William and James Voitlein

Contents

Illustrations

Preface

Sara Vaughn Gabbard

In the interest of full disclosure, I must admit that I was born and raised in Lincoln, Illinois. My hometown is the first named *for and by* Abraham Lincoln before he became famous, my forefathers making the decision in 1853 to name their prairie settlement after a gangly, circuit-riding lawyer who frequently visited the area. When informed of the request, the young attorney advised against it on the grounds that "Nothing named Lincoln ever amounted to much." When the settlers remained adamant, he then christened the town by breaking a watermelon and sprinkling the juice on the courthouse steps.

When, after submitting the manuscript for *Lincoln and Freedom: Slavery, Emancipation, and the Thirteenth Amendment* (coedited with Harold Holzer), I was given the opportunity to work once again with Southern Illinois University Press, I eagerly agreed to participate in this project, which is dedicated to the concept that Abraham Lincoln must be studied in the context of his times. The purpose of this book is to correct the assumption that we can judge historical figures by the standards of our time, the present, rather than by the time in which they actually lived.

Howard L. and Elizabeth W. Chapman, the M. E. Raker Foundation, the Edward M. and Mary McCrea Wilson Foundation, and Lincoln Financial Foundation offered the generous financial support that is required for such a project. As in the past, Sylvia Frank Rodrigue and other staff members of Southern Illinois University Press gave us their professional and personal support.

Joe Fornieri, coeditor, and nine other leading Lincoln scholars agreed to contribute chapters to this book. I hold these authors in the highest esteem not only for their obvious intellectual capacity and writing skills but also for their shared belief that history in general, and the story of Abraham Lincoln in particular, must continue to be told "to the latest generation."

Lincoln's America

Introduction: Interpreting Lincoln the Man and His Times

Joseph R. Fornieri

> For it is only in an atmosphere of freedom that the qualities of mind indispensable to true statesmanship can mature and fructify.
>
> When great perils threaten the state, one often sees the people fortunately choose the most appropriate citizens to save it.
> —Alexis de Tocqueville, *Democracy in America*

*D*o the times make the man, or does the man make the times? Is history begotten by the conscious actions of heroic leaders, or are human agents the product of historical forces beyond their control? Though it may be something of a cliché (like asking, "what comes first, the chicken or the egg?"), the question is nonetheless worth pursuing as we celebrate the life, times, and legacy of Abraham Lincoln on the occasion of the bicentennial of his birth in 2009. Because Lincoln epitomizes our idea of democracy, being at once its greatest teacher and practitioner, his bicentennial provides us with a unique opportunity to reflect upon our democratic experiment. Indeed, Lincoln is at the very center of our national myth, the sustaining narrative or story that defines us as a common people.[1] He provides the clearest articulation of what it means to be an American, reminding us that our national identity is not based upon a common race, religion, or color but upon our shared fidelity to an idea—the equal dignity and freedom of all human beings.[2] The effort to comprehend Lincoln and his time is therefore an exercise in civic self-understanding.

This volume, which consists of new and original essays from some of the leading Lincoln scholars of our generation, explores the interplay between the man and his time. It considers such diverse topics as religion, education, middle-class family life, the antislavery movement, and the wider intellectual, political, and legal milieu of mid-nineteenth-century America that shaped the character and leadership of our greatest president. Though Lincoln's greatness is of enduring significance and cannot simply be reduced to the flux of history or to the vicissitudes of time and place, he was nonetheless a product of the nineteenth-century America that formed him. This is not to deny the importance of either timeless truths or historical context in studying our sixteenth president. Rather, it is to recognize the combination of both, much like the complex roles that both nature and nurture play in explaining human behavior. It is to recognize both the universal import of Lincoln's thought and its particular embodiment in life and history.

In chapter 1, Allen C. Guelzo explores Lincoln's place in nineteenth-century intellectual history by tracing the influence of liberal political economists of the Enlightenment like Francis Wayland upon his political outlook. In chapter 2, I compare Lincoln and Tocqueville on the contribution of religion to American public life. It is my contention that Lincoln's view of religion and politics embodies Tocqueville's description of the compatibility between the spirit of religion and liberty in America. Myron Marty provides an overview of the educational context of nineteenth-century America in chapter 3 and reveals Lincoln's pedagogical influences and his extraordinary self-schooling. In chapter 4, Mark Noll examines the religious context of the Civil War era, pointing out the continuities and discontinuities between Lincoln's personal piety and nineteenth-century belief. In chapters 5 and 6, Kenneth J. Winkle and Frank J. Williams take the reader to central Illinois during Lincoln's lifetime. Winkle reports on life in Springfield, the growth of that region's middle class, and the nineteenth-century ideal of Victorian marriage as it applied to Abraham and Mary Lincoln. Williams first describes the development of Lincoln's legal career as a circuit-riding prairie lawyer and then notes how this experience prepared the sixteenth president for his subsequent role as "Attorney-in-Chief" during the Civil War. Chapters 7 and 8 concentrate on Lincoln and the slavery question. James Oakes focuses specifically on the debate over the right to property in a slave and the political origins of Lincoln's case against this alleged right. Meanwhile, historian Richard Striner examines more broadly Lincoln's pivotal role in the antislavery movement of the nineteenth century. In chapter 9, Harold Holzer discusses the growth of the visual arts in nineteenth-century America and demonstrates their effect upon Lincoln and his times. Finally, in chapter 10, constitutional scholar and historian Herman Belz places Lincoln within the antebellum debate over the meaning of federalism and the Union. In response to those who claim that Lincoln's understanding of the Union was novel, Belz argues that the sixteenth president affirmed and defended a "more perfect Union" that was intrinsic to the founding.

We offer no apology for affirming Lincoln as a model of greatness for succeeding generations to imitate. To deprive ourselves of Lincoln as a guide would be to sever our link to the permanent things that speak to us both as human beings and as citizens. To reduce Lincoln to the historical context of his times would confine us to a sterile antiquarianism that has no bearing on how we live today. Lincoln himself objected to such a hermetically sealed historicism by consistently affirming the *transhistorical* truths of the Declaration of Independence as the moral compass of the nation. He criticized Chief Justice Roger Taney's contextualization of the Declaration as a document that applied exclusively to the particular circumstances of those in power at the time of the Revolution. According to Lincoln, this narrow interpretation did violence to the plain, unmistakable language and universal import of the document as an aspiration that applied in the abstract to all human beings at all times. Indeed, Lincoln's exposition of the Founders' intent of the universal meaning of equality compels each of us to answer the same question that he put to Taney one hundred and fifty years ago: "Are you really willing that the Declaration shall be thus frittered away?—thus left no more at most, than an interesting memorial of the dead past? thus shorn of its vitality, and practical value; and left without the *germ* or even the *suggestion* of the individual rights of man in it?"[3]

While the historicist reduction of Lincoln to his time and place is problematic, the failure to appreciate adequately the historical context of Lincoln's leadership produces similar distortions of his thought and legacy. The focus upon Lincoln's greatness in the abstract, apart from the concrete social, legal, and political circumstances that defined the boundaries of his leadership, may lapse into hagiography. The pitfalls of such an ahistorical approach make it vulnerable to deconstructionist and revisionist objections that are based on half-truths. For example, critics who seek to debunk the myth of Lincoln "the Great Emancipator" point to the fact that the Emancipation Proclamation exempted the border states as proof that it was all a farce and that Lincoln was actually a fraud.[4] Though it makes use of selective facts and partial truths, this revisionist interpretation is insufficiently historical because of what it fails to mention. It conveniently

leaves out certain salient facts: that prior to the Thirteenth Amendment, the
Constitution prevented the federal government from interfering with slavery
in states that remained within the Union; that the Emancipation Proclamation was justified constitutionally as a war measure and therefore applied
only to belligerents; and that barring the use of force, Lincoln nonetheless
made several attempts at compensated emancipation in the border states,
which they consistently rejected.[5] The mythical Lincoln of folklore may be
a suitable place to begin our study of the sixteenth president; but we must
go beyond this surface image toward a more critical engagement with the
rich complexity of the man and his times if we are to understand his actions as the Great Emancipator. Such an engagement appreciates the way
that Lincoln prudentially applied the principle of equality under a myriad
of social and political circumstances.

If Lincoln's greatness cannot simply be reduced to a product of his times,
how may his teachings and example be applied to our unique circumstances
of twenty-first-century America? The effort of each generation to discern
and apply Lincoln's teaching to the circumstances of its own time can be
compared to the Supreme Court's use of precedent, or *stare decisis*. Like the
Court's jurisprudence, we may begin with a philosophical consideration of
Lincoln's speech and action on key concepts or core principles, such as equality, prudent statesmanship, religion in American public life, democracy,
constitutionalism, the rule of law, balancing civil liberties and security in
wartime, and the inseparability between liberty and union. Consider how,
for example, if the Court had given greater attention to Lincoln's critique
of *Dred Scott* and to his administration's conferral of the privileges and
immunities of equal citizenship to free blacks, the nation might have been
spared the moral and legal abomination of *Plessy v. Ferguson* (1896).[6] Instead
of following Lincoln's precedent on equal citizenship and the culmination
of this precedent in the Fourteenth Amendment, the Court reversed course
and adopted a novel legal principle ("separate but equal") that provided the
legal basis for segregation.[7] It would require another landmark decision,
Brown v. Board of Education (1954), for the Court to remedy its self-inflicted
wound in *Plessy*.

The appeal to Lincoln's thought and legacy as a standard against which
to judge events of our own time may legitimately raise concerns that he is
being exploited for ideological purposes. The concern is valid. However, if
rigidly adhered to, the reluctance to judge the present in view of the past
may stifle normative evaluation altogether. The attempt to study Lincoln
under the pretense of complete moral neutrality, without assigning praise

or blame and without drawing lessons for our own time, is either futile or disingenuous. It labors under the false precept that social science is completely "value free." This supposition, in turn, is based upon the dubious distinction between objective "facts" and subjective "values," a distinction that is itself self-defeating and internally contradictory. It must be noted that one's very commitment to the distinction between fact and value presupposes a choice in value that cannot be justified in terms of the fact/value distinction's criterion of objectivity. That is to say, the historian's preference for facts over values in the study of history is itself a value judgment. Moreover, the very decision to write on a particular topic about Lincoln presupposes a choice in "values." Presumably, one chooses a particular aspect of Lincoln's thought and legacy over another because he or she thinks that it is important and therefore "worthy" of greater attention; that it sheds light on an enduring problem or question about human nature, politics, or society. Could we really take seriously a clinically detached study of Lincoln that evades a compelling justification as to why the subject is worthwhile and relevant to our own time?

So as not to be misunderstood, it must be emphasized that to make normative or evaluative judgments about history does not mean that the study of history is purely subjective or relative. Moral judgments, as Lincoln fully believed, may be defended by reasoned argument.

Finally, in exploring Lincoln and his times, we would do well to consult the ancient wisdom of Plato, who observed that the republic is "the soul of man writ large."[8] By this, Plato meant to reveal the profound correspondence between the order of the individual citizen's soul and the order of the wider state and society (the regime) that formed it. Given Plato's insight, we are compelled to ask whether or not the political culture of twenty-first-century America promotes or inhibits those qualities that nurtured the character of an Abraham Lincoln in the nineteenth century. It is our earnest hope that the sixteenth president remains a model of democratic statesmanship that will continue to inspire new generations of American leaders of all kinds—local board members, teachers, parents, priests, ministers, rabbis, imams, managers, administrators, coaches, counselors, social workers.[9] Notwithstanding the problems and challenges we face as a nation today, the fact that interest in Lincoln and the Civil War still appeals to large sections of the American public suggests that there is some reflection occurring on the central figure and pivotal event in American history. We hope that this volume contributes in some modest way to furthering such reflections.

Notes

1. Andrew DelBanco, *The Real American Dream: A Meditation on Hope* (Cambridge: Harvard University Press, 2000).

2. Benjamin J. Barber, *An Aristocracy for Everyone: The Politics of Education and the Future of America* (New York: Ballantine Books, 1992).

3. Abraham Lincoln, "Speech at Springfield, Illinois," June 26, 1857, in Roy P. Basler, ed., *The Collected Works of Abraham Lincoln*, 9 vols. (New Brunswick, N.J.: Rutgers University Press, 1953–55), 2:407.

4. Lerone Bennett, *Forced into Glory: Abraham Lincoln's White Dream* (Chicago: Johnson Publishing, 2000).

5. Allen Guelzo, *Lincoln's Emancipation Proclamation: The End of Slavery in America* (New York: Simon and Schuster, 2004), 157–81; Joseph R. Fornieri, "Lincoln and the Emancipation Proclamation: A Model of Prudent Leadership," in *Tempered Strength: Studies in the Nature and Scope of Prudential Leadership*, ed. Ethan Fishman (Lanham, Md.: Rowman and Littlefield, 2002), 125–49.

6. I discuss in greater detail the civil rights implications of Lincoln's critique of *Dred Scott* and his view of black citizenship in "Lincoln on Negro Citizenship," *Lincoln Lore*, no. 1885 (Summer 2006): 6–17. Also see Harold Holzer and Sara Vaughn Gabbard, eds., *Lincoln and Freedom: Slavery, Emancipation, and the Thirteenth Amendment* (Carbondale: Southern Illinois University Press, 2007).

7. See Frank J. Williams, "The End of the Beginning: Abraham Lincoln and the Fourteenth and Fifteenth Amendments," in Holzer and Gabbard, *Lincoln and Freedom*, 213–32.

8. Quoted in Eric Voegelin, *Order and History*, vol. 3, *Plato and Aristotle* (Baton Rouge: Louisiana State University Press, 1957), 70.

9. See, for example, Donald T. Phillips, *Lincoln on Leadership: Executive Strategies for Tough Times* (New York: Warner Books, 1992).

1

A. Lincoln, Philosopher: Lincoln's Place in Nineteenth-Century Intellectual History

Allen C. Guelzo

The nineteenth century in Europe and America was an era of second thoughts. Those second thoughts were largely about the Enlightenment, which had been born in the mid-1600s as a scientific revolution and blossomed into the Age of Reason in the 1700s, when it seemed that no puzzle was beyond the grasp of scientific rationality. That blossom was snipped all too quickly by the French Revolution, which drowned rationality in human politics in a spray of Jacobin-terrorized blood, then by the revulsion of European art and music from the Enlightenment's canons of balance and symmetry in favor of the Romantic glorification of the sublime and the irrational, and finally by the rage and contempt that the Enlightenment's most rationalized offspring—its bourgeois capitalist entrepreneurs, inventors, and managers—inspired in the hearts of intellectuals and aristocrats alike. This does not mean that the Enlightenment was herded off the scene entirely by the Romantic reaction. The scientists had dug themselves firmly into a position from which they refused to be dislodged, and the bourgeoisie of France and England continued their relentless struggle to wrest control of their nations' politics from its nobles and emperors. So, there remained men and women of the nineteenth century who lashed themselves firmly to the mast of the Enlightenment, disregarding the sirens of Romantic passion in art and literature, as well as politics. And it is among the latter that we must classify Abraham Lincoln.

Lincoln was born on February 12, 1809, at almost the very end of what is sometimes called the "long Enlightenment" (from the publication of John Locke's *Essay concerning Human Understanding* in 1690 until Waterloo and the fall of the first Napoleon in 1815). On that day in 1809, Thomas Jefferson, that quintessential American man of Reason, was in the last weeks of his presidency; Tom Paine, that quintessential pamphleteer of American revolution and American deism, was (appropriately enough) living in Greenwich Village; and twelve of the signers of the Declaration of Independence, that quintessential document of Enlightenment political rationality, were still alive. The intellectual universe that these men inhabited had been shaped by the consequences of the scientific discoveries of Galileo and Isaac Newton, whose achievement, if it could be condensed into one sentence, would be that they taught Europeans to look upon the contents of the universe as things that *were moved*, rather than things that *moved* on their own. Physical objects—and for Galileo, this started with observations of the planets—did not possess occult forces within themselves that produced physical movement, nor were they creations obeying the invisible direction of God. They were simply inert material substances that lumbered into motion only because some other material substance caused them to, and whose motion was entirely governed by the laws of indifferent but calculable forces (for Newton, this meant *gravity*). If anyone wanted proof of this, he had only to watch Galileo's sensational public experiments in the 1630s or consult the mathematical proofs offered by Newton in his *Philosophiae Naturalis Principia Mathematica* (1687). The scientific discoveries of Galileo and Newton forced Europeans to criticize every theory about the physical world they had inherited from the Christian or classical past. Everything, from politics to religion, was now open to criticism, reevaluation, and "enlightenment."

The Enlightenment developed a series of convictions about what the future might hold for a suitably enlightened Europe, and we can organize those convictions around three basic topics: God and natural religion, man and natural society, and history and hope.

Christianity was the largest of the Enlightenment's targets: it asked for a belief in miracles and Divine Providence that ran completely counter to scientific discoveries that described the mechanism and uniformity of nature, and it asked for faith in personalities and events that no reasonable human being could ever expect to encounter in normal life. On the other hand, the Enlightenment did not rush to embrace atheism. Newton and Galileo could tell people *how* the world operated, but they could offer no clues as to *where* it had come from; in fact, Newton himself insisted repeatedly on the need for the creative activity of God as the cause of the universal system he was describing. What the Enlightenment wanted was to forge some kind of accommodation with Christianity, based on several shared, generic assumptions about God that are based upon the operation of reason upon nature. This "natural religion" took classic form in the hands of another Enlightenment American, Benjamin Franklin, who thought he could distill the true essence of religion to a few, simple propositions:

> That there is one God who made all things.
> That he governs the World by his Providence.
> That he ought to be worshiped by Adoration, Prayer & Thanksgiving.
> But that the most acceptable Service of God is doing Good to Man.
> That the Soul is immortal.
> And that God will certainly reward Virtue and punish Vice either here or hereafter.[1]

It became common very early on to label this thinly tailored brand of religion as *deism*, and its practical implication was that what people needed was not grace but an understanding of the moral laws God had hardwired into them. Stories from the Bible were useless for guiding human behavior; instead, one could safely and reasonably base ethics on self-love and the pursuit of happiness.

The pursuit of happiness, however, was a social, and not just a strictly personal and private, matter; and so the Enlightenment sought to transfer the neatness, simplicity, and rationality found in the natural sciences to the untidy and messy affairs of human government and society. The Enlightenment's political philosophers believed that, like the physical universe, there were several constant forces in human behavior that could be organized toward a better society. One of these was self-love, the search for individual satisfaction and contentment. And the way to organize society so as to allow self-love its proper operation was to guarantee personal liberty and personal property, for how could anyone pursue self-love without property? This, in turn, threw the Enlightenment entirely against controlled economic systems and toward market capitalism, whose "hidden hand" seemed to function in exactly the same way gravity did in the physical world. "Commerce," wrote Voltaire in his *Philosophical Letters* (1732), "which has brought wealth to the citizenry . . . has helped to make them free, and freedom has developed commerce in its turn."[2]

If the physical universe was not a moral stage-play that God had written, then there could be no divine playwright either. Other, more rational causes had to be found to explain the historical past; hence, economics, geography, and psychology had to be called in to offer an entirely new set of clues for deciphering the historical record. Edward Gibbon dismissed the notion that the ancient Roman Empire had fallen because God had judged it for its persecution of the early Christians, and in his massive *History of the Decline and Fall of the Roman Empire* (in six volumes, 1776–88), Gibbon explained the collapse of the Romans in entirely natural terms. The Enlightenment had no use for morality plays about struggle or sin. It looked at the vast improvements that the scientific discoveries of the 1600s had wrought and concluded that there was no reason why matters ought not to continue to improve and progress upwards. Even Gibbon (whose acquaintance with the barbarians ought to have taught him better) confidently predicted that human history was now to become a tale of ever-increasing progress, guided by reason, liberty, and wealth. We cannot be certain, he wrote, "to what height the human species may aspire in their advances toward perfection; but it may safely be assumed that no people, unless the face of nature is changed, will relapse into their original barbarism. . . . We may therefore acquiesce in the pleasing conclusion that every age of the world has increased, and still increases, the real wealth, the happiness, the knowledge, and perhaps the virtue of the human race."[3]

—

The Romantics weighed in the balances the Enlightenment's vast preoccupation with reason and order and found it wanting. Rather than the regularized dullness of classical symmetry, they were excited by passion and conflict, and they discussed in heated terms the contrast between the civilized and the authentic, between thought and feeling, between consciousness and spontaneity. In 1808 the Romantic poet and painter William Blake read over a copy of Sir Joshua Reynolds's lectures on art, in which Reynolds (the president of the Royal Academy) had laid out a classical theory of art. Blake scribbled furious rebuttals into the margins, like "God forbid that Truth should be Confined to Mathematical Demonstration." Where Reynolds declared that mere enthusiasm "will carry you but a little way," Blake replied, "Meer Enthusiasm is the All in All."[4]

The Romantics found in nature not order but grandeur; not sunny, well-manicured gardens and lawns, but terrible deep mountain chasms, the power of storms, and the beauty of the simplest of wild things. But the most obvious way in which Romanticism differed from the Enlightenment was in its preference for emotion, "heart, warmth, blood, humanity, life," and the experience of the sublime, over against enlightened reason. Victor Hugo, the French Romantic, in his novel *The Hunchback of Notre Dame* (1831), which, like Scott's *Ivanhoe*, glorified the Middle Ages, shocked and titillated the jaded classical tastes of France when he selected the grotesque, twisted hunchback Quasimodo as a heroic figure. (Although deformed in body and a walking violation of classical forms of art, Quasimodo is nevertheless the only character in the novel with deep and authentic feelings, and it is for him that the reader winds up having the greatest sympathy.) And in politics, Romanticism declared that societies were not built on propositions but on experience. Joseph de Maistre argued in his *Study on Sovereignty*, "One of the greatest errors of this age is to believe that the political constitution of nations is the work of man alone and that a constitution can be made as a watchmaker makes a watch." The natural political state of humanity, he claimed, was monarchy: "it can be said in general that all men are born for monarchy" and "even those nations destined to be republics have been constituted by kings."[5]

If the Enlightenment had its American acolytes in Franklin, Jefferson, and Tom Paine, Romanticism had its American followers in the philosopher Ralph Waldo Emerson, the poets Edgar Allan Poe and Walt Whitman, and the painters Thomas Cole and Frederick Edwin Church (by no means an exhaustive list). They shared in many ways Romanticism's aversion to imposing human logic on nature. Religion and ethics, Emerson complained, usually end up degrading nature and suggesting its dependence on spirit. God refuses to be recorded in propositions; the happiest man is the one who learns from nature the lessons of worship. And in the hands of John C. Calhoun and George Fitzhugh, they invented a new political attitude that dismissed the universal equality of the entire human race in favor of a politics built around a *volkish* racial solidarity of whites—and the enslavement of blacks. It was a "great and Dangerous" error, wrote Calhoun in 1849, to have believed "that all men are born free and equal—than which nothing can be more unfounded and false." And it is equally "great and dangerous" to believe that "all people are equally entitled to liberty," especially those "too ignorant, degraded and vicious, to be capable either of appreciating or of enjoying it." Every nation embodied some impalpable *gestalt*, which grew up, plantlike, in all its people and was neither universal nor transferable. Theorizing in the abstract about the logic of equality was, to Fitzhugh, of "little worth; for all government is the gradual accretion of Nature, time and circumstances," not constitutions, declarations, and other ink-tracks on paper. Nations are built up over centuries, as a distinct national character is built up in the people of each nation, and not merely by signing-on to a collection of political propositions.[6]

And yet, it was in politics that Romanticism had its hardest struggle for dominance. (In art and literature, it won the day overwhelmingly; in science and economics, it barely made a dent, although it has to be said that in both Marx and Darwin, some decidedly very Romantic impulses lurked beneath what was presented as a rigorously logical and scientific surface.) On the one hand, with the fall of Napoleon, a reactionary Romanticism, magnifying monarchy and nationality, asserted itself through the Congress of Vienna and the crushing of the revolutions of 1848 and the imperial coup d'état of Napoleon III. On the other hand, the politics of the Enlightenment, in the form of classical liberalism, found powerful and persuasive exponents (in Britain) in John Stuart Mill, John Ramsay McCulloch, and the "Manchester School," whose polestars were Richard Cobden and John Bright. In America, Henry Carey, Richard Hildreth, and Francis Wayland still hewed to liberalism's description of "civil government" strictly as a means to "the security of persons, property, and reputation." Aristocrats and other traditional forms of power could, and ought, to be swept aside. "Such a government, proceeds upon the principle that the people are the fountain of power, and are competent to govern themselves." They were also competent to govern their economic lives. Hildreth caustically attacked the "mystic moralists" who repudiate "the pursuit of mercantile wealth" as "a low, base, groveling occupation, fatal to the dignity and virtue of man" when it was really "an essential preliminary to the pursuit of the true, the beautiful, and the good" and had "a principal influence in determining the form and character of governments." People who professed a Romantic yearning for a return to medieval hierarchy, Hildreth snorted, were almost always "those children of good fortune whom some lucky accident of birth or position enables to pass a life of leisure in the gardens of Epicurus" or "amid the groves of the Academy."[7]

———

Abraham Lincoln is not usually given much of a place in the context of the nineteenth century's struggle of ideas—apart, of course, from having said some very eloquent things about democracy and a new birth of freedom. Lincoln neither looked like an intellectual (Henry Clay Whitney thought "he had the appearance of a rough intelligent farmer") nor did he encourage people to think of him that way. Lincoln "was said to be a very simple-minded man, devoid of the silences and ambitions in life." His favorite entertainment was "negro minstrelsy and [Lincoln] seemed to extract the greatest delight from the crude jokes and harmless fun of the black-faced and red-lipped performers." He never wrote a book (unless we count the edition of the debates he staged with Stephen A. Douglas in 1858, and even that was assembled from newspaper cuttings). Lincoln was, by preference, a politician, a profession not ordinarily esteemed among great thinkers; and the political persona he crafted for himself was humble Abraham Lincoln. "I was born and have ever remained in the most humble walks of life," he said in his first political appeal in 1832, and even his political views were "Short & Sweet Like an old womans dance." He was, by vocation, a lawyer—but "purely and entirely a case lawyer, nothing more," whose practice was mostly concentrated on property litigation. "I am not an accomplished lawyer," he stated bluntly in the 1850s, and the distribution of his caseload bears this out: ordinary trespass and assumpsit cases accounted for 26 percent of his entire practice, with another 42 percent taken up with the humdrum proceedings of ejectment, debt, mortgage foreclosure, replevin, and divorce. His entire schooling amounted to no more than a year's worth of on-again, off-again attendance in "A.B.C. schools" and some tutoring in elementary grammar; whatever else he needed, as a surveyor and then as a lawyer, he taught himself from the standard textbooks of the day. (Even at the end of his legal career, in 1860, Lincoln's best advice for "obtaining a thorough knowledge of the law" was simply to "Begin with [Sir William] Blackstone's Commentaries, and after reading it carefully through, say twice, take up [Joseph] Chitty's Pleadings, [Simon] Greenleaf's Evidence & [Justice Joseph] Story's Equity &c. in succession.") He did not attempt to conceal the limits of his education. The entry he wrote for a biographical dictionary of Congress in 1858 described his education as simply "defective." If anything, he was remarkably forthcoming about those defects, when he had to be. "I have not a fine education," Lincoln said at the beginning of the 1858 campaign against Douglas. "I am not capable of entering into a disquisition upon dialectics." In his youth, "There was absolutely nothing to excite ambition for education," and all he gleaned from attending school for less than "one year" was how to "read, write, and cipher to the Rule of Three." But, like his jokes about his own homely looks, Lincoln did not belittle his education because he was indulging some populist fantasy; he simply felt it was wiser if *he* made fun of it, rather than others.[8]

All of this was true—as far as it goes. But it did not go very far.

The embarrassment with which Lincoln shrouded his meager education also contained a substantial amount of anger: *first*, because his prospects for education had been foreclosed against his will by a father who treated "eddication" with contempt; and *second*, because he was conscious of possessing more-than-average intellectual powers, which would have benefited mightily from the "eddication" that his father was unwilling to pay for. William Herndon, his third law partner, understood from years of partnership that

Lincoln "had great reason, pure and strong" and "was a persistent thinker, and a profound analyzer of the subject which engaged his attention." John Todd Stuart, who was Lincoln's first law partner and his mentor in lawyering from the time Lincoln was admitted to the bar, thought Lincoln had a "Mind of a metaphysical and philosophical order" who, by 1860, had "made Geology and other sciences a special study." He had nothing to speak of in the way of "the languages"—the Greek and Latin that were still the staple of American collegiate curriculums—"but in other respects I consider [Lincoln] a man of very general and varied knowledge" who was "always studying into the nature of things." But even then, recalled his longtime associate on the Eighth Judicial Circuit, David Davis, Lincoln tried to remedy his lack of classical learning by studying "the Latin grammar" in between cases "on the [court] circuit." Nevertheless, Lincoln preferred the harder-edged precision of geometry and "the exact sciences," and his basic intellectual instinct was "to arrive at moral and physical, mathematical demonstration of things." Milton Hay, another law colleague of Lincoln's in Springfield, remembered that Lincoln's "mind ran to a mathematical exactness about things. Exactness in the statement of things was a peculiarity with him."[9]

And instinct does seem to have played the major role in Lincoln's self-education. Lincoln's garrulous cousin, Dennis Hanks, told Herndon that by the time Lincoln was "12 years old," he had become "a Constant and I may Say Stubborn reader, his father having Sometimes to slash him for neglecting his work by reading." That reading included "Websters old Spelling Book—The life [of] Henry Clay. Robinson Crusoe—Weems Life of Washington—Esops fables—Bunyan's Pilgrim's progress." Piecing together the reminiscences of others who knew the young Lincoln, his reading also embraced Asa Rhoads's *An American Spelling Book, Designed for the Use of Our Common Schools* (1802), Nicholas Pike's *A New and Complete System of Arithmetic, Composed for the Use of the Citizens of the United States* (1788), William Grimshaw's *History of the United States* (1820), David Ramsay's *Life of George Washington* (1807), *The Kentucky Preceptor, Containing a Number of Useful Lessons for Reading and Speaking* (1812), *The American Speaker* (1811), Caleb Bingham's *The Columbian Orator* (1794), and William Scott's *Lessons in Elocution; or, A Selection of Pieces in Prose and Verse* (1779). But more than just being "much Devoted to Reading," Lincoln brought to his reading a near-photographic memory for what he read. He "had the Best memory of any man i Ever Knew," recalled J. Rowan Herndon, "he Never forgot any thing he Read." As a storekeeper in New Salem, Illinois, in the 1830s, Lincoln impressed his neighbors, not just with his books, but with how "He mastered them rapidly. . . . He read very thoroughly, and had a most wonderful memory" and "Would distinctly remember almost every thing he read." As he told Noah Brooks years later, "If I like a thing, it just sticks after once reading it or hearing it." And when his lifelong friend Joshua Speed "once remarked to him that his mind was a wonder to me" because "impressions were easily made upon his mind and never effaced," Lincoln gently corrected him. "I am slow to learn," he insisted, but also "slow to forget that which I have learned—My mind is like a piece of steel, very hard to scratch any thing on it and almost impossible after you get it there to rub it out."[10]

These instincts all turned to Lincoln's advantage when he began reading law in the mid-1830s under John Todd Stuart's tutelage, since most of his legal education consisted of little more than reading the basic legal source-books and observing Stuart in action. "Mr Lincoln turned his attention Exclusively to the law" and "read so much—was so studious—took so little physical exercise—was so laborious in his studies that he became Emaciated & his best friends were afraid that he would craze himself—make himself derange from his habits of study which were incessant." This did not, however, prevent him from undertaking at least some "miscellaneous reading," on "surveying" in order to earn a living, and on "History—Biography & general newspaper reading." He mastered surveying as he mastered everything else, by reading the standard textbooks, Abel Flint's *A System of Geometry and Trigonometry: Together with a Treatise on Surveying* (1804), and Robert Gibson's *The Theory and Practice of Surveying; Containing All the Instructions Requisite for the Skilful Practice of This Art* (1803). And he gave philosophy its due by working through "[Thomas] Browns Philosophy [*Lectures on the Philosophy of the Human Mind*] or [William] Paley." But the real passion Lincoln developed was for "History and poetry." Poetry meant "Burns & Shakespeare," with a helping of "Byron [and] Milton." Charles Maltby said that "it was usual for him, after reading and studying [Lindley] Murray [or, more likely, William Russell's 1818 American "abridgement" of Murray's *English Grammar*] or [Sir William] Blackstone for two or three hours, to take up Burns' poems . . . his favorite selections being Tom O'Shanter, Address to the Dial, Highland Mary, Bonny Jeane and Dr. Hornbook." All of this kept bobbing to the surface throughout the rest of Lincoln's life, so "that people in his later life were amazed at his wonderful familiarity with books, even those so little known by the great mass of readers."[11]

———

Much as Lincoln loved Burns and Shakespeare and even tried his own hand at writing poetry, the most important intellectual influences on his development came from history, political economy, and religion. History, for Lincoln, especially meant the history of the American Revolution. In 1861, he remembered that "away back in my childhood, the earliest days of my being able to read, I got hold of . . . 'Weem's Life of Washington,'" and it burned into his imagination "the battle fields and struggles for the liberties of the country. . . . I recollect thinking then, boy even though I was, that there must have been something more than common that those men struggled for . . . something that held out a great promise to all the people of the world to all time to come." He claimed that he had "never had a feeling politically that did not spring from the sentiments embodied in the Declaration of Independence," and he praised the Founders of the Republic as "the pillars of the temple of liberty" and "a fortress of strength." Out of all the Founders, though, it was Washington and Jefferson who set the most profound example to Lincoln. "Washington is the mightiest name of earth—long since mightiest in the cause of civil liberty; still mightiest in moral reformation," Lincoln said in 1842. "To add brightness to the sun, or glory to the name of Washington, is alike impossible." Likewise, he added in 1859, "The principles of Jefferson are the definitions and axioms of free society." So it should be no surprise to find Lincoln's own political rhetoric containing numerous echoes of Washington's and Jefferson's writings.[12]

———

It is said that every man has his portion of ambition. I may have mine, I suppose, as well as the rest, but if I know my own heart my ambition would not lead me into public life. My only ambition is to do my duty in this world as I am capable of performing it and to merit the good opinion of all men.—Washington to Benjamin Lincoln, October 26, 1788

> Every man is said to have his peculiar ambition. Whether it be true or not, I can say for one that I have no other so great as that of being truly esteemed of my fellow men.—Lincoln, Communication to the People of Sangamo County, 1832

I cannot omit the occasion to congratulate you and my country on the success of the experiment nor to repeat my fervent supplications to the Supreme Ruler of the Universe . . . that his providential care may still be extended to the United States.—Washington, Eighth Annual Address, December 7, 1796

> Our popular government has often been called an experiment.
> —Lincoln, Message to Congress in Special Session, 1861

To take a single step beyond the boundaries thus specially drawn around the powers of Congress is to take possession of a boundless field of power.—Thomas Jefferson, "Opinion against the Constitutionality of a National Bank," 1791

Would I not thus give up all footing upon constitution or law? Would I not thus be in the boundless field of absolutism?—Lincoln to Salmon Chase, 1863

Of course, adulation and even imitation of Washington and Jefferson were scarcely unique in Lincoln's time, nor did Lincoln restrict himself just to them (Lincoln cited Henry Clay, his "beau ideal of a statesman," over forty times). What gave Lincoln's thinking about the history of the Revolution its unique torque was his connection between the Revolution and the classical political economy of the Enlightenment. The underlying purpose Lincoln discerned in "the toils that were endured by the officers and soldiers of the army, who achieved . . . Independence" was not "the mere matter of the separation of the colonies from the mother land; but something . . . which gave promise that in due time the weights should be lifted from the shoulders of all men, and that all should have an equal chance." That something was equality; and the equality Lincoln saw in the Declaration was an equality of economic opportunity that encouraged social mobility and self-transformation for everyone. "We stand at once the wonder and admiration of the whole world," Lincoln said in 1856, because in the United States, "every man can make himself." There are neither artificial hierarchies based on status nor inherent national or racial discriminations within the promise of the Declaration, but a universal equality based upon natural rights. "Most governments have been based, practically, on the denial of equal rights of men" because "they said, some men are too ignorant, and vicious, to share in government. Possibly so, said we; and, by your system, you would always keep them ignorant, and vicious. We proposed to give all a chance; and we expected the weak to grow stronger, the ignorant, wiser; and all better, and happier together."[13]

So universal and foundational were these natural rights that, despite ignorance, nationality, or race, anyone who had not deliberately closed his eyes could see and understand them. "Perhaps half our people . . . are men who have come from Europe—German, Irish, French and Scandinavian—men that have come from Europe themselves, or whose ancestors have come hither and settled here." They have no Romantic "connection . . . by Blood" with the Revolutionary Founders; but "when they look through that old Declaration of Independence they find" a proposition, *that all men are created equal*, and based on that proposition, "they feel that that moral sentiment taught in that day evidences their relation to those men, that it is the father of all moral principle in them, and that they have a right to claim it as though they were blood of the blood, and flesh of the flesh of the men who wrote that Declaration." In fact, what Lincoln admired most in Henry Clay was that Clay "loved his country" not just because "it was his own country" but for its purposeful determination to be "a free country." Liberty was not a provincial cultural invention of white, English-speaking Americans; the liberty Clay advanced, as an American, was "the advancement, prosperity and glory, of human liberty, human right and human nature." And if he "desired the prosperity of his countrymen," it was "chiefly to show to the world that freemen could be prosperous."[14]

The connections Lincoln made between natural rights and economic and social mobility aligned him perfectly with Clay's Whig Party in the 1830s and 1840s. It also made Lincoln a natural enemy of slavery, since the two fundamental facts that characterized slavery in John Calhoun's South were its identification with race and its absolute annihilation of mobility, not only for the enslaved, but even for free whites who were encouraged to see their society as a *herrenvolk* democracy in which thousand-bale planters and white yeomen would accept economic stasis in the interest of promoting racial solidarity. His enmity against slavery was reinforced by his ambitious program of reading in political economy, all of which was a choir in praise of bourgeois capitalism: "Mill's political economy, Carey's political economy, social science. McCullough's [McCulloch's] political economy." Lincoln "liked political economy, the study of it," Herndon remembered, and Shelby Cullom was even more emphatic: "Theoretically, Mr. Lincoln was strong on financial questions. On political economy he was great." But of them all, it was Francis Wayland's *Elements of Political Economy* (1837) that Lincoln liked best. "Lincoln ate up, digested, and assimilated Wayland's little work." And as with Washington and Jefferson, scraps of Wayland's writings, great and small, frequently embedded themselves in Lincoln's writings.[15]

———

The competition which exists in a free country, is all that is necessary to bring wages to their proper level. Hence, combinations among capitalists or laborers are not only useless, but expensive, and unjust.—Wayland, Elements of Political Economy, 303

> If the gentleman from Fulton thought that he was paying too high for his bread and meat, let him go home and invite his constituents to come over and set up a competition in this line of business. This was a matter that would always regulate itself.—Lincoln, "Speech in Illinois Legislature on Bill to Provide Payment for Work on State House," 1841

Internal improvements, such as roads, canals, railroads, &c., may, in general, be safely left to individual enterprise. . . . The only case in which a government should assume such works, is that in which their magnitude is too great for individual enterprise, or that in which the power they confer, is too great to be entrusted to private corporations.—Wayland, Elements of Political Economy, 405

> The legitimate object of government, is to do for a community of people, whatever they need to have done, but can not do, at all, or can not, so well do, for themselves—in their separate, and individual capacities.—Lincoln, "Fragment on Government," 1854

[I]f A, on the ground of intellectual superiority, have a right to improve his own means of happiness, by diminishing those which the Creator has given to B, B would have the same right over A, on the ground of superior muscular strength; while C would have a correspondent right over them both, on the ground of superiority of wealth; and so on indefinitely.—Wayland, Elements of Moral Science, 191

> If A. can prove, however conclusively, that he may, of right, enslave B. why may not B. snatch the same argument, and prove equally, that he may enslave A?—
>
> You say A. is white, and B. is black. It is color, then; the lighter, having the right to enslave the darker? Take care. By this rule, you are to be slave to the first man you meet, with a fairer skin than your own.
>
> You do not mean color exactly? You mean the whites are intellectually the superiors of the blacks, and, therefore have the right to enslave them? Take care again. By this rule, you are to be slave to the first man you meet, with an intellect superior to your own.
>
> But, say you, it is a question of interest; and, if you can make it your interest, you have the right to enslave another. Very well. And if he can make it his interest, he has the right to enslave you.—Lincoln, "Fragment on Slavery," 1854

[I]f a thing need to be done today, we have no means which shall enable us to estimate the loss that may ensue, by putting it off until tomorrow.—Wayland, Elements of Political Economy, 377

> The leading rule for the lawyer, as for the man of every other calling, is diligence. Leave nothing for tomorrow which can be done today.—Lincoln, "Fragment: Notes for a Law Lecture," 1850

Lincoln was (in a phrase) a classical liberal democrat—an enemy of artificial hierarchy, a friend to trade and business as ennobling and enabling, and an American counterpart to Mill, Cobden, and Bright (whose portrait Lincoln hung in his White House office).[16]

There was, at the end of the day, almost nothing about Lincoln that anyone could decisively pinpoint as Romantic. He glorified the operation of reason and shunned appeals to passion. He was repelled by "the growing disposition to substitute the wild and furious passions, in lieu of the sober judgement of Courts" and suspected that it was tyrants, not lovers of liberty, who "naturally seek the gratification of their ruling passion," which is the lust for power. "Reason, cold, calculating, unimpassioned reason" was the best material for creating "general intelligence, [sound] morality and, in particular, a reverence for the constitution and laws." His taste in philosophy ran in the path of Enlightenment logic—toward Joseph Butler's *Analogy of Religion, Natural and Revealed, to the Constitution and Nature* (1736), for instance, or Jeremy Bentham's Utilitarianism—rather than Chateaubriand or Schleiermacher. Noah Brooks learned that Lincoln "was a lover of many philosophical books, and particularly liked Butler's Analogy of Religion [and] Stuart Mill on Liberty." He "never read Novels," apart from having once tried to penetrate Sir Walter Scott's *Ivanhoe* (another Romantic celebration, like *The Hunchback of Notre Dame*, of medieval chivalry) "but never finished it." He was more curious about geology, even to the point of reading through Sir Charles Lyell's epochal *Principles of Geology* (1830–33) and Robert Chambers's *Vestiges of the Natural History of Creation* (1844). But he had no interest in finding the sublime in a

> deep romantic chasm which slanted
> Down the green hill athwart a cedarn cover!
> A savage place! as holy and enchanted
> As e'er beneath a waning moon was haunted
> By woman wailing for her demon-lover!

When Lincoln returned from Congress by way of Niagara Falls in 1849, Herndon eagerly quizzed him about his thoughts "in the presence of the great natural wonder?" Lincoln, partly to tease the overeager Herndon, but also in truth, said, "The thing that struck me most forcibly when I saw the Falls, was, where in the world did all that water come from?" Lincoln simply had no eye "for the magnificence and grandeur of the scene, for the rapids, the mist, the angry waters, and the roar of the whirlpool. . . . It was in this light he viewed every question." Shortly thereafter, the Great Lakes steamer Lincoln was traveling upon ran aground on a sandbar, and Lincoln's first reaction was what might have been expected from Benjamin Franklin rather than Samuel Taylor Coleridge: "Mr. Lincoln was very attentive in watching the movements of the hands and the effect of what they did; he occasionally made suggestions that profited the commander." Eventually, he even developed a device for floating "stranded boats," which he patented.[17]

But at no point did Lincoln depart further from the Romantic sensibility than in his firm refusal to be drawn into the vortex of American Protestant evangelicalism. The Founders of the Republic might have been men of the

Enlightenment, and they wrote the American Constitution with a view toward zoning the unpredictable energies of religion off the public square; but in the two decades after Lincoln's birth, a renascent evangelicalism reconquered large stretches of American culture, and it did so, in large measure, through cultivating the most passionate commitments of "the religious affections" in revival meetings and "disinterested benevolence" in various reform societies. The conservative Old School Calvinism, "which did very well in the days of our fathers," complained Princeton's Albert Baldwin Dod, "will not answer now. . . . This is an age of great excitement," and "we must have something more exciting," something "grand. Terrible, &c." which "will fever the blood, quicken the pulse, blanch the cheek, and agitate the whole frame." Lincoln had grown up with this on the frontier and wanted no part of it. His parents' church, the Separate Baptists, repudiated revivals and "excitement" in favor of an absolute Calvinist predestination, but Lincoln rejected that, too. As an adolescent, Lincoln "had no particular religion—didn't think of that question at that time, if he ever did—He never talked about it." And as much as his head was drilled full of memorized Scripture, his preferred reading on religion was in the two most popular religious skeptics of the Enlightenment, "Tom Pain[e] & [Constantin] Volney." When Lincoln moved to Springfield in 1837 to practice law under John Todd Stuart, Stuart thought "he was an avowed and open Infidel" who "Sometimes bordered on atheism" and "went further against Christian beliefs—& doctrines & principles than any man I ever heard."[18]

Lincoln soon enough discovered that a reputation for "infidelity" was not going to win him many votes among the faithful of central Illinois, and the "whispering . . . levied a tax of considerable per cent" on his electability. He issued a number of ambiguous statements about religion, admitting what he could not deny, but denying that this created any crisis for voters' confidence. "That I am not a member of any Christian Church, is true; but I have never denied the truth of the Scriptures; and I have never spoken with intentional disrespect of religion in general, or of any denomination of Christians in particular." Herndon suspected that, "to avoid the disgrace, odium, and unpopularity" that "infidelity" would bring down on him, Lincoln advertised himself "openly to the world as a seeker." If so, the seeking was not very energetic. "I never heard of his entering a place where God is worshipped, and I have never yet found a person who could give me any evidence that he ever went to a [religious] meeting in the town," complained one Springfield minister. "He often goes to the railroad shop and spends the Sabbath in reading Newspapers, and telling stories to the workmen, but not to the house of God." And yet, Lincoln *did* consider himself to be at least some parts of a seeker. To Aminda Rogers Rankin, he candidly confessed his "shadows and questionings"; but he had been schooled in the hard logic of Calvinist predestination, and if God did exist, he was a God who did the choosing of people by his own will, not the other way round. "I am a fatalist," Lincoln admitted, and until God chose to enlighten him, Lincoln thought "it was my lot to go on in a twilight, feeling and reasoning my way through life, as questioning, doubting Thomas did."[19]

He did not consider himself an optimist. All human beings, Lincoln believed, behave according to self-interest; provide them with a set of "motives" that appeal to that self-interest, and they will respond predictably. To Herndon, he "contended that motives moved the man to every voluntary act of his life. . . . Man is compelled to feel, think, will, and to act subject to the influences of these conditions." Nor did he exempt himself from that rule. "I claim not to have controlled events," he declared to Albert G. Hodges, "but confess plainly that events have controlled me." Reflecting on the series of splits, twists, and maneuvers that had led to his dark-horse nomination and election to the presidency, Lincoln concluded "from the fact of his having made a race for the Senate of the United States with Judge Douglas in the state of Illinois, his name became prominent, and he was accidentally selected and elected afterwards as president of the United States." Fundamentally, Lincoln was conscious that his "melancholy" was a temperamental characteristic. "You flaxen men with broad faces are born with cheer and don't know a cloud from a star," Lincoln remarked to Iowa congressman Josiah Grinnell. "I am of another temperament." The Civil War only deepened that melancholy. "When I think of the sacrifices of life yet to be offered and the hearts and homes yet to be made desolate before this dreadful war is over," he said to a military staffer on the way to the Gettysburg Soldiers' Cemetery dedication in November 1863, "my heart is like lead within me, and I feel, at times, like hiding in deep darkness."[20]

And yet, for all the certainty with which Lincoln spoke of feeling certain that "I should meet with some terrible end," in the *longue durée* of human progress toward liberty, he was as much a man of hope as Gibbon. "The struggle of today," he wrote to Congress in his first annual presidential message in December 1861, was "for a vast future also." As burdened as he was by the struggles of the war, "the great republic" and "the principle it lives by" were the guarantee "for man's vast future." He described emancipation as a "motive" for rallying black enlistment, since "negroes, like other people, act upon motives." But once they were enlisted, Lincoln was also certain, black soldiers would "with silent tongue, and clenched teeth, and steady eye, and well-poised bayonet" be instrumental in helping "mankind on to this great consummation." Even after four years of civil bloodletting, "the national resources, then, are unexhausted, and, as we believe, inexhaustible." Provide only an "increased devotion to that cause for which" the Union's dead had given "the last full measure of devotion," and "this nation" will enjoy "a new birth of freedom." And more than just *this nation*, the principle of "government of the people, by the people, for the people, shall not perish from the earth."[21]

Helen Nicolay wrote about the man her father had served as principal White House secretary that "the truth is that Lincoln was no prophet of a distant day. . . . His early life was essentially of the old era." Intellectually, he belonged much more to the world of Washington and Franklin—and Paine and Volney—than to the soon-dawning era of William James. It has been difficult to appreciate the importance of that world because the one that succeeded it—the intellectual world of James's pragmatism—represented such a stark intellectual break with Lincoln's. Richard Hofstadter once wrote that "had [Lincoln] lived to seventy, he would have seen the generation brought up on self-help come into its own, build oppressive business corporations, and begin to close off those treasured opportunities for the little man." It was actually worse than that, because Hofstadter saw Lincoln only through the lens of an American evasion of class struggle; what would have been just as painful would be an intellectual world in which questions of truth and validity could be settled only by an appeal to practice and experience, which sounds oddly similar to Stephen A. Douglas's doctrine of "popular sovereignty." The hallmark of Enlightenment thought was its confidence that whatever questions there are in the universe, precise answers exist somewhere for them, and that they are all part of a single natural system. The aesthetic of Romanticism was built around the suspicion that there were no such answers, but that passion might supply a satisfactory substitute. Even granting that Lincoln was not an intellectual but a politician, it is hard to believe that, even as a politician, he would be comfortable living with that.[22]

Notes

1. Benjamin Franklin, *The Autobiography and Other Writings*, ed. L. Jesse Lemisch (New York: New American Library, 1961), 106.

2. Voltaire, *Philosophical Letters*, ed. Ernest Dilworth (Indianapolis: Bobbs-Merrill, 1961), 39; Daniel Defoe, "The Complete English Tradesman" (1727), in *Commerce, Culture, and Liberty: Readings on Capitalism before Adam Smith*, ed. H. C. Clark (Indianapolis: Liberty Fund, 2003), 242.

3. Gibbon quoted in Robert Nisbet, *History of the Idea of Progress* (New York: Basic Books, 1980), 187.

4. Blake quoted in Kenneth Clark, *The Romantic Rebellion: Romantic versus Classical Art* (New York: Scribner's, 1973), 45.

5. Joseph de Maistre, "Study on Sovereignty," in *The Works of Joseph de Maistre*, ed. Jack Lively (New York: Schocken Books, 1971), 103, 107, 113; Paul Johnson, *The Birth of the Modern: World Society, 1815–1830* (New York: HarperCollins, 1991), 142–51; Richard Wolin, *The Seduction of Unreason: The Intellectual Romance with Fascism from Nietzsche to Postmodernism* (Princeton, N.J.: Princeton University Press, 2004), 115.

6. John C. Calhoun, "Disquisition on Government," in *Union and Liberty: The Political Philosophy of John C. Calhoun*, ed. R. M. Lence (Indianapolis: Liberty Fund, 1992), 42, 44; George Fitzhugh, *Cannibals All! or, Slaves without Masters*, ed. C. Vann Woodward (Cambridge: Harvard University Press, 1960), 246; Isaiah Berlin, *The Roots of Romanticism*, ed. Henry Hardy (Princeton, N.J.: Princeton University Press, 1999), 61; Eugene Genovese and Elizabeth Fox-Genovese, *The Mind of the Master Class: History and Faith in the Southerners' Worldview* (New York: Cambridge University Press, 2005), 62–68.

7. Francis Wayland, *Elements of Political Economy* (Boston, 1837), 391; Richard Hildreth, "Theory of Wealth," in *An American Utilitarian: Richard Hildreth as a Philosopher*, ed. M. M. Pingel (New York: Columbia University Press, 1948), 45, 48, 49.

8. Statement of Henry Clay Whitney (1887), and letter of James Herndon (May 29, 1865), in *Herndon's Informants: Letters, Interviews, and Statements about Abraham Lincoln*, ed. Douglas L. Wilson and Rodney O. Davis (Urbana: University of Illinois Press, 1998), 16, 648; Jesse Weik, *The Real Lincoln: A Portrait* (1922), ed. Michael Burlingame (Lincoln: University of Nebraska Press, 2002), 75; Herndon to Jesse Weik (November 24, 1882), and Herndon's essay "Lincoln the Lawyer," in Emmanuel Hertz, *The Hidden Lincoln: From the Letters and Papers of William H. Herndon* (New York: Viking, 1938), 88, 427; *Lincoln Legal Briefs*, no. 41 (January–March 1997) and no. 44 (October–December 1997); Abraham Lincoln, "Communication to the People of Sangamo County" (March 9, 1832), "Fragment: Notes for a Law Lecture" (July 1, 1850), "Brief Autobiography" (June 15, 1858), "Speech at Chicago, Illinois" (July 10, 1858), "To Jesse W. Fell, Enclosing Autobiography" (December 20, 1859), and "Autobiography Written for John L. Scripps" (June 1860), in *Collected Works of Abraham Lincoln*, ed. Roy P. Basler, 9 vols., hereafter referred to as *Collected Works* (New Brunswick, N.J.: Rutgers University Press, 1953–55), 1:8–9, 2:81, 459, 491, 3:511, 4:62; Mark Steiner, *An Honest Calling: The Law Practice of Abraham Lincoln* (DeKalb: Northern Illinois University Press, 2006), 52–53.

9. Michael Burlingame, *The Inner World of Abraham Lincoln* (Urbana: University of Illinois Press, 1994), 39; Herndon to C.O. Poole (January 5, 1886) and David Davis to Herndon, in Hertz, *Hidden Lincoln*, 120, 426; Stuart, in *The Lincoln Papers*, ed. David C. Mearns (Garden City, N.Y.: Doubleday, 1948),

159; Hay, in *An Oral History of Abraham Lincoln: John G. Nicolay's Interviews and Essays*, ed. Michael Burlingame (Carbondale: Southern Illinois University Press, 1996), 26.

10. Letters of J. Rowan Herndon (May 26, 1865), William H. Greene (May 30, 1865), Dennis F. Hanks (June 13 and September 8, 1865), N. W. Branson (August 3, 1865), and Joshua Speed (December 6, 1866) to William Herndon, in Wilson and Davis, *Herndon's Informants*, 7, 18, 41, 90, 105, 499; Josiah G. Holland, *The Life of Abraham Lincoln* (Springfield, Mass.: Gurdon Bill, 1866), 31–32; Michael Lind, *What Lincoln Believed: The Values and Convictions of America's Greatest President* (New York: Random House, 2004), 44–45, 47; Louis A. Warren, *Lincoln's Youth: Indiana Years, Seven to Twenty-three, 1816–1830* (Indianapolis: Indiana Historical Society, 1991), 76–79, 87, 103–11; Stewart Winger, *Lincoln, Religion, and Romantic Cultural Politics* (DeKalb: Northern Illinois University Press, 2003), 202–3; Noah Brooks, quoting Lincoln, in *Recollected Words of Abraham Lincoln*, ed. Don Fehrenbacher and Virginia Fehrenbacher (Stanford, Calif.: Stanford University Press, 1996), 54.

11. Letters of Mentor Graham (May 29, 1865), Henry McHenry (May 29, 1865), and Joshua Speed (December 6, 1866) to Herndon, in Wilson and Davis, *Herndon's Informants*, 10, 14, 499; William G. Green, in Mearns, *Lincoln Papers*, 154; Charles Maltby, *The Life and Public Services of Abraham Lincoln* (Los Angeles: Daily Independent Steam Power Print, 1884), 31–32; Elihu Washburne, in *Reminiscences of Abraham Lincoln by Distinguished Men of His Time*, ed. Allen Thorndike Rice (New York: North American Press, 1886), 7.

12. Lincoln, "Communication to the People of Sangamo County" (March 9, 1832), "Address before the Young Men's Lyceum of Springfield, Illinois" (January 27, 1838), "An Address, Delivered before the Springfield Washington Temperance Society" (February 22, 1842), "Farewell Address at Springfield, Illinois" (February 11, 1861), "Address to the New Jersey Senate at Trenton, New Jersey" (February 21, 1861), "Speech in Independence Hall, Philadelphia, Pennsylvania" (February 22, 1861), "Message to Congress in Special Session" (July 4, 1861), and "To Salmon P. Chase" (September 2, 1863), in *Collected Works*, 1:8, 115, 279, 4:190, 235, 240, 439, 6:429; Willard Sterne Randall, *George Washington: A Life* (New York: Owl Books, 1997), 437, 468; George Washington, "Eighth Annual Address" (December 7, 1796), in *A Compilation of the Messages and Papers of the Presidents, 1789–1897*, ed. James D. Richardson (Washington, D.C.: Government Printing Office, 1896), 1:204; Thomas Jefferson, "Opinion against the Constitutionality of a National Bank" (February 15, 1791), in *The Complete Jefferson: Containing His Major Writings, Published and Unpublished, except His Letters*, ed. Saul K. Padover (New York: Buell, Sloan and Pierce, 1943), 342; Warren, *Lincoln's Youth*, 162–64.

13. Lincoln, "Fragment on Slavery" (July 1, 1854), "Speech at Kalamazoo, Michigan" (August 27, 1856), and "Speech in Independence Hall, Philadelphia, Pennsylvania" (February 22, 1861), in *Collected Works*, 2:222, 364, 4:240; Edgar DeWitt Jones, *The Influence of Henry Clay upon Abraham Lincoln* (Lexington, Ky.: Henry Clay Memorial Foundation, 1952), 19.

14. Lincoln, "Eulogy on Henry Clay" (July 6, 1852), and "Speech at Chicago, Illinois" (July 10, 1858), in *Collected Works*, 2:126, 499–500; J. David Greenstone, *The Lincoln Persuasion: Remaking American Liberalism* (Princeton, N.J.: Princeton University Press, 1993), 250.

15. Herndon to Jesse Weik (January 1, 1886), in Hertz, *Hidden Lincoln*, 117; Cullom, in Walter B. Stevens, *A Reporter's Lincoln*, ed. Michael Burlingame (Lincoln: University of Nebraska Press, 1998), 154; Lincoln, "Speech in Illinois Legislature on Bill to Provide Payment for Work on State House" (January 25, 1841), "Fragment: Notes for a Law Lecture" (July 1, 1850), "Fragment on Government" (July 1, 1854), and "Fragment on Slavery" (July 1, 1854), in *Collected Works*, 1:230, 2:220, 222–23; Wayland, *Elements of Political Economy*, 303, 377, 405; Francis Wayland, *The Elements of Moral Science* (Boston: Gould and Lincoln, 1851), 191; William Lee Miller, *Lincoln's Virtues: An Ethical Biography* (New York: Knopf, 2002), 278.

16. The single major exception to Lincoln's adherence to the political economy of the Manchester liberals concerned free trade, since Lincoln (like the rest of the Whig Party) was an ardent apostle of protection and tariffs; the difference, however, lay largely in the relative positions of the American and British economies, with American industry still requiring some form of shelter while it grew to proportions capable of competing in world markets with British goods. Wayland, however, frankly sympathized with free trade and endorsed the Anti–Corn Law League (see Wayland, *Elements of Political Economy*, 343; and Lind, *What Lincoln Believed*, 92–94).

17. Lincoln, "Address before the Young Men's Lyceum of Springfield, Illinois" (January 27, 1838), and "Speech to the Jury in the Rock Island Bridge Case, Chicago, Illinois" (September 22, 1857), in *Collected Works*, 1:109, 113, 115, 2:418; Francis B. Carpenter, *Six Months at the White House with Abraham Lincoln* (New York: Hurd and Houghton, 1867), 115; Noah Brooks, "Personal Recollections of Abraham Lincoln," in *Lincoln Observed: Civil War Dispatches of Noah Brooks*, ed. Michael Burlingame (Baltimore: Johns Hopkins University Press, 1998), 219; William H. Herndon and Jesse W. Weik, *Herndon's Lincoln*, ed. Douglas L. Wilson and Rodney O. Davis (Urbana: University of Illinois Press, 2006), 187–88; Herndon, "Lincoln's Boat," in Hertz, *Hidden Lincoln*, 397. The verses are from Samuel Taylor Coleridge's *Kubla Khan*.

18. Albert Baldwin Dod, "On Revivals of Religion," in *Essays, Theological and Miscellaneous, Reprinted from the Princeton Review* (New York, 1847), 118, 133; interview with Sarah Bush Lincoln (September 8, 1865), letter of Abner Ellis (January 6, 1866), and interview with John Todd Stuart (March 2, 1870), in Wilson and Davis, *Herndon's Informants*, 107, 179, 576.

19. Herndon and Weik, *Herndon's Lincoln*, 213; Lincoln, "Handbill Replying to Charges of Infidelity" (July 31, 1846), and "To Allen N. Ford" (August 11, 1846), in *Collected Works*, 1:382, 383; G. W. Pendleton, quoted in Burlingame, *Oral History*, 155; Rankin, quoting Lincoln, in Fehrenbacher and Fehrenbacher, *Recollected Words*, 373.

20. Lincoln, "To Albert G. Hodges" (April 4, 1864), in *Collected Works*, 5:35; Lind, *What Lincoln Believed*, 59; Charles Morehead and Josiah Grinnell, quoted in Fehrenbacher and Fehrenbacher, *Recollected Words*, 186, 334; E. W. Andrews in Thorndike, *Reminiscences of Abraham Lincoln*, 511; Herndon to Jesse Weik (November 14, 1885, and February 25, 1887), in Hertz, *Hidden Lincoln*, 103, 180; Winger, *Lincoln, Religion, and Romantic Cultural Politics*, 78.

21. "Annual Message to Congress" (December 3, 1861), "To James C. Conkling" (August 26, 1863), "Gettysburg Address" (November 19, 1863), and "Annual Message to Congress" (December 6, 1864), in *Collected Works*, 6:410, 7:23, 281, 8:151.

22. Helen Nicolay, *Personal Traits of Abraham Lincoln* (New York: Century, 1912), 381–82; Richard Hofstadter, "Abraham Lincoln and the Self-Made Myth," in *The American Political Tradition and the Men Who Made It* (1948; reprint, New York: Knopf, 1973), 105; Berlin, *Roots of Romanticism*, 21–22.

2

Tocqueville and Lincoln on Religion and Democracy in America

Joseph R. Fornieri

> I had seen the spirit of religion and the spirit of freedom almost always move in contrary directions. Here I found them united intimately with one another: they reigned together on the same soil.
>
> —Alexis de Tocqueville, *Democracy in America*

The French aristocrat Alexis de Tocqueville and the American statesman Abraham Lincoln provide comparable wisdom about the moral and religious foundations of American democracy. Tocqueville, a foreign observer, is the famed author of *Democracy in America*, a work that has been aptly described as "at once the best book ever written on democracy and the best book ever written on America."[1] Lincoln, a native citizen, is the savior of the American democratic experiment and its most eloquent spokesman. While there are notable differences between the two, both Lincoln and Tocqueville view religion as an indispensable source of moral instruction that ennobles and preserves democracy. Tocqueville speaks for both when he says, "the reign of freedom cannot be established without mores, nor mores founded without beliefs" (*Democracy,* 11). Indeed, Lincoln's ultimate moral justification of American democracy, what I have elsewhere described as his political faith, embodies Tocqueville's memorable description of religion as "the first of [America's] political institutions . . . necessary to the maintenance of republican institutions" (280).[2] In what follows, I seek to compare Tocqueville and Lincoln on the compatibility between religion and democracy in American public life.[3] In concluding, I will explore their contemporary relevance as well as some of the areas of divergence between them. What guidance do these two teachers of democracy provide us on the perennial question of religion and politics in America?

Alexis de Tocqueville was born in 1805 to a noble family that was caught up in the tumultuous events of the French Revolution. His parents were imprisoned and spared the guillotine's blade at the last moment. Tocqueville lived through a series of revolutions that convulsed France and Europe in the nineteenth century: the fall of Napoleon; the Restoration of the Bourbon monarchy; the abdication of Charles X during the July Days of 1830; the Second Republic in 1848; the fall of the Second Republic; Napoleon II's coup d'état of 1851; and the Second Empire. He thus had firsthand experience of the turbulence of democracy in France and its unhappy tendency to vibrate between the extremes of tyranny and anarchy.

Though he was an aristocrat, Tocqueville may be characterized politically as a moderate liberal who sought to reconcile the aristocratic concern for greatness of the few with the democratic concern for equal justice for all.[4] His foremost intent, one that recurs throughout his writings, was to preserve the precious inheritance of political liberty—namely, the responsible governance of free, self-determining citizens. Americans, he believed, mistakenly conflate freedom and equality. They presume that greater equality in all areas of life necessarily translates into greater freedom. This is erroneous, according to Tocqueville. He maintained that liberty was threatened just as much by subtler forms of radical egalitarianism as by more overt forms of absolutism and aristocratic privilege. Indeed, part of his genius as a thinker is to emphasize the inherent tension between liberty and equality in democracies (*Democracy*, 52).[5]

After the July Days, Tocqueville and his friend Gustave Beaumont sailed to America with the ostensible purpose to study the prison system (both were lawyers). This was merely a pretext for their real purpose: to study America—the quintessence of democracy—up close and personal. The fruit of Tocqueville's ten-month journey to the United States was his classic work *Democracy in America*, published in two volumes, 1835 and 1840. The book was an immediate success in Europe. It was even reviewed by the great liberal thinker and reformer John Stuart Mill. Tocqueville died in 1859, on the eve of the American Civil War. More than two decades before Lincoln's "House divided against itself" speech of 1858, he similarly predicted a crisis over the incompatibility between freedom and slavery: "[W]hatever the efforts of Americans of the South to preserve slavery they will not succeed at it forever. Slavery contracted to a single point on the globe, attacked by

Christianity as unjust, by political economy as fatal; slavery, in the midst of democratic freedom and enlightenment of our age, is not an institution that can endure. It will cease by the deed of the slave or the master. In both cases, one must expect great misfortunes" (348).

In his introduction to *Democracy in America*, Tocqueville forthrightly announces his intent "[t]o instruct democracy, if possible to reanimate its beliefs, to purify its mores, to regulate its movements, to substitute little by little the science of affairs for its inexperience, and knowledge of its true interests for its blind instincts" (7). Convinced that, for better or worse, democracy was ordained by Divine Providence, he declared that "A new political science is needed for a world altogether new" (7). Tocqueville reasoned that if the tide of democracy was irresistible, then America was the paradigmatic place to study it, since democracy had developed there in pristine form, apart from the feudal hierarchies of Europe. He thus explains, "I confess that in America I saw more than America; I sought there an image of democracy itself, of its penchants, its character, its prejudices, its passions; I wanted to become acquainted with it if only to know at least what we ought to hope or fear from it" (13).

The above statement reveals the extent to which Tocqueville viewed the ascendancy of democracy as morally ambiguous. Unlike many of the utopian theorists of his time, he did not believe that democracy would inexorably lead to greater freedom and dignity for human beings. To be sure, if some of its more virulent tendencies were left unrestrained, it could spiral downward on a path of servitude and debasement. Tocqueville's own family experience during the French Revolution confirmed that there were both things "to hope" and "fear" from democracy.

Tocqueville envisioned himself standing at the crossroads between the twilight of the *ancien régime* and the dawn of a new, democratic era. The contrast between aristocracy and democracy is therefore a consistent theme in his writing. As one who inhabited both worlds, he points out to his readers the "trade-off," so to speak, between democracy and aristocracy, noting what is lost and gained in each case (*Democracy*, 234–35). In sum, Tocqueville's new political science seeks to ennoble democracy, to "attenuate its vices and make its natural advantages emerge" (8).

Tocqueville studies democracy not simply as a type of government but more broadly as a way of life. Throughout *Democracy in America*, he employs the theoretical construct of the *social state* to examine democratic society. The social state refers to the unique circumstances, origins, facts, laws, institutions, and conditions that shape a society's moral character and its development in a particular direction. Tocqueville thus defines the social state as "ordinarily the product of fact, sometimes of laws, most often of these two causes united; but once it exists, one can consider it as the first cause of most of the laws, customs, and ideas that regulate the conduct of nations; what it does not produce, it modifies" (45). As Harvey Mansfield notes in the introduction to *Democracy in America*, Tocqueville's social state eschews both a classical founding and a prepolitical state of nature (xliv). By contrast, it sees society and politics as intertwined. Tocqueville leaves unanswered the question of which comes first: society or politics. He notes the mutual influence between the social state and the mores, customs, and habits that spring from the social state.

By *mores*, Tocqueville means the "habits of the heart . . . the different notions that men possess . . . the various opinions that are current in their midst . . . the sum of ideas of which the habits of the mind are formed. . . . the whole moral and intellectual state of a people" (*Democracy*, 275). For Tocqueville, religion was not only crucial to the origins of the American social state of equality of conditions but also continues to play an important role in forming the mores of democratic society. Tocqueville states: "Freedom sees in religion the companion of its struggles and its triumphs, the cradle of its infancy, the divine source of its rights. It considers religion as the safeguard of mores; and mores as the guarantee of laws and the pledge of its own duration" (43–44).

Significantly, Tocqueville emphasizes that America was born equal, rather than having to become so through a democratic revolution that overturned its entire social state, as in France. In his view, then, the American Revolution was more of an *evolution* that furthered and extended the egalitarian social state that already existed on the North American continent. Tocqueville explains the various factors and conditions that led to the equality of conditions as America's social state—to name a few: the absence of feudal hierarchies that existed in Europe; the availability of land and property; the existence of a large middle class; a relatively equal distribution of fortunes and intelligence among the population; estate laws that equally partitioned land; and laws against primogeniture that precluded the emergence of a hereditary aristocracy.

Perhaps most important, however, Tocqueville points to America's religious origins as crucial to its democratic character and social state. He recalls that "it was the religious aspect of the country that first struck my eye" (*Democracy*, 282). In point of fact, America was settled by a group of people who were already democratic in character and who brought with

them democratic laws, traditions, and *mores*—namely, the Puritans. Tocqueville thus explains that "Puritanism was not only a religious doctrine;
it also blended at several points with the most absolute democratic and
republican theories" (32).

Moreover, Tocqueville contends that Puritanism was not merely a local phenomenon confined to New England. Rather, its mores permeated
the entire nation and had a lasting impact upon the regime's subsequent
development. As Myron Marty notes in his essay about education in pre-
Revolutionary America in this volume, "the most commonly used book
was *The New England Primer*, a ninety-page reader published initially in
1690 and eventually printed in all thirteen colonies. Perhaps as many as two
million copies were sold. Many of its religious maxims, reflecting Puritan
perspectives, were drawn from the King James translation of the Bible."

According to Tocqueville, the following democratic features of Puritanism contributed to the equality of conditions in America: its rejection of
ecclesiastical hierarchy; its presbyter system (a self-governing community
of church elders); its fidelity to written covenants among equal citizens before God; and its doctrines of the priesthood of all believers, *sola fide* (faith
alone), and *sola scriptura* (Bible alone). These doctrines all emphasized one's
individual encounter with God apart from the mediation of the clergy. The
Puritans were, in effect, democratic dissenters who opposed the intertwined
hierarchies of the British monarchy, the Anglican clergy, and the established
religion of the crown. Upon arriving in the New World, in place of this
hierarchy, they established the New England townships as a form of local,
participatory government. Indeed, Tocqueville regarded these townships as
the cradle and apprenticeship of democracy in America (*Democracy*, 40).[6]

Finally, the Puritan emigrants were themselves members of the middle
class, thereby reinforcing the equality of conditions in the New World. Tocqueville summarizes the Puritan contribution to democracy in these terms:
"The greatest part of English America has been peopled by men who, after
having escaped the authority of the pope, did not submit to any religious
supremacy; they therefore brought to the New World a Christianity that I
cannot depict better than to call it democratic and republican: this singularly
favors the establishment of a republic and democracy in affairs. From the
beginning, politics and religion were in accord, and they have not ceased
to be" (275).

Much has been written on the influence of Puritanism on American public life.[7] Despite its institutional decline by the mid-nineteenth century,
its originating role in shaping the social state and its lingering teachings

continued to exert an enduring influence on the political culture of the nation. In particular, the Puritan legacy endures in America's perennial self-understanding as a chosen people, a second Israel, called by God for a special mission. While this self-understanding of American exceptionalism carries with it the potential for both self-righteous triumphalism and higher moral purpose, it is nonetheless a firmly established part of America's history, political culture, and identity.

The origin of American exceptionalism can be traced, in turn, to the origins of the Massachusetts Bay Colony. Its first governor, John Winthrop, proclaimed the aspiration to establish a model Christian community in the New World that would serve as a "city upon a hill" (Matthew 5: 14), a spiritual exemplar to the rest of the world. This biblical symbol, used by Winthrop to express a unique mission or calling by God, would be subsequently applied to America's political destiny. The American nation, some believed, was called by Providence to serve as the model or standard-bearer of democratic government to the rest of the world. This self-understanding is manifest in the writings of Ezra Stiles,[8] Publius in the *Federalist Papers*, Jefferson, Webster, and Lincoln. It persists in the twentieth century with Woodrow Wilson's call to make "the world safe for democracy" and Ronald Reagan's reference to America as a "shining city on the hill." In each case, the American experiment in self-government was seen as providing hope for the future of freedom throughout the world.

Lincoln's rhetoric during the Civil War corresponds with Tocqueville's observations that "Puritanism . . . was almost as much a political theory as a religious doctrine" (35).[9] Consistent with the Puritan legacy, the sixteenth president characterized his fellow countrymen as God's "almost chosen people." However, by using the conditional term *almost*, he introduced a moral ambiguity and irony that was in keeping with his conscious efforts to guard against self-righteousness.[10] Further consonant with the foregoing symbol of American mission, Lincoln defined the Civil War in terms of a wider calling to preserve democracy for all mankind.[11] The fate of the American experiment in republican government would reverberate throughout the world. Accordingly, Lincoln explained, the Union's preservation "presents to the whole family of man, the question, whether a constitutional republic, or a democracy—a government of the people, by the same people—can, or cannot maintain its territorial integrity, against its own domestic foes."[12] In his annual message to Congress, on December 1, 1862, Lincoln likewise described the worldwide significance of the struggle: "Fellow-citizens, *we* cannot escape history. . . . The fiery trial through which we pass will light us down, in honor or dishonor, to the latest generation. . . . We shall nobly save, or meanly lose, the last, best, hope of earth."[13]

After tracing the religious origins of America and its influence on the social state, Tocqueville contrasts the compatibility between religion and democracy in the United States to their antipathy in France: "I had seen the spirit of religion and the spirit of freedom almost always move in contrary directions. Here I found them united intimately with one another: they reigned together on the same soil" (*Democracy*, 282). To appreciate more fully the difference between religion and democracy in France vis-à-vis America, it is instructive to consult another great work of Tocqueville's, *The Old Regime and the French Revolution*.[14] Here he explains how the Catholic Church in France became an inevitable target of the revolutionaries because it was inseparably wed to the power of the state and to the *ancien régime*. In seeking to usher in a new order, the revolutionaries sought to annihilate all vestiges of the old order, including the Church. For the revolutionaries, the power and privileges of the first estate (the clergy), its ties to the monarchy and the nobility, and its status as the official religion of France were intolerable reminders of the inequality of the *ancien régime*.

However, Tocqueville contends that the overthrow of the established church in France did not lead to the expulsion of religion altogether. Because to be human is to be a *homo religiosus* (a religious being by nature), human beings search for some ultimate meaning to their existence. Religion abhors a vacuum, according to Tocqueville (*Democracy*, 25–26). To use the metaphor of Richard John Neuhaus, the public square does not remain naked when traditional religion is expelled from it. The old garment is inevitably clothed with a substitute, "ersatz" religion that provides an alternative meaning and purpose to public life.[15] In France during the Revolution, the traditional religion of Roman Catholicism was replaced by the substitute religion of secular humanitarianism. Tocqueville maintains that this new creed fueled the immoderate passions of the revolutionaries: "The anti-religious spirit of the age had very various consequences, but it seems to me that what led the French to commit such singular excesses was not so much that it made them callous or debased their moral standards as that it tended to upset their mental equilibrium. When religion was expelled from their souls, the effect was not to create a vacuum or a state of apathy; it was promptly, if but momentarily, replaced by a host of new loyalties and secular ideals that not only filled the void but (to begin with) fired the popular imagination."[16] Tocqueville had made this very same point years earlier in *Democracy in America*: "In centuries of fervor, it sometimes happens that men abandon their religion, but they escape its yoke only to submit to that of another. Faith changes its object, it does not die" (286).

The evacuation of the old religion and its replacement by an ersatz religion had a corresponding effect upon the French psyche. Tocqueville notes that it "upset their mental equilibrium." The new religion entailed a belief in the "perfectibility of man" and "faith in his innate virtue." The revolutionaries were spurred by a "fanatical faith in their vocation . . . of transforming the social system, and regenerating the whole human race."[17] Such "faith" in human perfectibility has enormous political implications and consequences. For one thing, Tocqueville thought it explained why physiocrats like Quesnay rejected the separation of powers as a necessary brake upon the sovereign will of the people. Such checks were unnecessary, given his belief in human perfectibility. Once the corruption of the old regime was excised, the natural goodness of human beings would be realized through enlightenment. The only safeguard to be relied upon in constructing a new government was universal education. Quesnay thus declared that "when a nation is fully educated, tyranny is automatically ruled out."[18] Indeed, the political philosopher David Walsh refers to Tocqueville's characterization of the spiritual pathology of the French revolutionaries as "a brilliant dissection of the disorder of militant humanitarianism, of secular religion."[19] Following Tocqueville's footsteps, another Frenchman, Albert Camus, also pondered the ersatz religion of the French revolutionaries. Camus similarly noted in *The Rebel* that the enthusiasm of the revolutionaries to kill God ("deicide," as he refers to it), unhinged their own sense of human and political limitations.[20] For both Tocqueville and Camus, the human being's hubristic impulse to become god is at the very core of totalitarian schemes to recast human nature and society in the image of those who wield absolute power.

Unlike the militant humanitarianism described by Tocqueville, Lincoln's and the Founders' views of politics were informed by a biblical view of human nature that appreciated both the dignity and depravity of humankind. Perhaps the most memorable expression of human fallibility in American political thought (one that stands diametrically opposed to Quesnay's) comes from James Madison in *Federalist* no. 51: "It may be a reflection on human nature that such devices [checks and balances] should be necessary to control the abuses of government. But what is government itself but the greatest of all reflections on human nature? If men were angels, no government would be necessary. If angels were to govern men, neither external nor internal controls on government would be necessary."[21] Testifying to the extent to which revelation's teaching on human frailty was confirmed by common experience, Lincoln poignantly and humorously observed, "The Bible says somewhere that we are desperately selfish. I think we would have discovered that fact without the Bible."[22]

Lincoln's realistic view of human nature, one that recognized the potential for good and evil in each human heart, was inseparable from his prudent discernment that few things in human affairs are purely good or purely evil; most are a compound of both. Unlike the French revolutionaries, whose "mental equilibrium" was upset by their utopian longings, Lincoln's practical wisdom eschewed casting political conflict in dualistic terms, as a contest between the forces of light and the forces of darkness.[23] Unlike some of the radicals of his own time, Lincoln refused to demonize his opponents and enemies in view of his recognition that all human beings are equally flawed. His corresponding compassion and lack of self-righteousness towards others was, in part, based upon this Christian insight into human nature: we are equal not only in our dignity but in our depravity. For example, in his temperance address of February 22, 1842, Lincoln appeals to the moral authority of Christianity against the reformers' self-righteousness:

> "But," say some, "we are no drunkards; and we shall not acknowledge ourselves such by joining a reformed drunkard's society, whatever our influence might be." Surely no Christian will adhere to this objection. If they believe, as they profess, that Omnipotence condescended to take on himself the form of sinful man, and, as such, to die an ignominious death for their sakes, surely they will not refuse submission to the infinitely lesser condescension, for the temporal, and perhaps eternal salvation, of a large, erring, and unfortunate class of their own fellow creatures. Nor is the condescension very great.
>
> In my judgment, such of us as have never fallen victims have been spared more from the absence of appetite, than from any mental or moral superiority over those who have. Indeed, I believe, if we take drunkards as a class, their heads and their hearts will bear an advantageous comparison with those of any other class.[24]

Lincoln consistently affirmed this realistic view of human frailty throughout his public life. For instance, at Peoria in 1854, he confessed, "I have no prejudice against the Southern people. They are just what we would be in their situation."[25] Six years later, on the eve of the Civil War, he likewise declared, "Human nature is the same—people at the South are the same as those at the North, barring the differences in circumstances."[26] And after winning a bitter election campaign in 1864, he magnanimously declared,

"Human-nature will not change. In any future great national trial, compared with the men of this, we shall have as weak, and as strong; as silly and as wise; as bad and as good."[27] Finally, in his Second Inaugural Address, upon the eve of the Union's victory over a prostrated South, Lincoln punctured the self-righteousness of his Northern audience by reminding them that "the prayers of both could not be answered; that of neither has been answered fully."[28] In this speech, which was thoroughly imbued with biblical symbolism, he called not for revenge but for the superabundant force of Christian charity to heal the nation's wounds: "With malice toward none; with charity for all; with firmness in the right, as God gives us to see the right, let us strive to finish the work we are in; to bind up the nation's wounds."[29] Thus, Lincoln's prudence as informed by his Christian realism in the Second Inaugural Address stands in sharp relief to both the radicals of his own time and to the radicals of the French Revolution, whose secular religious impulses, according to Tocqueville, motivated the cruelty of the "reign of terror."[30]

Whereas Tocqueville observed the spirits of freedom and religion in France were at war, he noted their compatibility in America. His view is confirmed by John Adams, who likewise distinguished the anti-Christian spirit of the French Revolution from the Christian influence upon the underpinnings of equality in the American regime: "If [the] empire of superstition and hypocrisy should be overthrown, happy indeed will it be for the world; but if all religion and morality should be overthrown with it, what advantage will be gained? The doctrine of human equality is founded entirely in the Christian doctrine that we are all children of the same Father, all accountable to Him for our conduct to one another, all equally bound to respect each other's love."[31]

Though he understood the contribution of religion to American public life, Tocqueville was well aware of the dangers of mixing the sacred and the secular. The bloodletting of the French Wars of Religion in the sixteenth century provided him with a ready example of state-sponsored persecution. What, then, accounted for the harmonious combination of religion and politics in America as opposed to France? How did America avoid both the wars of religion that plagued Europe for centuries, as well as the secular backlash that sought to overthrow traditional religion in the name of the new religion of humanity?

Tocqueville attributed the relative harmony between religion and democracy in America to the institution of the separation of church and state, an institution that itself can be traced to the puritan dissenter and founder of Rhode Island, Roger Williams. By preventing the state from abridging or privileging the rights of one religious sect over another, the separation of church and state was itself a condition of equality in American democratic society. It should be remembered that Charles Carroll of Maryland, signer of the Declaration and a Roman Catholic, supported the prohibition against religious tests in the Constitution not out of an antireligious spirit but because he was well aware of how state religious establishments in Britain had discriminated against Catholics, barring them from public life.[32] Tocqueville also maintained that, in addition to the separation of church and state (perhaps even because of it), religious pluralism in America further contributed to freedom on the continent.

For Tocqueville, the indirect yet essential role of religion within the context of the separation of church and state strikes the mean between the antireligious secularism of the French revolutionaries on the one hand, and the dangerous commingling of church and state under the *ancien régime* on the other (286–87). Tocqueville fully recognized that too intimate a union of religion and politics tends to undermine religion's spiritual integrity, thereby making it vulnerable to political fortunes: "As long as a religion finds its force in the sentiments, instincts, and passions that one sees reproduced in the same manner in all periods of history, it defies the effort of time, or at least it can only be destroyed by another religion. But when religion wishes to be supported by the interests of this world, it becomes almost as fragile as all the powers on earth. Alone, it can hope for immortality; bound to ephemeral powers, it follows their fortune and often falls with the passions of a day that sustain them" (285).

For Tocqueville, the mores of Christianity played a crucial role in advancing equality and liberty. Indeed, he maintains that "Christianity destroyed slavery . . . by asserting the rights of the slave" (334). He notes further that "Christianity, which has rendered all men equal before God, will not be loath to see all citizens equal before the law" (10). Perhaps because our own Civil War settled the issue, we take for granted the utter incompatibility between democracy and slavery. Yet this was not always the case. We need only to consider the existence of slavery in Athens—the cradle of democracy in the West. The city-states of Athens, Sparta, and the Roman Republic all depended upon the institution of slavery.

Significantly, both Tocqueville and Lincoln pointed to the incompatibility between the Christian view of equality that was implicit to democracy and the institution of slavery. Slavery was condemned by the liberal principle of equality, which, in turn, was based upon the Christian teaching of the dignity of free and rational beings created in the image of God. Consonant with

Tocqueville's teaching, political philosopher Maurizio Viroli notes that the confluence of Christianity and republicanism during the Middle Ages led to the first republics without slaves in the Italian city-states.[33] Viroli shows how these republics combined Christian and pagan teachings to justify their political self-determination against the absolutism of both the pope and the Holy Roman emperor.[34] Speaking of the eighteenth century, historian Mark Noll similarly notes the "unusual convergence of republicanism and Christianity in the American founding."[35]

If Christianity and slavery were so antithetical, how, then, does Tocqueville account for servitude's presence on the American continent and its subsequent justification by Southern clergymen? Why was it not extinguished prior to the nineteenth century, before the time of Lincoln and Tocqueville? In response, Tocqueville explains that, indeed, "Christianity had destroyed servitude; [but] Christians of the sixteenth century reestablished it; they nevertheless accepted it only as an exception in their social system, and they took care to restrict it to a single one of the human race. They thus made a wound in humanity less large, but infinitely more difficult to heal" (326–27). Though condemned in principle by the teachings of both republicanism and Christianity, slavery was reestablished out of greed to enrich Europe's colonial empires and excused because it was perpetrated against a particular non-European race.

Notably, Tocqueville distinguishes between ancient slavery, which was universally practiced without regard to race, and modern slavery, which was restricted to the African race and concentrated in the southern part of the New World (327). Indeed, given the "peculiar" conditions of modern slavery in America, Tocqueville prophetically warned that "The most dreadful of all evils that threaten the future of the United States arises from the presence of blacks on its soil" (326). And like Lincoln, he ironically noted the hypocrisy of Americans who preached equality but practiced slavery: "They have violated all the rights of humanity towards the black, and then they have instructed him in the worth and inviolability of these rights" (348). Indeed, this statement bears comparison to Lincoln's repeated invocation of Jefferson's warning about slavery in *Notes on the State of Virginia*: "And can the liberties of a nation be thought secure when we have removed their only firm basis, a conviction in the minds of the people that these liberties are of the gift of God? That they are not to be violated but with His wrath? Indeed I tremble for my country when I reflect that God is just."[36]

Slavery was viewed by both Tocqueville and Lincoln as an anomaly that was ultimately incompatible with the spirit of America's founding principles and culture. Tocqueville even described Southern culture as a remnant of Old World feudal aristocracy. Like the *ancien régime* in France, its mores, slavery among them, were antithetical to the burgeoning force of equality. Indeed, in *Democracy in America*, Tocqueville reserves his greatest scorn for Southerners who had revived slavery, a relic of barbarism, and thereby reversed the moral strides Western civilization had made towards equality over the past thousand years: "What is taking place in the South of the Union seems to me at once the most horrible and most natural consequences of slavery. When I see the order of nature reversed, when I hear humanity crying and struggling in vain under the laws, I avow that I cannot find the indignation to stigmatize the men of our day, authors of these outrages; but I gather all my hatred against those who, after more than a thousand years of equality, introduced servitude into the world once again" (348).

As we have seen, Tocqueville contended that "whatever the efforts of Americans of the South to preserve slavery they will not succeed at it forever." This pertained to the efforts of the Southern clergy and intellectual elite to justify the institution. Though Tocqueville clearly believed that slavery was antithetical to the moral foundations of liberal democracy, he was not sanguine about the prospects of a peaceful resolution to the problem of slavery and race in America. He foresaw a national calamity.

Tocqueville and Lincoln alike appeal to religion in perpetuating the nation's republican institutions. Tocqueville explains, "I sought the cause to which one must attribute the maintenance of America's political institutions, and religion appeared to me one of the principal ones" (*Democracy*, 518). Religion plays a crucial role for both men in restraining the excesses of democracy, particularly the tyranny of the majority. Tocqueville had famously warned:

> It is of the very essence of democratic governments that the empire of the majority is absolute; for in democracies, outside the majority there is nothing that resists it. . . . The moral empire of the majority is also founded on the principle that the interests of the greatest number ought to be preferred to those of the few. . . . The majority in the United States therefore has an immense power in fact, and a power in opinion almost as great; and once it has formed on a question, there are so to speak no obstacles that can, I shall not say stop, but even delay its advance, and allow it the time to hear the complaints of those it crushes as it passes. (235–42)

Likewise, in his Lyceum Address of 1838, Lincoln called for a "political religion" that was essential to the "perpetuation" of America's "political institutions." In this much-studied speech, he argued that the greatest threat to American self-government was internal, stemming from the Republic's own democratic excesses. After recounting examples of the "mobocratic spirit" that was sweeping the land, Lincoln explained:

> I hope I am over wary; but if I am not, there is, even now, something of ill-omen amongst us. I mean the increasing disregard for law which pervades the country; the growing disposition to substitute the wild and furious passions, in lieu of the sober judgment of the Courts; and worse than savage mobs, for the executive ministers of justice. . . . Accounts of outrages committed by mobs, form the every-day news accounts of the times. . . . Such are the effects of mob law; and such are the scenes, becoming more and more frequent in this land so lately famed for love of law and order. . . . By such examples, by instances of the perpetrators of such acts going unpunished, the lawless in spirit, are encouraged to become lawless in practice. . . . Thus, then, by the operation of this mobocratic spirit, which all must admit, is now abroad in the land, the strongest bulwark of any Government, and particularly those constituted like ours, may effectually be broken down and destroyed—I mean the *attachment* of the people.[37]

Perhaps it is no coincidence that Tocqueville's and Lincoln's reflections on tyranny of the majority are written around the same time and directed, in part, towards the same perceived threat to republican liberty—namely, Jacksonian Democracy. Consonant with the Whig political philosophy of the time, Lincoln invoked the moral restraint and sanctioning power of religion as a check upon the plebiscitarian impulses of the Jacksonian Democrats.[38]

Tocqueville's political sympathies accorded with the Whig Party as well. In *Democracy in America*, he consults the Federalist interpretation of the American Constitution as recorded by Joseph Story in his *Commentaries on the Constitution of the United States*, a work that likewise influenced the constitutional thought of Whigs like Daniel Webster and Abraham Lincoln.[39] Moreover, his scathing critique of President Jackson reads like it was written by Lincoln and the Whig Party: "General Jackson is the agent of provincial jealousies. . . . He maintains himself and prospers by flattering these passions daily. General Jackson is the slave of the majority: he follows it in its wishes, its desires, its half-uncovered instincts, or rather he divines it and runs to place himself at its head" (*Democracy*, 377–78).[40]

The parallels between Tocqueville's and Lincoln's repudiation of mob rule may also be attributed to the fact that both were lawyers, deeply committed to an ordered liberty that respected constitutional government and the rule of law.[41] To be sure, Tocqueville viewed lawyers as a semi-aristocratic class in America, one poised to restrain the tyranny of the majority. The following observations in *Democracy in America* could have been made by the young Whig and lawyer who penned the Lyceum Address: "The lawyer belongs to the people by his interest and by his birth, and to the aristocracy by his habits and his tastes; he is like a natural liaison between the two things, like the link that united them. . . . The more one reflects on what takes place in the United States, the more one feels convinced that the body of lawyers forms the most powerful and so to speak the lone counterweight to democracy in this country."[42] Indeed, Lincoln the Whig, lawyer, and statesman embodied the reconciliation between greatness and equality that Tocqueville thought was essential to the ennobling of democracy.

Notably, both Tocqueville and Lincoln regarded slavery as an expression of the unbridled tyranny of the majority. To deny the principle of consent to one group of human beings, thereby investing some human beings with absolute power over others, was despotism in whatever form it took. As a champion of ordered liberty, Tocqueville repudiated this unbounded power: "Therefore, when I see the right and the ability to do everything granted to any power whatsoever, whether it is called people, or king, democracy or aristocracy, whether it is exercised in a monarchy or in a republic, I say: there is the seed of tyranny, and I seek to go live under other laws" (*Democracy*, 241). Given the Christian teaching that humans are equally fallible and imperfect beings in comparison to Divine perfection, no one can be entrusted with absolute power. Tocqueville thus explains: "Omnipotence seems to be an evil and dangerous thing in itself. Its exercise appears to me above the strength of man, whoever he may be, and I see only God who can be omnipotent without danger, because of his wisdom" (235–42).

Lincoln similarly inveighed against the wielding of absolute power by the white majority over the black minority in his celebrated Peoria Address of October 16, 1854:

> The doctrine of self-government is right—absolutely and eternally right—but it has no just application here, as here attempted [by Douglas]. Or perhaps I should say that whether it has such just application depends upon whether a negro is *not* or *is* a man. If he is *not* a man, why in that case, he who *is* a man may, as a matter of self-government, do just as he pleases with him. But if the negro is a man, is it not to that extent a total destruction of self-government, to say that he too shall not govern *himself.* When the white man governs himself that is self-government; but when he governs himself, and also governs *another* man, that is *more* than self-government—that is despotism. If the negro is a man why then my *ancient faith* teaches me that "all men are created equal;" and that there can be no moral right in connection with one man's making a slave of another.[43]

Just as he had invoked a "political religion" in his Lyceum Address in 1838 to support the nation's republican institutions against mob rule, so in 1854 at Peoria, Lincoln appealed to the "ancient faith" of the Declaration against the threat of slavery's extension. At Peoria, Lincoln similarly traced the underlying moral justification of popular sovereignty to divine right, the very antithesis of the nation's ancient faith: "But this argument strikes me as not a little remarkable in another particular—in its strong resemblance to the old argument for the 'Divine right of Kings.' By the latter, the King is to do just as he pleases with his white subjects, being responsible to God alone. By the former the white man is to do just as he pleases with his black slaves, being responsible to God alone. The two things are precisely alike; and it is but natural that they should find similar arguments to sustain them."[44]

For his part, Tocqueville further contended that the tyranny of the majority extended its empire over the thoughts, opinions, and minds of those in a democracy: "When one comes to examine what the exercise of thought is in the United States, then one perceives very clearly to what point the power of the majority surpasses all the powers that we know in Europe" (*Democracy*, 243). He deplored the conformity of thought he found in America.

Tocqueville's concern with public opinion and its impact upon the moral character of citizens in a democracy was shared by Lincoln. Both men called for the ennobling of public opinion through the mores of religion. Indeed, Lincoln attacked popular sovereignty because it corrupted public opinion, impressing the belief upon the public mind that there was nothing morally questionable in legislating about slavery, that its rightness or wrongness was relative to the interests of the white majority:

> Now let me call your attention to one thing that has really happened, which shows this gradual and steady debauching of public opinion, this course of preparation for the revival of the slave trade, for the territorial slave code, and the new Dred Scott decision that is to carry slavery into the free States. Did you ever five years ago, hear of anybody in the world saying that the negro had no share in the Declaration of National Independence; that it did not mean negroes at all; and when "all men" were spoken of negroes were not included? . . . If you think that now, and did not think it then, the next thing that strikes me is to remark that there has been a *change* wrought in you, and a very significant change it is, being no less than changing the negro, in your estimation, from the rank of a man to that of a brute. They are taking him down, and placing him, when spoken of, among reptiles and crocodiles, as Judge Douglas himself expresses it. Is not this change wrought in your minds a very important change? *Public opinion in this country is everything.* In a nation like ours

this popular sovereignty and squatter sovereignty have already wrought a change in the public mind to the extent I have stated. There is no man in this crowd who can contradict it. (Emphasis mine)[45]

Like Tocqueville, Lincoln emphasized the reciprocity between opinions and mores in a democracy. The moral relativism of popular sovereignty was especially pernicious because it dehumanized African Americans in the public mind, stripping them of any claim to either inalienable or constitutional rights. Once widely held in a democracy where "public opinion is everything," such debauched opinions tended to acquire a spurious legitimacy and authoritativeness. The enactment of such opinions into policy only served to reinforce their authoritativeness upon the public mind.

Lincoln's political faith was not formulated as an abstract doctrine but rather as a concrete response to competing interpretations of American public life that affirmed the compatibility between slavery and democracy.[46] Though the term *political religion* made its first notable appearance in the Lyceum Address as a call for reverence for the laws against the unrestrained passions of the mob, as noted, Lincoln used comparable expressions like "the national faith," the "political faith," "the early faith of the republic," the "ancient faith of the Republic," and "those sacred principles enunciated by our fathers." The creed of this political faith was enshrined in the Declaration of Independence, which Lincoln interpreted as an American moral covenant. For Lincoln, the Declaration of Independence was, in effect, a declaration of natural law.[47] The principles of equality, liberty, and consent in the Declaration of Independence were rationally accessible to all and confirmed by God's revelation in the Bible.

Indeed, the Declaration of Independence, which Lincoln viewed as the creed of the nation's political faith, can itself be seen as an expression of the complementary spirit of religion and freedom in America described by Tocqueville. According to Lincoln, the principles of the Declaration were inspired by "truth, and justice, and mercy, and all the humane and Christian virtues."[48] The Declaration makes four references to the Divinity: "the laws of nature and of nature's God," "the Creator," "The Supreme Judge of the World," and "Divine Providence." These various references were broad enough to accommodate the beliefs of those who subscribed to the rational religion of the Enlightenment and to those who held more traditional views about the Deity. In America, unlike France, the Enlightenment rationalism of Thomas Jefferson and Benjamin Franklin blended with the more traditional faith in the providential God of Israel to justify the Revolution on moral grounds, thereby confirming Tocqueville's observations.[49] Indeed, the following statement by Benjamin Rush to Thomas Jefferson in 1800 is exemplary of the Christian republicanism of the American founding, which was clearly described by Tocqueville and reaffirmed by Lincoln: "I have always considered Christianity as the *strong ground* of republicanism. The spirit is opposed, not only to the splendor, but even to the very forms of monarchy, and many of its precepts have for their objects republican liberty and equality as well as simplicity, integrity, and economy in government."[50]

In the allegorical drama of Lincoln's political faith, the subjugation of the thirteen colonies under England corresponded to the servitude of the Hebrew tribes under Egypt; the American people, whom Lincoln ironically referred to as God's "almost chosen people," represented the Jews, God's chosen people. The divine rights of kings symbolized Pharaoh's claim to mastery over the Israelites. The Founders collectively played the role of Moses, the deliverer of his people from slavery and their lawgiver, who established a more perfect union among the Hebrew tribes. The Declaration and its affirmation of equality represented an American Decalogue, or Ten Commandments, the moral covenant handed down from God promulgating the basic principles of the nation's political faith. The Fourth of July symbolized an American Passover, a sacred day of political renewal. The challenge of proslavery theology was tantamount to an idolatry, forsaking the ancient faith of the Fathers for divine right. Lincoln thus represented the nation's prophet and its political savior—the preacher of his nation's political faith who called his errant people back to their ancestral ways.[51]

As we have seen, Tocqueville emphasized that slavery was "attacked by Christianity" and was incompatible with its egalitarian teaching, despite efforts to justify the "peculiar institution" as ordained of God.[52] The fact that the Bible was exploited by proslavery theologians did not lead Lincoln to repudiate its moral authority. Rather, he observed that Scripture itself warns against the twisting of the word for evil purposes. In a letter to a Baptist group, dated May 30, 1864, he compared the Southern clergy's manipulation of the Bible to Satan's exploitation of scripture to tempt Jesus Christ: "When a year or two ago, those professedly holy men of the South, met in semblance of prayer and devotion, and . . . appealed to the Christian world to aid them in doing to a whole race of men, *as they would have no man do unto themselves* [Matthew 7:12], to my thinking, they contemned and insulted God and His church, far more than did Satan when he tempted the Savior with the kingdoms of the earth. The devil's attempt was no more false and far less hypocritical."[53]

Lincoln's allusion to Matthew 4:1–11 would have been clear to the Bible-reading public in nineteenth-century America. Just as Jesus exposed Satan's manipulative efforts as sophistry and offered an alternative interpretation that was true in both letter and spirit, Lincoln implies, so Northerners must recognize the sophistry of proslavery and do the same. In sum, Lincoln upholds the moral authority of scripture, while at the same time warning against its abuse. It would be hard to find a more cogent teaching on the use and abuse of the Bible in politics in American history.

Lincoln's case against slavery appealed to the following teachings from the Bible: the message that "man [was] created in the image of God" (Genesis 1:26–27); the "Great Commandment" to "love one's neighbor as oneself" (Matthew 22:37–40); the Golden Rule "to do unto others" as one would want to be treated (Matthew 7:12); and God's command that "In the sweat of thy face thou shalt eat bread" (Genesis 3:19).[54] More specifically, Lincoln invoked the passage in Genesis when he declared that "nothing stamped with the Divine image and likeness was sent into the world to be trodden on, and degraded, and imbruted by its fellows."[55] The self-evident truth of human equality was based on the Christian teaching of the dignity of all human beings. Lincoln alluded to the "Great Commandment" in Matthew 22 when he stated that "'Give to him that is needy' is the Christian rule of charity; but Take from him that is needy is the rule of slavery."[56] He appealed to the Golden Rule of Matthew 7 when he warned, "This is a world of compensations; and he who would be no slave, must consent to have no slave. Those who deny freedom to others, deserve it not for themselves; and under a just God, can not long retain it."[57] Indeed, his terse definition of democracy, "As I would not be a slave, so I would not be a master," was itself an expression of the Golden Rule.[58]

Perhaps the biblical passage that Lincoln cited most against slavery was Genesis 3:19: "As Labor is the common burthen of our race so the effort of some to shift their share of the burthen on to the shoulders of others, is the great, durable, curse of the race." Richard Carwardine has explained that, based upon this precept, Lincoln developed a "theology of labor," whereby God ordained "the burden of work, the individual's duty to engage in it, and the moral right to enjoy the fruits of his labor."[59]

Though there are remarkable parallels between the views of Tocqueville and Lincoln on the contribution of religion to American public life, there are some interesting divergences as well.[60] First, Tocqueville does not explicitly point to the Declaration as the creed of the nation's political faith, as Lincoln does. Instead, he emphasizes the role of religion as an intermediary institution between the individual and the state. Second, Tocqueville focuses much more upon the dangers of materialism and individualism than Lincoln does. He fears that democratic citizens will no longer strive for greatness but will retreat increasingly into a private, solitary life of creature comforts. Americans have an inordinate taste for "material well being." Third, Tocqueville underscores the tension between freedom and equality more than Lincoln. Notwithstanding their mutual repudiation of mob rule, Tocqueville highlights the dangers of equality to freedom more than Lincoln.

Are these differences irreconcilable? Perhaps they can be attributed to the different roles that each played in confronting the promise and perils of American democracy. As a leader who faced the concrete challenge of slavery and disunion, it would have been absurd, if not cruel, for Lincoln as a leader to discourse on the future dangers of materialism when he was striving to extend equality to large segments of the population who had been shut out of the American dream. Furthermore, to say that Lincoln emphasized a common political creed based on the ancient faith of the Declaration is not to say that he ignored or rejected the role of religious communities as intermediary institutions in shaping democratic mores. Indeed, as Richard Carwardine has noted, Lincoln and the Republican Party's success depended, in part, upon their mobilization and support of America's Protestant religious communities.[61] To be sure, Lincoln's many proclamations of days of prayer and fasting were an accommodation to the faith of the various religious communities and to the crucial role they played in American public life.[62] Finally, as James Oakes shows in his essay in this volume, Lincoln was by no means blind to the greedy materialism implicit to the American dream. Rather, his critique of American greed was focused on the concrete debate over the right to property in a slave. In sum, the differences between the two are therefore not necessarily contradictions but may be differences in emphasis and context that express valid concerns from the particular standpoint of an outside commentator versus an inside participant. We would do well to pay attention to the concerns of both sages.

In conclusion, what lessons do these two teachers of democracy offer for our own time? Tocqueville's and Lincoln's views of the compatibility of religion and democracy in America present challenges to both sides in the "culture war." They challenge those secularists who make war on religion, seeking to drive it out of public life, and those religious zealots whose triumphalism blinds them to the limits of politics by confounding the sacred with the secular. Given Tocqueville's diagnosis of the antireligious spirit of his time, he would perhaps not be surprised by European efforts to expunge all reference to Christianity in the E.U. constitution. By so doing, he would remind them, they are undermining the moral grounding of the liberal values they purport to uphold.[63] The transcendent value of free, self-governing individuals who are equal in both their dignity and depravity was a profound revelation and development in Western civilization derived from Christianity. Tocqueville envisions Christianity as providing a dual role in democracy: it morally underpins the very idea of equal rights and liberty; and it enlarges and ennobles citizens by calling them to duties beyond themselves. Given religion's role in restraining some of democracy's more dangerous tendencies, like tyranny of the majority and materialism, he declares, "one must maintain Christianity within the new democracies at all cost" (*Democracy*, 521). Based on what he had experienced in France and what he had seen in America, Tocqueville further cautioned, "Therefore when any religion whatsoever has cast deep roots within a democracy, guard against shaking it; but rather preserve it carefully as the most precious inheritance from aristocratic centuries; do not seek to tear men from their old religious opinions to substitute new ones, for fear that, in the passage from one faith to another, the soul finding itself for a moment empty of belief, the love of material enjoyments will come to spread through it and fill it entirely." (519).

Despite the loud voices of those on the political extremes, the teachings of Tocqueville and Lincoln on religion and politics are recognized by both sides of the political spectrum in the United States. For example, in *God's Politics*, Jim Wallis convincingly dispels the myth that conservatives have a "monopoly" on religion in American public life.[64] Moreover, in his most recent book, *Consumed*, liberal progressive Benjamin R. Barber reiterates Tocqueville's call for religion as a restraint upon the unbridled materialism and consumerism that is corrupting our democratic culture and government: "Religion may be the sector with the most potential for resistance from the outside to the infantilist ethos and its consumer culture. Despite America's deep engagement in consumerism and the materialist ethos it entails Americans remain the most religious people in the developed world."[65]

To acknowledge the contribution of Christianity to American democracy is not to embrace theocracy or to exclude other religions from the pluralism affirmed and cherished by our regime. Ecclesiastical power in politics is incompatible with the spirit of American liberalism and dangerous to the integrity of both the sacred and secular, as Tocqueville well recognized and explained. Though Lincoln's political faith draws deeply upon the teachings of Christianity and the Bible for confirmation, it is translated into the common language of reason within the context of the separation of church and state.[66] It may therefore be accepted by all religious groups who acknowledge the authority of reason. As Mark Noll has shown in his essay in this volume, Lincoln's view of the compatibility between faith and reason was consistent with the theological trends of the nineteenth century. Lincoln's political faith is not a substitute for religion; rather, it publicly articulates the minimum, moral consensus required to sustain a liberal order. The success of the American experiment in pluralism has been the extent to which various sects and ethnic groups have accepted and assimilated the American creed. No less a liberal progressive and stalwart defender of pluralism than Barber states, "When civic identity is local and embedded in a long civic tradition and the patriotic trappings of a civil religion (e.g., the Declaration of Independence, the Constitution, the Gettysburg Address, the Emancipation Proclamation, Martin Luther King's "I have a Dream" speech), it can at least begin to provide an approximation of a social glue that holds a citizenry together."[67]

Yet implicit to the freedom and pluralism of liberal democracy is the danger (also foreseen by Tocqueville) that religion will become corrupted by the materialistic values of the regime, thereby losing its vitality as an ennobling and restraining force. Another potential danger stems from the threat of a religious extremism that repudiates liberalism altogether and the Christian civilization that gave rise to it. The liberal pretense of moral neutrality is philosophically mute and incoherent before such a challenge to its core principles. In response, Lincoln and Tocqueville provide us with articulate and defensible voices that acknowledge the positive contribution of religion to American public life in the context of the separation of church and state.

Notes

The author would like to thank Angelo Valente for his clerical assistance in the preparation of this chapter.

1. Alexis de Tocqueville, *Democracy in America*, ed. and trans. Harvey C. Mansfield and Delba Winthrop (Chicago: University of Chicago Press, 2000), xvii. Hereafter cited in text and notes as *Democracy*.

2. I explore Lincoln's political faith as a combination of reason, revelation, and republicanism in *Abraham Lincoln's Political Faith* (DeKalb: Northern Illinois University Press, 2003).

3. I have found Carson Holloway's book *The Right Darwin? Evolution, Religion, and the Future of Democracy* (Dallas: Spence Publishing, 2006) especially helpful and enriching. This work provides a Tocquevillian defense of religion in

American public life and a critique of current Darwinian theories of morality that seek to replace it. Also see Bruce Frohnen, *Virtue and the Promise of Conservatism: The Legacy of Burke and Tocqueville* (Lawrence: University Press of Kansas, 1993); Peter Augustine Lawler, *The Restless Mind* (Lanham, Md.: Rowman and Littlefield, 1993); Doris S. Goldstein, *Trial of Faith: Religion and Politics in Lincoln's Thought* (New York: Elsevier, 1975); Sanford Kessler, *Tocqueville's Civil Religion: American Christianity and the Prospects for Freedom* (Albany: State University of New York Press, 1994).

4. Peter Lawler, "Alexis de Tocqueville," in *An Invitation to Political Thought*, ed. Kenneth L. Deutsch and Joseph R. Fornieri (Belmont, Calif.: Wadsworth-Thomson, 2008).

5. Tocqueville states:

> There is in fact a manly and legitimate passion for equality that incites men to want all to be strong and esteemed. This passion tends to elevate the small to the rank of the great; but one also encounters a depraved taste for equality in the human heart that brings the weak to want to draw the strong to their level and that reduces men to preferring equality in servitude to inequality in freedom. It is not that peoples whose social state is democratic naturally scorn freedom; on the contrary, they have an instinctive taste for it. But freedom is not the principal and continuous object of their desire; what they love with an eternal love is equality; they dash toward freedom with a rapid impulse and sudden efforts, and if they miss the goal they resign themselves; but nothing can satisfy them without equality, and they would sooner consent to perish than lose it.

6. Tocqueville states, "In the heart of the township one sees a real, active, altogether democratic and republican political life reigning. The colonies still recognize the supremacy of the metropolis; monarchy is the law of the state, but a republic is already very much alive in the township" (40).

7. Mark A. Noll, *America's God* (Oxford: Oxford University Press, 2002); Sidney E Ahlstrom, *A Religious History of the American People* (New Haven: Yale University Press, 1972), 70–165; Perry Miller, *Errand into the Wilderness* (Cambridge: Harvard University Press, 1956); David Gelernter, *Americanism: The Fourth Great American Religion* (New York: Doubleday, 2007).

8. See: Dr. Ezra Stile's election sermon, "The United States Elevated to Glory and Honor" (May 8, 1783), http://www.belcherfoundation.org/united_states_elevated.htm (accessed April 15, 2008).

9. See John P. Diggins, *The Lost Soul of American Politics: Virtue, Self-Interest, and the Foundations of Liberalism* (New York: Basic Books, 1984).

10. Douglas L. Wilson, *Lincoln's Sword: The Presidency and the Power of Words* (New York: Knopf, 2006), 100.

11. William D. Pederson, "The Impact of Abraham Lincoln's Constitutional Legacy: A Global Outlook.," Twenty-sixth annual Gerald McMurty Lecture,

Lincoln Lore, no. 1885 (Summer 2006): 18–22; Joseph R. Fornieri, "The Global Significance of Abraham Lincoln's Mission," *International Abraham Lincoln Journal* 2 (2001): 1–26.

12. Abraham Lincoln, "Message to Congress in Special Session (July 4, 1861), in *The Collected Works of Abraham Lincoln*, ed. Roy P. Basler, 9 vols., hereafter referred to as *Collected Works* (New Brunswick, N.J.: Rutgers University Press, 1953–55), 4:426–27.

13. Abraham Lincoln, "Annual Message to Congress" (Dec. 1, 1862), in *Collected Works*, 5:537.

14. Alexis de Tocqueville, *The Old Regime and the French Revolution*, trans. by Stuart Gilbert (New York: Doubleday, 1983).

15. Richard J. Neuhaus, *The Naked Public Square: Religion and Democracy in America* (Grand Rapids, Mich.: William B. Eerdmans, 1986).

16. Tocqueville, *Old Regime*, 156.

17. Ibid.

18. Ibid., 160.

19. David Walsh, *The Growth of the Liberal Soul* (Columbia: University of Missouri Press, 1997), 190.

20. Albert Camus, *The Rebel: An Essay on Man and Revolt,* ed. Anthony Bower (1951; reprint, New York: Vintage Books, 1992), 112–64.

21. James Madison, Alexander Hamilton, and John Jay, *Federalist Papers*, No. 51, ed. Clinton Rossiter, introd. and notes by Charles R. Kesler (New York: Mentor, 1999), 290.

22. Abraham Lincoln, "Seventh and Last Debate with Stephen A. Douglas at Alton, Illinois" (October 15, 1858), in *Collected Works*, 3:310.

23. For a discussion of Lincoln and the virtue of prudence, see Joseph R. Fornieri, *The Language of Liberty: The Political Speeches and Writings of Abraham Lincoln* (Washington, D.C.: Regnery, 2003); and Ethan Fishman, "Under the Circumstances: Abraham Lincoln and Classical Prudence," in *Abraham Lincoln: Sources and Styles of Leadership*, ed. Frank J. Williams, William D. Pederson, and Vincent J. Marsala (Westport, Conn.: Greenwood, 1994).

24. Abraham Lincoln, "Temperance Address" (February 22, 1842), in *Collected Works*, 1:278.

25. Abraham Lincoln, "Speech at Peoria, Illinois" (October 16, 1854), in ibid., 2:255.

26. Abraham Lincoln, "Speech at Hartford, Connecticut" (March 5, 1860), in ibid., 4:9.

27. Abraham Lincoln, "Response to a Serenade, (November 10, 1864), in ibid., 8:101.

28. Abraham Lincoln, "Second Inaugural Address" (March 4, 1865), in ibid., 8:333.

29. See Ronald C. White Jr., *Lincoln's Greatest Speech* (New York: Simon and Schuster, 2003).

30. See Reinhold Niebuhr, "The Religion of Abraham Lincoln," in *Lincoln's American Dream*, ed. Kenneth L. Deutsch and Joseph R. Fornieri (Washington, D.C.: Potomac Books, 2005); and Noll, *America's God.*

31. Adams quoted in David McCullough, *John Adams* (New York: Simon and Schuster, 2001), 619.

32. A. James Reichley, *Religion in American Public Life* (Washington, D.C.: Brookings Institution, 1985), 112–13.

33. Maurizio Viroli, *Republicanism,* trans. Antony Suggar (Vancouver: Douglas and McIntyre, 2002), 25–26.

34. Maurizio Viroli, *Machiavelli* (New York: Oxford University Press, 1998), 21–24.

35. Noll, *America's God,* 57, 73–92.

36. Thomas Jefferson, *The Life and Selected Writings of Thomas Jefferson*, ed. Adrienne Koch and William Peden (1944; reprint, New York: Modern Library, 1993), 257–58.

37. Abraham Lincoln, "Address before the Young Men's Lyceum of Springfield, Illinois" (January 27, 1838), in *Collected Works,* 1:109.

38. See Stewart Winger, *Lincoln, Religion, and Romantic Cultural Politics* (DeKalb: Northern Illinois University Press, 2003).

39. See Tocqueville, *Democracy in America*, 105–6, 112, 113, 130, 134, 136, 138, 259, 323.

40. For an analysis of the Whigs, see Michael Holt, *The Rise and Fall of the American Whig Party: Jacksonian Politics and the Onset of the Civil War* (New York: Oxford University Press, 1999).

41. Brian Dirck, *Lincoln the Lawyer* (Urbana: University of Illinois Press, 2007); Mark Steiner, *An Honest Calling: The Law Practice of Abraham Lincoln* (DeKalb: Northern Illinois University Press, 2006). See also the essays by Herman Belz and Frank J. Williams in this volume.

42. I leave it to the reader to decide whether Tocqueville's description of lawyers is still apt today. See also *Collected Works*, 3:220, 410.

43. Abraham Lincoln, "Speech at Peoria, Illinois" (October 16, 1854), in *Collected Works,* 2:265–66. Emphasis mine.

44. Ibid., 2:278.

45. Abraham Lincoln, "Speech at Columbus, Ohio" (September 16, 1859), in *Collected Works,* 3:423–24.

46. Fornieri, *Abraham Lincoln's Political Faith*, 70–91.

47. Joseph R. Fornieri, "Lincoln, the Natural Law, and Prudence," in *Language of Liberty*, xix–lxiii. Also see Harry V. Jaffa, *A New Birth of Freedom: Abraham Lincoln and the Coming of the Civil War* (Lanham, Md.: Rowman and Littlefield, 2000), 509.

48. Abraham Lincoln, "Speech at Lewistown, Illinois" (August 17, 1858), in *Collected Works*, 2:544–47. Also cited in Richard J. Carwardine, *Lincoln: Profiles in Power* (London: Pearson and Longman, 2003), 81–83.

49. I agree with Noll (*America's God*, 211), who explains that American political thought in the early nineteenth century blended elements of what we now call liberalism and republicanism, and that a rigid distinction between these two traditions would have been alien to the Founders. "Once it is understood that America's increasing liberalism did not necessarily obliterate a broad commitment to republican values—in other words, that a simple antithesis between republicanism and liberalism is a modern construct rather than a historical reality—much else becomes clear about the early national period. Americans of almost all political convictions did embrace stronger notions of individual rights, and most of them also wanted to see the powers of government limited to one degree or the other. But these commitments did not represent a repudiation of the republican heritage of the Revolutionary era."

50. Rush quoted in Noll, *America's God*, 65.

51. Lucas Morel, *Lincoln's Sacred Effort: Defining Religion's Role in American Self-Government* (Lanham, MD.: Lexington Books, 2000).

52. Frederick A. Ross, *Slavery Ordained of God* (1857; reprint, Miami: Mnemosyne, 1969). For Lincoln's reply to Ross and proslavery theology, see Fornieri, *Abraham Lincoln's Political Faith*, 70–91.

53. Lincoln to George B. Ide, James R. Doolittle, and A. Hubble, May 30, 1864, in *Collected Works*, 7:368.

54. I have summarized this argument in the introduction to Deutsch and Fornieri, *Lincoln's American Dream*, 25–32, though it is worth repeating in this context.

55. Abraham Lincoln, "Speech at Lewistown, Illinois" (August 17, 1858), in *Collected Works*, 2:544–47.

56. Abraham Lincoln, "Fragment on Pro-Slavery Theology" (October 1, 1858), in ibid., 3:204–5.

57. Abraham Lincoln to Henry L. Pierce and others, April 6, 1859, in ibid., 3:376.

58. Abraham Lincoln, "Definition of Democracy" (August 1, 1858), in ibid., 2:532.

59. Carwardine, *Lincoln*, 38.

60. Though well worth pursuing, a more detailed analysis of these differences is beyond the scope of this essay, which focuses upon the similarities between their view of the compatibility between religion and democracy in American public life. For a fine essay that compares and contrasts Lincoln and Tocqueville on Democratic leadership, see Brian Danoff, "Lincoln and Tocqueville on Democratic Leadership and Self-Interest Properly Understood," in *Review of Politics* 67 (2005): 687–719.

61. Carwardine *Lincoln*, 124–30, 271.

62. See Morel, *Lincoln's Sacred Effort*.

63. Walsh, *Growth of the Liberal Soul*, 13–45.

64. Jim Wallis, *God's Politics: Why the Right Gets It Wrong and the Left Doesn't Get It* (San Francisco: HarperSanFrancisco, 2005).

65. Benjamin R.Barber, *Consumed: How Markets Corrupt Children, Infantilize Adults, and Swallow Citizens Whole* (New York: Norton, 2007), 315.

66. Fornieri, *Abraham Lincoln's Political Faith*, 37–69, 92–131. Also see Harry V. Jaffa, *Crisis of the House Divided: An Interpretation of the Issues in the Lincoln-Douglas Debates* (Garden City, N.Y.: Doubleday, 1959); and Hadley Arkes, *First Things: An Inquiry into the First Principles of Morals and Justice* (Princeton, N.J.: Princeton University Press, 1986).

67. Barber, *Consumed*, 334–35.

3

Schooling in Lincoln's America and Lincoln's Extraordinary Self-Schooling

Myron Marty

Abraham Lincoln's climb to the peak of what Kenneth J. Winkle calls the "occupational ladder" characteristic of nineteenth-century Illinois shows that, from early in life, he was a person to be reckoned with. At age twenty-two, after living and working as a farmer, he served a stint as a flatboatman on the Mississippi River. He was also a miller and a store clerk at that age. At age twenty-eight, he was officially enrolled as an attorney by the clerk of the Illinois Supreme Court. In overlapping episodes along the way, he was also a militia captain, a merchant, a postmaster, a surveyor, and a legislator.[1] Schooling played a part in his climb, of course, but he aptly referred to it on one occasion as "defective." It was something he and his peers got "by littles."[2]

From the mid-1830s through the 1850s, while engaging in systematic self-schooling, Lincoln made a name for himself in the Illinois legislature and his law practice. By 1859, he was attracting attention beyond Illinois, and that year he sent a sketch of his life to Jesse W. Fell, secretary of the Illinois Republican state central committee, who had requested it on behalf of a Pennsylvania newspaper. "There is not much of it," Lincoln wrote, "for the reason, I suppose, that there is not much of me." Here is how he recalled his schooling on this occasion:

> My father, at the death of his father, was but six years of age; and he grew up, literally without education. He removed from Kentucky to what is now Spencer county, Indiana, in my eighth year. We reached our new home about the time the State came into the Union. It was a wild region, with many bears and other wild animals, still in the woods. There I grew up. There were some schools, so called; but no qualification was ever

required of a teacher beyond "readin, writin, and cipherin," to the Rule of Three. If a straggler supposed to understand latin happened to sojourn in the neighborhood, he was looked upon as a wizzard [*sic*]. There was absolutely nothing to excite ambition for education. Of course when I came of age I did not know much. . . . The little advance I now have upon this store of education, I have picked up from time to time under the pressure of necessity.

Whatever the newspaper wrote about him, Lincoln suggested, should be modest, in keeping with the modesty of his sketch, although incorporating material from his speeches would be acceptable.[3]

By June 1860, Lincoln and others were contemplating the possibility that he might be chosen as the Republican Party's candidate for president that year, and, as he was relatively unknown beyond Illinois, it was natural for prospective biographers to pursue him for information. He evidently prepared a form letter to be sent by his secretary, John G. Nicolay, to such persons stating that "applications of this class are so numerous that it is simply impossible for him to attend to them." Nonetheless, he recognized the need for a campaign biography, and when John L. Scripps, a writer for the *Chicago Press and Tribune,* sought his assistance in preparing *Life of Abraham Lincoln,* he responded. Writing in the third person, he was again self-effacing about his schooling: "A. now thinks that the aggregate of all his schooling did not amount to one year. He was never in a college or Academy as a student; and never inside of a college or academy building till since he had a law license. What he has in the way of education he has picked up."[4]

Admire as we must Lincoln's intellect and accomplishments, his meager schooling notwithstanding, it is useful to recall that other middle-aged men in his times, particularly those reared in the rural South and Midwest, could have described their schooling in similar terms. Not that their parents and communities discounted the need for learning. In fact, they encouraged it, particularly in families, as learning on countless matters was passed on from generation to generation. Learning occurred also in workplaces, whether on farms or through apprenticeships in the shops of the towns and cities, and in churches. And schools had always been a part of American life.

In pre-Revolutionary America, schools were typically church-sponsored or otherwise privately operated. Attendance was voluntary, as was the financial support on which they depended. In these schools, as well as in homes, the most commonly used book was *The New England Primer*, a ninety-page reader published initially in 1690 and eventually printed in all thirteen colonies. Perhaps as many as two million copies were sold. Many of its religious maxims, reflecting Puritan perspectives, were drawn from the King James translation of the Bible. Although it was eventually displaced, *The New England Primer* established precedents for later textbooks.

Sentiment for public support for schools late in the eighteenth century resulted in a key provision of the Land Ordinance of 1785, the law that laid the foundation for landownership in the Great Lakes region. The land was to be divided into townships six miles square, with revenue produced by one of the thirty-six sections in each township to be reserved for the maintenance of public schools.[5] The Northwest Ordinance enacted two years later provided for the formation of five states in this region, their governance, and their projected admission to the United States.

This laid a promising foundation, but it applied only to Northern states. More was required, as Thomas Jefferson, then in retirement, stated in a proposal to Virginia's governor, John Tyler, in 1810: "I have indeed two great measures at heart, without which no republic can maintain itself in strength: 1. That of general education, to enable every man to judge for himself what will secure or endanger his freedom. 2. To divide every county into hundreds, of such size that all the children of each will be within reach of a central school in it. . . . Every hundred, besides a school, should have a justice of the peace, a constable and a captain of militia. . . . These little republics would be the main strength of the great one."[6]

Jefferson's proposal seems to have had little traceable effect, but whatever the reason, common schools appeared in many locales. According to Louis Warren, when Lincoln was five years old his mother, Nancy Hanks Lincoln, taught him letters, perhaps preparing him to attend school, although her reading and writing abilities, if any, were limited.[7] Lincoln, then living in rural Kentucky, attended school for a short period in the fall of 1815, when he was six, and similarly the following autumn. Around then his father, Thomas Lincoln, beset by problems with titles to land he had purchased, moved his family to Perry County (later Spencer County) in Indiana, where landownership was more secure and the Northwest Ordinance proscribed slavery.

In 1818, three months after Abraham Lincoln's mother's died, his father married Sarah Bush Johnston. His stepmother encouraged young Lincoln's learning and nourished his ambitions. In the early 1820s, while helping his father with farming and working as a hired hand for neighbors, he attended school in several brief periods. These were no doubt "subscription schools," with the teachers being paid by their pupils' parents in skins or farm produce.[8]

At home, reading the family Bible contributed to Lincoln's learning, as did reading borrowed books with titles that were familiar in such schools as existed in those years and probably in those Lincoln attended, including, among others: *The Life and Memorable Actions of George Washington,* a fanciful work by Parson Mason Locke Weems; Noah Webster's *American Spelling Book* (known as the "Blue-Backed Speller"); Daniel Defoe's *Robinson Crusoe*; *Aesop's Fables*; John Bunyan's *Pilgrim's Progress*; William Grimshaw's *History of the United States*; James Riley's *Narratives*; Nicolas Pike's *A New and Complete System of Arithmetic*; Murray Lindley's *The English Reader*; books of hymns and spiritual songs by Isaac Watts and Starke Dupuy; and most significant for Lincoln's literary future, Thomas Dilworth's *Spelling Book.*[9]

Abundant legends surround Lincoln's learning in his childhood and youthful years, but the extent of his schooling and precisely what he read and when he read it is uncertain. Yet, as Douglas Wilson has remarked, "the Lincoln of history, insofar as can be determined from the testimony of those who knew him, proves in many respects worthy of the legend."[10] That Lincoln was a voracious reader with a remarkable capacity for absorption and that in these years he laid the groundwork for his later self-education are beyond question.

As Lincoln entered adulthood, so, in a sense, did America. By 1830, schools of some sort were available to most white children in the North, less so in the South. In rural areas, according to Carl Kaestle, schools had not changed much since 1780.[11] The growth of cities between 1830 and 1860 persuaded many that free public schools were essential. In those three decades, the population in America's ten largest cities increased from fewer than 600,000 to approximately 2,700,000.

The arrival of immigrants also pointed to the need for publicly supported schools. In the 1830s, about 600,000 men, women, and children came to America from other countries; in the 1840s, more than 1,700,000; and in the 1850s, the number rose to nearly 2,600,000. Many were attracted by what they believed was America's promise, but others fled circumstances in their homelands—the famine caused by the potato blight in Ireland in 1847, for example, and the revolutions of 1848 that spread across Europe. Between 1847 and 1854, the immigrant total reached about 2,675,000.[12]

Horace Mann (1796–1859) and Henry Barnard (1811–1900) were among the leaders in efforts to create common schools that were intended to educate all children at public expense. Their vision for establishing common schools in their respective states, Massachusetts and Connecticut, called for local and state governments to share responsibility for the operation and financing of schools, the certification of teachers, and various other reforms, such as requiring attendance and placing children in graded classrooms. Their states established standards in the common-school movement, and their efforts were gradually emulated in other states.

It must be noted, of course, that the movement to establish free public schools was not driven strictly by the desire to help children learn. Additionally, and perhaps most compellingly, schools were seen as instruments of social control. Reformers believed that schools provided a means of quelling discontent among those who saw old ways of life changing and of coping with immigrants uncertain about how to make their way in the new land. Not least in importance, schools were expected to provide workers for the growing industries.

It is also important to note that the efforts to establish free, publicly supported schools met with fierce opposition. Lawrence Cremin, the preeminent historian of American education, described the situation in *The Transformation of the School*:

> The fight for free schools was a bitter one, and for twenty-five years the outcome was uncertain. Local elections were fought, won, and lost on the school issue. . . . Legislation passed one year was sometimes repealed the next. State laws requiring public schools were ignored by the local communities that were supposed to build them. Time and again the partisans of popular education encountered the bitter disappointments that accompany any effort at fundamental social reform.
> Yet by 1860 a design had begun to appear, and it bore the marks of Mann's ideal.[13]

Another complicating factor arose from Mann's determination that common schools should be nonsectarian—this at a time when religious revivals spurred the evangelizing efforts of sectarian Christians. His challenge was to demonstrate that *nonsectarian* did not mean *anti-Christian*. That the materials used by evangelicals in their schools were largely the same as those in common schools minimized the differences that might have thrown barriers on the path of the common-school movement.

One additional consideration in Mann's school-reform efforts merits mention: Despite his progressive views on "the woman question," he seems to have made little effort to engage women in his cause. In commenting on this, Cremin notes the involvement of women in reforming women's education—Emma Willard, Sarah and Angelina Grimké, Sarah Josepha Hale, and Catherine Beecher, for example. Maybe, Cremin speculates, Mann was guided by a simple prudence that made him "loath to raise questions that might have endangered the fragile coalition he had put together in favor of the schools."[14]

Learning materials in the common schools would be required, of course, and a measure of standardization was considered desirable. Both were introduced with the publication in 1836 of the first two in a series of texts known as the McGuffey Eclectic Readers. Like *The New England Primer,* these books, begun under the guidance of William Holmes McGuffey (1800–1873), stressed citizenship and morality and reflected religious influences. As the number of volumes in the series grew to six, they gained sufficient popularity to result in sales of more than one hundred million copies before the end of the century. Another widely used book was Noah Webster's *The American Spelling Book: Containing an Easy Standard for Pronunciation*, published in 1783 and republished many times in subsequent years.

Ripple effects of urbanization were slow in reaching rural areas, particularly in the South, but as movement of the population, including immigrants, to the West from Eastern states accelerated, the new settlements also faced the challenge of creating publicly supported schools. Andrew Gulliford provides a good summary of the situations prevailing there. School terms, he wrote, varied from a few weeks to a few months. If a traveling schoolteacher failed to appear, a widow or young woman took charge of the teaching. Revenues from land grants for schools were sequestered by state treasurers, leaving parents with the challenge of providing for their children's schooling. Teachers' salaries depended on the wealth and stability of the families supporting the local schools. Because rural schools were often isolated, they failed to attract qualified teachers and were forced to accept, in some instances, unqualified ones who "simply perpetuated the narrow beliefs and ignorance of the community." The schools were frequently overcrowded, short on learning materials, and subject to the whims of parsimonious school boards for their maintenance. The teaching method was rote recitation and memorization.[15]

This brief history of schooling in the first half of the nineteenth century confirms that, for his times, Lincoln's schooling was much like that of other children in similar circumstances. How then to explain his extraordinary learning? Honest teachers are well aware that, if teaching means *making* students learn something, it is nearly impossible for one person to teach another anything. Perhaps Lincoln benefited from not having ineffective teachers stand in his way. Moreover, learning theorists have shown that there are different modes of learning and that matching teachers' styles and students' modes of learning is problematic. Facing this reality, what teachers *can* do is to make it possible for their students to learn in the modes best suited to them and to provide inspiration, discipline, examples, and learning materials. When students' intrinsic inspiration and discipline move them to learn, and when learning materials are available, they can do as Lincoln did after his childhood years, that is, educate themselves.

Indeed, if Lincoln had been asked to name his best teacher, his response might well have been the same as Frank Lloyd Wright's when someone posed that question for him: "I will have to give that honor to myself." Here is how Lincoln described his continuing education in the autobiographical sketch cited earlier: "After he was twenty-three and had separated from his father, he studied English grammar, imperfectly of course, but so as to speak and write as well as he now does. He studied and nearly mastered the six books of Euclid since he was a member of Congress. He regrets his want of education, and does what he can to supply the want."[16]

We can be cautiously specific about some experiences in Lincoln's education, despite the paucity of verifiable records. How he mastered the English language, for example, can be inferred from the texts he used for that purpose. In his school days, and perhaps later while living in New Salem, he studied Thomas Dilworth's *A New Guide to the English Tongue*, published initially in England in 1740. This compact book taught its users how to spell by having them progress from single-syllable words to those with five syllables. This established a general pattern, observed in other parts of the book, of progression from the elementary to the more complex. It also advised readers on matters of punctuation, accent, parts of speech, syntax, analogy, comparison, abbreviations, and the effective use of monosyllabic words, as well as on spelling proper names. It included rules of grammar, pronunciation, and debate, and it provided materials for practice in oration, mainly in the form of forty-two admonitions for upright living, most of them with reference to teachings from Christianity; for example, number 12: "Gold, tho' the noblest of Metals, loseth its Lustre when continually worn in the same Purse with Copper, or Brass; and the best Men, by associating themselves with the Wicked, are often corrupted with their Sins, and partake of their Punishments." Dilworth's book concluded with thirty-six "sentences in verse"; a dozen brief fables, with interpretations; and a number of prayers for public and private uses.[17]

Another source in Lincoln's self-education, for which Dilworth prepared him very well, was William Scott's *Lessons in Elocution*. Advice he found there is evident in his speeches, as they demonstrated the importance of speaking distinctly and deliberately and pronouncing words boldly and forcibly and with propriety and elegance. "An insipid flatness," Scott wrote, "is almost the universal fault in reading, and even public speakers often suffer their words to drop from their lips with such a faint and feeble utterance, that they appear neither to understand or feel what they say themselves, nor to have any desire that it should be understood or felt by their audience. This is a fundamental fault; a speaker without energy is a lifeless statue." Also important were acquiring "a compass and variety in the Height of [one's] voice"; accenting words properly; distinguishing in every sentence the more significant words "by a natural, forcible, and varied emphasis"; accompanying emotions and passions with corresponding tones, looks, and gestures; and acquiring a variety of pause and cadence.

The lessons included 120 passages from literature for practice in reading and 57 from sermons, speeches, and soliloquies, including a goodly number from Shakespeare, for practice in speaking. Additionally, Scott gave detailed instructions, with illustrations, on how orators can appear to be at ease, and he suggested specific practices in the art of gesture. Through the years, Lincoln, reflecting his genius for absorbing and retaining lessons like Scott's, became an expert practitioner in this art, and those who saw his long sweeping arms and other body movements as they emphasized the words he was speaking were treated to experiences denied those who simply read his speeches.[18]

Lincoln also studied grammar, devoting himself to a book by Samuel Kirkham, published in an eleventh edition in 1829. The title page reveals the book's comprehensive contents:

English Grammar
in
Familiar Lectures;
Accompanied by
a Compendium
Embracing
A New Systematic Order of Parsing
a New System of Punctuation,
Exercises in False Syntax,
and
A System of Philosophical Grammar,
in Notes:
to which are added,
An appendix and a Key to the exercises,
Designed
for the Use of Schools and Private Learners.
By Samuel Kirkham
Stereotype Edition
New York:

Collins & Brother,
254 Pearl Street

Some methods, Kirkham said, "require the teacher to *interrogate* the pupil as he proceeds; or else he is permitted to parse without giving any explanations at all." Others, he continued, "hint that the learner ought to apply definitions in a general way, but they lay down no systematic arrangement of questions as his guide." By contrast, the "*systematic* order laid down in this work, if pursued by the pupil, compels him to apply every definition and every rule that appertains to each word he parses without having a question put to him by the teacher. . . . This course enables the learner to proceed independently . . . [and] obviates the necessity of pursuing . . . a stupid course of drudgery; for the young beginner who pursues it, will have, in a few weeks all the most important definitions and rules perfectly committed, simply by applying them in parsing." Several pages later, Kirkham concedes that it might be possible to acquire "that knowledge of language which will enable him to avoid those glaring errors that offend the ear by perusing good authors and conversing with learned persons," but he insists that other errors, equally gross, can only be detected by those who have a knowledge of the rules they violate.[19]

Kirkham's *Grammar* is a well-designed labyrinth of lectures, explanations, definitions of countless grammatical terms, exercises, examples, rules, and more rules. It would have taken dedication indeed to work one's way through its twists and turns, but those who mastered it no doubt had a grasp of grammar that few could match.

Lincoln's self-education did not end, of course, with Dilworth, Scott, and Kirkham. Fortunately, New Salem gave him opportunities to further the intellectual development that would be needed to move up the occupational ladder. In 1831, shortly after Lincoln arrived in town, James Rutledge, one of New Salem's founders, organized the New Salem Debating Society. This provided a forum for debating issues in religion, philosophy, and literature. Before long, Lincoln, who from childhood had aspired to be a speaker, was given a chance to speak before members of this society. Rutledge noted that in his first speech Lincoln pursued the question being debated "with reason and argument so pithy and forcible that all were amazed."[20]

Meanwhile, a movement known as the National American Lyceum spread from New England into many other states and became a contributor to the education of adults. A local lyceum would host guest lecturers and also invite members to speak. In 1833 some of Lincoln's friends and associates founded the Springfield Young Men's Lyceum.[21] It is likely that Lincoln joined soon after moving to Springfield on April 15, 1837. On January 27, 1838, he presented a speech titled "The Perpetuation of Our Political Institutions," described by Mark Neely as "a young lawyer's call for orderly procedures in an unruly republic and as the classic document of Lincoln's early intellectual style, before he became an impassioned political foe of slavery."[22]

While his liberal learning would prove immensely valuable in his eventual political career, Lincoln needed knowledge and skills that would equip him for earning a living. So, in 1833, when John Calhoun, surveyor of Sangamon County, offered to make him deputy surveyor in his part of the county, as he recalled in the third-person, autobiographical sketch sent to John L. Scripps in 1860, "He accepted, procured a compass and chain, studied Flint, and Gibson a little, and went at it. This procured bread, and kept body and soul together."[23]

Lincoln's approach to acquiring practical knowledge in the art of surveying exemplifies how he advanced himself: He borrowed books and studied them. He may have received some assistance from Mentor Graham, a marginally qualified teacher in the area, but mostly he was on his own. The "Flint" he referred to was a compilation of information and guidance titled *System of Geometry and Trigonometry, together with a Treatise on Surveying.* The compiler, Abel Flint, designed his book to equip surveyors with the expertise in mathematics that the art of surveying requires. On page 26, readers begin to learn about logarithms; then come lessons in geometry and trigonometry. After detailed descriptions of the tools and practices of surveying, there are an appendix and 137 pages of tables.[24]

Robert Gibson's *The Theory and Practice of Surveying: Containing all the Instructions Requisite for the Skillful Practice of This Art* is larger, longer, and more substantial than Flint's compilation. It almost *had* to be that to justify the boast in its title. Here, too, exercises in mathematics are the starting point, with sections on decimal fractions, logarithms, geometry, and trigonometry. Lengthy treatises on instruments and methods of surveying follow, and the book concludes with several hundred pages of tables.[25]

M. L. Houser, who devoted his life to identifying books that played a part in Lincoln's learning, speculated that Lincoln had been tutored in these two popular books in Indiana by James Blair and that his studying "Flint and Gibson a little" in 1833 amounted to reviewing his earlier experiences with them. Houser suggested "that a person who examined the 750 pages . . . in these two books, and then supposed that any young man who was unacquainted with the subjects discussed, could master them 'in six weeks,' would be, at the least, a liberal supposer."[26]

Lincoln's climb up the occupational ladder continued in 1834. He described it briefly in the autobiography he wrote for Scripps:

> The election of 1834 came, and he was then elected to the Legislature by the highest vote cast for any candidate. Major John T. Stuart, then in full practice of the law, was also elected. During the canvass, in a private conversation he encouraged A. [to] study law. After the election he borrowed books of Stuart, took them home with him, and went at it in good earnest. He studied with nobody. He still mixed in the surveying to pay board and clothing bills. When the Legislature met, the law books were dropped, but were taken up again at the end of the session. He was reelected in 1836, 1838, and 1840. In the autumn of 1836 he obtained a law licence, and on April 15, 1837 removed to Springfield and commenced the practice, his old friend, Stuart taking him into partnership.[27]

That he "studied with nobody" set Lincoln apart from his contemporaries, many of whom had some college education or had attended law school. Unlike them, as well, according to his partner William Herndon, he "was never a law clerk for any man in the law business in Springfield or elsewhere." Rather, said his friend Joshua Speed, Lincoln read books at "his humble home on the banks of the Sangamon, without a preceptor or fellow student."[28]

There are differing accounts concerning the books Lincoln used at the beginning of his studies in the law. David Turnham, an Indiana friend and neighbor, claimed that he lent Lincoln *The Statutes of Indiana* and that Lincoln "fairly devoured the book in his eager efforts to abstract the store of knowledge that lay between the lids." This, he said, "led Abe to think of the law as his calling in maturer years." Lincoln's cousin, the often-unreliable Dennis Hanks, said that he had bought this volume and "from that [Lincoln] Lerned the principles of Law and allso My self."[29] For more systematic study of the law, Lincoln's first books were Sir William Blackstone's *Commentaries* (five volumes), which had notes of reference to the Constitution and laws of the federal government of the United States and of the Commonwealth of Virginia. There are different versions of how he acquired the *Commentaries*, but he most likely bought them at a sheriff's auction.

Lincoln's advice to an inquirer regarding "the best mode of obtaining a thorough knowledge of the law" no doubt reflects what he had done: "The mode is very simple, though laborious and tedious. It is only to get the books, and read, and study them carefully. Begin with Blackstone's Commentaries, and after reading it carefully through, say twice, take up Chitty's Pleading, Greenleaf's Evidence, & Story's Equity &c. in succession.

Work, work, work, is the main thing."[30] To another acquaintance, who had apparently asked him to be an instructor for a law student, he wrote that what the young man should do is "read the books for himself without an instructor . . . get a license, and go to the practice, and still keep reading." That, he said was the "cheapest, quickest, and best way" for the young man "to make a lawyer of himself."[31]

Lincoln's contemporaries recalled that when he lived in New Salem he seemed to read all the time, often aloud, sometimes when walking the streets. He read, among others, Shakespeare, Robert Burns, and Alexander Pope. His interest in Thomas Paine's *Age of Reason* and Constantin de Volney's *The Ruins: A Survey of the Revolutions of France,* fed the belief of his critics that he was a religious skeptic.[32] A number of historians have compiled lists of books Lincoln is presumed to have owned or read. Some show the books checked out of the Library of Congress in his name. However, evidence concerning what he actually read is scant.[33]

Any uncertainties about such things notwithstanding, it is obvious that the mature Lincoln, his own best student, had made himself a bona fide intellectual, a man of ideas, equipped with deep and profound learning in literature, history, philosophy, and science, as well as in practical matters. Allen Guelzo, in *Abraham Lincoln: Redeemer President,* describes Lincoln's grasp of the powerful currents of religion, philosophy, and political economy that shaped the outcome of the Civil War. Lincoln, he says, absorbed and assimilated the ideas of classical liberalism, the Enlightenment, Victorian skepticism, and Calvinist spirituality. Perhaps that blend is what kept him from making a commitment to Christianity, despite the earnest efforts of clergymen in his acquaintance to entice him to do so.[34]

What did the self-taught Lincoln do for subsequent generations, particularly those who lacked the intrinsic motivations, the self-discipline, and the intellectual gifts that had enabled him to be his own teacher? How did he help those who required education in formal settings? In his first run for office, on March 9, 1832, just after his twenty-third birthday, one of the twelve paragraphs in a document he apparently distributed as a handbill in Sangamon County stated his commitment to education:

> Upon the subject of education, not presuming to dictate any plan or system respecting it, I can only say that I view it as the most important subject which we as a people can be engaged in. That every man may receive at least, a moderate education, and thereby be enabled to read the histories of his own and other countries, by which he may duly appreciate the value of our free institutions, appears to be an object of vital

importance. . . . For my part, I desire to see the time when education, and by its means, morality, sobriety, enterprise and industry, shall become much more general than at present, and should be gratified to have it in my power to contribute something to the advancement of any measure which might have a tendency to accelerate the happy period.[35]

This time his bid for office was unsuccessful, but he had opportunities to honor his commitment later. In the Illinois legislature, however, he rarely provided leadership on matters concerning education, and Paul Simon, who studied closely Lincoln's years there, concluded, "Somewhat surprisingly, Lincoln's record in the field of education was not particularly good."[36]

During his presidency, there were only two significant actions affecting education, but both were highly significant. The first was the Morrill Act of 1862, perhaps the most important legislative act in support of education ever passed. It provided for the granting of some thirteen million acres of the public domain to the states for establishing mechanical and agricultural colleges. Since then, the act has been expanded, and there are now more than one hundred land grant colleges and universities, with at least one in each state, one in the District of Columbia, and four in territories.[37] Lincoln apparently paid little attention to the Morrill Act and did not mention it in his annual message to Congress. "There was some ambiguity," says Phillip Paludan, "about formal education in a man who had had little of it himself."[38] That ambiguity, however, did not prevent him from enrolling his eldest son, Robert Todd Lincoln, at Harvard.

The second action was the Emancipation Proclamation. Although education was not its initial purpose, it was a first step toward granting educational opportunities to African Americans. In *Forever Free: The Story of Emancipation and Reconstruction,* Eric Foner quotes a member of a North Carolina education society established by former slaves as saying that he thought "a school-house would be the first proof of *independence.*" His white contemporaries were astonished by the freedmen's "avidity for learning," as they flocked to schools created by Northern missionary societies, the Freedmen's Bureau, and their own initiative.[39]

Regrettably, the desires of former slaves to advance themselves through education were successfully thwarted by their former owners and by indifference elsewhere. Consequently, the dreams of the freedmen were deferred too long and inexcusably, but they could not be denied forever. Today, sixteen of the institutions enjoying land grant status are historically black, and other land grant institutions that excluded the descendants of slaves for almost a century no longer do so.

In the post-Lincoln years of the nineteenth century, the common-school movement continued to evolve along the lines established by midcentury. By then, amid battles over school funding and other issues, according to Lawrence Cremin, a majority of states had established public school systems.[40] At least half the children of school age were getting some formal education. The school systems continued to adapt to the ongoing challenges of urban growth resulting from industrialization and immigration. More than fourteen million immigrants arrived during the decades 1860 to 1900.[41]

But by the late 1870s, reformers were calling for change. Styling themselves progressives, they sought, according to Cremin, to broaden the programs and functions of schools to encompass concerns for health, vocation, and the quality of family and community life; to apply in the classroom pedagogical principles derived from research in psychology and the social sciences; to tailor instruction to the changing school populations; and to democratize culture without vulgarizing it.[42] Debates over these matters remained unsettled for decades. Also in these years, some reformers began to advocate programs of vocational education in the school—the subject of heated debates that continued well into the twentieth century.

As for Lincoln, his self-education continued throughout his life. During the Civil War, as commander-in-chief, he studied manuals on military matters, but he learned mainly by trial and error, prompting this perceptive judgment by Woodrow Wilson: "[Lincoln] was not fit to be President until he actually became President. He was fit then because, learning everything as he went, he had found out how much there was to learn, and had still an infinite capacity for learning. . . . Lincoln was always a-making, he would have died unfinished if the terrible storms of war had not stung him to learn in those four years what no other twenty could have taught him."[43]

Had he lived in the postwar years, his learning in other areas would no doubt have followed patterns established earlier in his life. What he might have done to provide school-based education for others in the Reconstruction years and after is impossible to say.

Notes

1. Kenneth J. Winkle, *The Young Eagle* (Dallas: Taylor, 2001), 121–22.
2. *The Collected Works of Abraham Lincoln*, ed. Roy P. Basler, 9 vols., hereafter referred to as *Collected Works* (New Brunswick, N.J.: Rutgers University Press, 1953–55), 2:459 (June [15?] 1858), 4:62 (c. June 1860). For a searchable on-line edition of the *Collected Works*, see http://www.hti.umich.edu/l/lincoln/ (accessed February 20, 2007).

3. *Collected Works,* 3:511 (December 20, 1859). This is the sort of self-derogation that apparently influenced Richard Hofstadter's interpretation of Lincoln in "Abraham Lincoln and the Self-Made Myth," in *The American Political Tradition* (New York: Knopf, 1948), 92–134. His depiction of Lincoln as a slick politician and expert propagandist has been largely discredited.

4. *Collected Works,* 4:62 (c. June 1860).

5. Indiana Historical Bureau, http://www.statelib.lib.in.us/www/ihb/resources/docldord.html (accessed February 20, 2007).

6. Thomas Jefferson, *Writings* (New York: Library of America, 1984), 1226–27. Jefferson had more ideas on schooling. In an 1813 letter to John Adams, Jefferson called for a bill to promote "a more general diffusion of learning." From free schools in each region, the best students would be selected to "receive at the public expense a higher degree of education at a district school"; the most promising ones could then complete their education at a university. Jefferson to Adams, October 28, 1813, in Lester J. Cappon, ed., *The Adams-Jefferson Letters: The Complete Correspondence between Thomas Jefferson and Abigail and John Adams* (1959; reprint, Chapel Hill: University of North Carolina Press, 1987), 390.

7. Louis A. Warren, *Lincoln's Youth: Indiana Years, Seven to Twenty-one, 1816–1830* (Indianapolis: Indiana Historical Society Press), 10. Albert Beveridge wrote that Nancy Hanks Lincoln was "absolutely illiterate," in *Abraham Lincoln, 1809–1858,* vol. 1 (Boston and New York: Houghton Mifflin, 1928), 16.

8. Beveridge, *Abraham Lincoln,* 55. A number of books attempt to identify schools Lincoln attended and describe his experiences there. See, e.g., William H. Herndon and Jesse W. Weik, *Herndon's Lincoln,* ed. Douglas L. Wilson and Rodney O. Davis (Urbana and Chicago: University of Illinois Press, 2006), 33–41.

9. Don Fehrenbacher provides a succinct chronology of these years in *Abraham Lincoln: Speeches and Writings, 1859–1865* (New York: Library of America, 1989), 703–4. See also Warren, *Lincoln's Youth* for more chronological data. For Herndon's interviews with Lincoln's contemporaries who mention books that Lincoln studied, see Douglas L. Wilson and Rodney O. Davis, eds., *Herndon's Informants: Letters, Interviews, and Statements about Abraham Lincoln* (Urbana and Chicago: University of Illinois Press, 1998), 105, 109, 112, 121.

10. Douglas L. Wilson, *Honor's Voice: The Transformation of Abraham Lincoln* (New York: Knopf, 1998), 54.

11. Carl F. Kaestle, *Pillars of the Republic: Common Schools and American Society, 1780–1860* (New York: Hill and Wang, 1983), 22, 60.

12. Senate documents, 61st Cong., 3rd sess., December 5, 1910–March 4, 1911, p. 14, http://www.uscis.gov/graphics/shared/aboutus/statistics/IMM03yrbk/IMM2003list.htm (accessed February 20, 2007).

13. Lawrence A. Cremin, *The Transformation of the School: Progressivism in American Education, 1876–1957* (New York: Knopf, 1968), 13.

14. Lawrence A. Cremin, *American Education: The National Experience, 1783–1876* (New York: Harper and Row, 1980), 142–43.

15. Andrew Gulliford, *America's Country Schools* (Washington, D.C.: Preservation Press, 1984), 38–39.

16. *Collected Works*, 4:62 (c. June 1860).

17. Thomas Dilworth, *A New Guide to the English Tongue*, 13th ed. (Leeds, U.K.: Scholars' Facsimiles and Reprints, 1967), 128–29. Apparently no copies of the first through the fourth editions of this book have survived; copies of the fifth and eighth editions (1744 and 1746) exist in imperfect condition. The publisher estimates that at least a million copies of the more than one hundred editions were printed before 1800.

18. William Scott, *Lessons in Elocution: or, A Selection of Pieces in Prose and Verse for the Improvement of Youth in Reading and Speaking* (Boston: Isaiah Thomas, June 1811), 47, 50, 53–55.

19. Samuel Kirkham, *English Grammar* (New York: Collins & Brother, 1829), 11, 14.

20. Benjamin P. Thomas, *Lincoln's New Salem* (Springfield, Ill.: Abraham Lincoln Association, 1934), 29 (organization of the Society), 47 (Rutledge quotation).

21. Winkle, *Young Eagle*, 181.

22. Mark E. Neely Jr., *The Abraham Lincoln Encyclopedia* (New York: McGraw-Hill, 1982), 198.

23. *Collected Works*, 4:65 (c. June 1860).

24. Abel Flint, ed., *System of Geometry and Trigonometry, together with a Treatise on Surveying*, 5th ed., with additions by George Gillet (Hartford: Oliver Cooke, 1825). Which edition Lincoln used is uncertain.

25. Robert Gibson, *The Theory and Practice of Surveying: Containing All the Instructions Requisite for the Skillful Practice of This Art* (New York: Evert Duychunck, 1821).

26. M. L. Houser, *Lincoln's Education and Other Essays* (New York: Bookman Associates, 1957), 70.

27. *Collected Works*, 4:65 (c. June 1860). In fact, Lincoln had received the second-highest number of votes in the 1834 election, fourteen behind the leader.

28. Speed and Herndon quoted in Mark E. Steiner, *An Honest Calling: The Law Practice of Abraham Lincoln* (DeKalb: Northern Illinois University Press, 2006), 31.

29. David C. Mearns, "Mr. Lincoln and the Books He Read," in *Three Presidents and Their Books* (Urbana: University of Illinois Press, 1955), 58–59; Herndon and Weik, *Herndon's Lincoln*, 42;. Wilson and Davis, *Herndon's Informants*, 773. John Nicolay, in *A Short Life of Abraham Lincoln* (New York: Century, 1903), 14, says that Turnham was a constable who allowed Lincoln to come to his home to study this book.

30. *Collected Works*, 4:121 (September 25, 1860).

31. Ibid., 2:344 (December 2, 1857).

32. Wilson, *Honor's Voice*, 53–85.

33. Louis A. Warren, author of *Lincoln's Youth*, cited earlier, was the founding editor of *Lincoln Lore*, in which role he published a number of issues on Lincoln and books, listed here by number and year of publication: 71, 76, 80 (1930); 129 (1931); 167 (1932); 511 (1939); 567 (1940); 619, 622, 629, 634, 647 (1941); 769 (1944); 908, 909 (1946); 1073 (1949); 1190 (1952). See also Houser, *Lincoln's Education*; Mearns, *Three Presidents*. Also see Rufus Rockwell Wilson, *What Lincoln Read* (Washington, D.C.: Pioneer Publishing, 1932).

34. See Allen C. Guelzo, *Abraham Lincoln: Redeemer President* (Grand Rapids, Mich.: William B. Eerdmans, 1999), especially 18–21 and 461–63.

35. *Collected Works*, 1:8.

36. Paul Simon, *Lincoln's Preparation for Greatness: The Illinois Legislature Years* (Urbana and Chicago: University of Illinois Press, 1971), 277.

37. Answers.com, http://www.answers.com/topic/morrill-land-grant-colleges-act (accessed February 20, 2007).

38. Phillip Shaw Paludan, *The Presidency of Abraham Lincoln* (Lawrence: University Press of Kansas, 1994), 135.

39. Eric Foner, *Forever Free: The Story of Emancipation and Reconstruction* (New York: Knopf, 2005), 88–89.

40. Cremin, *Transformation of the School*, 13.

41. Senate documents, 61st Cong., 3rd sess., December 5, 1910–March 4, 1911, p. 14.

42. Cremin, *Transformation of the School*, viii–ix.

43. Quoted by Louis Warren, *Lincoln Lore*, no. 908 (September 2, 1946).

4

American Religion, 1809–1865

Mark Noll

The two specifically historical questions required for treating the subject of this chapter are, first, what was the nature of Abraham Lincoln's own religion? And, second, how did Lincoln's personal religion reflect (or stand out from) what was characteristic of American religion during his era more generally? Answering these already knotty questions is made more difficult because of another persistent question that has been anything but historical: how can Lincoln's life, including his religion, be useful for advancing political or ideological purposes today? As William Miller once put it, "the topic of Lincoln's religious views is caught in a great tug-of-war of interpretation because of the immense value he represents in the wars of culture."[1] Thankfully, careful research by a host of outstanding historians has made progress possible on the first two questions without becoming overly entangled in the third.

On Lincoln's own religion, historically considered, widely separated pioneering efforts by William Barton and David Hein set a promising course, defined by careful verification of Lincoln's purported words and deeds joined with sensitive attention to the contexts within which the words were uttered and the deeds took place.[2] Painstaking efforts to separate myths, which almost always serve present-day ideological purposes, from plausibly verified reality have recently helped greatly in the search for Lincoln's faith.[3] The result has been a flourishing of reliable writing on Lincoln's religion that, while it has not resolved all conundrums, has made possible a much clearer picture than before.[4] A review of the well-grounded picture of Lincoln's own religion leads naturally into the more complex question of how Lincoln's faith related to the general religious situation in the United

States. In that broader perspective, Lincoln's religion was still distinctive, but not because of any particular trait that differed greatly from what his peers believed and practiced, or because he was so exemplary in excelling the religious norms of his day. Rather, it was the way Lincoln combined ordinary beliefs and practices that made him unusual in his own day and an object of great religious interest (with controversy) in the years after he passed from the scene.

The Religion of Abraham Lincoln

Lincoln's earliest religious influences were evangelical, Calvinist, and strongly sectarian. During his youth in Kentucky and Indiana, he heard a great deal of Calvinist Baptist preaching at the churches his parents attended—in fact, several contending subvarieties of Calvinist Baptist preaching.[5] The dominant theme in the theology of these churches was God's sovereign control over every human life and for every human eventuality (including eternal salvation or damnation). Almost as strong in these Baptist churches was an emphasis on congregational autonomy, which grew out of a lively Dissenting Protestant rejection of control by historical precedents, outside denominational influences, or any kind of authority except local approval. When Lincoln moved to New Salem, he experienced a different manifestation of democratized religion in the clamor of competing Protestant preachers. In a strange way, he seems to have both absorbed and been repelled by these early influences.

In New Salem, Lincoln expressed heretical religious beliefs, as defined by most of the period's Christian churches. His views then included, at least, a belief in the universal salvation of all people, which represented a serious heresy by Protestant (or Catholic) standards of the time. At most, he may have followed the religious writings of Tom Paine and other avatars of Enlightenment rationalism, to the point of speaking publicly about the unreliability of the Bible. Witnesses credibly reported some continued expression of such skeptical views during Lincoln's early years in Springfield, where he removed in 1837. But at some relatively early point in his Springfield years, Lincoln began to keep his religious opinions to himself, though considerable dispute exists as to why he did so—whether from a desire not to offend more orthodox clients and voters or from an actual change of heart.

In 1846, and for the only time in his life, Lincoln wrote about his faith directly when supporters of his opponent in a race for Congress, the Methodist circuit-rider Peter Cartwright, accused him of religious infidelity. The handbill that Lincoln produced in response contained these carefully chosen but noncommittal words: "That I am not a member of any Christian Church, is true; but I have never denied the truth of the Scriptures; and I have never spoken with intentional disrespect of religion in general, or of any denomination of Christians in particular."[6]

After the death of the their sons (Eddie, nearly age four, in 1850; Willie, age eleven, in 1862), Abraham and Mary Lincoln were comforted by two Old School Presbyterian ministers. Among Presbyterians, the Old School party was more firmly committed to the denomination's traditional teachings on predestination than the New School, but those views were expressed with more education and more logical sophistication than the Baptists' predestinarian teaching of Lincoln's youth. James Smith of Springfield's First Presbyterian Church and Phineas D. Gurley of the New York Avenue Presbyterian Church in Washington may have read more into Lincoln's behavior than was actually there, but both were also probably on solid ground when they testified that, after these traumatic experiences, they witnessed a deepening of Lincoln's faith.[7]

In Washington, especially after the death of Willie, Lincoln regularly attended Gurley's church, perhaps even the midweek prayer service (though, if he did so, he remained in a side room, out of view of the congregation). At the same time, Lincoln did not live an overtly pious life. Thus, for example, although he abstained from drink and tobacco along with many of the era's evangelical Protestants, he kept his religious views to himself and never hid his love of the theater, of sometimes ribald verbal horseplay, and of other frivolities frowned upon by most evangelical leaders. To a European audience in the summer of 1865, the immigrant Swiss theologian and historian Philip Schaff needed to defend his own high praise for Lincoln, since "the pious folk in America were upset that Abraham Lincoln was shot in a theater, the pious of Germany that he was shot on Good Friday in a theater."[8]

Throughout his White House years, Lincoln's religious practice was reserved. Yet it does seem that he eventually expressed a belief in the value of prayer. On more than one occasion, he told the story of the Quaker women who were discussing the outcome of the war. "I think," said the first, "Jefferson [Davis] will succeed." The second asked, "Why does thee think so?" The reply came, "Because Jefferson is a praying man." "And so is Abraham a praying man," was the immediate rejoinder. "Yes," said the first, "but the Lord will think Abraham is only joking."[9] The witticism was poignant, because it reflected a truth. Many instances are recorded in diaries and letters, written before Lincoln's death, where the president either allowed White House visitors to pray with him or actually solicited their prayers. There are also several accounts, though less securely based and usually written down after 1865, that record Lincoln himself praying.

Well-considered documentary evidence offers solid support for the conclusion that Lincoln's personal faith evolved over time. However much he took in from the Calvinist Baptist beliefs of his own family, he clearly gave up conventional views to embrace advanced opinions during his years in New Salem. But by the time Lincoln married in 1842, his religion had become a much more private affair. Later in the 1850s, and especially during his years as president, he seems to have moved closer to orthodoxy. On the subject of "Lincoln's religion," in other words, it makes a considerable difference when and under what circumstances Lincoln made any particular affirmation of religious belief or unbelief.

The exact nature of Lincoln's religious evolution remains a matter of scholarly dispute. Differences center on the character of Lincoln's belief in Providence. As Allen Guelzo frames one possible answer: "Especially for those who had not known Lincoln before the war, Lincoln's comfortable resort to biblical language made it easy to impute some form of piety to him. . . . But he never spoke, in the language of evangelical Christianity, of Jesus as *my* Savior, and his repertoire of biblical citations was more a cultural habit rather than a religious one. . . . He remained a Victorian child of the Enlightenment, of Paine and Burns and Mill . . . , the Enlightenment [that] could nestle quite comfortably inside the hollow shell of Lincoln's ancestral Calvinism."[10] Among those who are convinced that more change had taken place are scholars like Richard Carwardine: "Lincoln avoided complete immersion in [the] evangelical waters swirling around him, but under the pressure of wartime events he was without doubt swept along to a new religious understanding, one much closer to the historic Calvinism that had profoundly shaped most northern Protestantism."[11] Conflicting opinions from such genuine experts make it necessary to speak with nuance, as, for example, Mary Todd Lincoln did shortly after her husband's death, when she affirmed that he was "a religious man always" but not "a technical Christian."[12]

If the precise shape of Lincoln's own religion must remain a mystery, more than enough has been reliably documented about its component parts to probe the question of how Lincoln's faith was situated in the cauldron of religious excitements that the nation experienced in its early decades.

The Religion of Lincoln's America

The years of Lincoln's life came very near to defining a specific era in American religious history. When he was born in 1809, the emerging character of the new nation's main religious trajectory was just coming into view. That trajectory was Protestant, but also democratic and tending toward the sectarian, rather than establishmentarian and dominated by the churchly, as had been the case in the colonial era. The nation's religion was strongly evangelical and Trinitarian, not rationalist or Unitarian, even though the religious views of the nation's main Founding Fathers had been closer to the latter than the former. Most remarkably, by the year of Lincoln's birth, evangelical Protestantism was growing rapidly both in numbers and as a force of cultural influence, despite the fact that into the 1790s, church attendance was continuing a long decline and the cultural impact of religion was decidedly shrinking in comparison to the influence of political and economic forces.

For the duration of Lincoln's life, characteristics prominent in the rising evangelical tide dominated the nation's religion. That religion was Protestant, as defined first by Methodists, Baptists, and Disciples—with strong intellectual and cultural influences also from Presbyterians and Congregationalists. It was evangelical in stressing personal conversion and personal piety. It was biblical, often under the slogan "the Bible alone," as opposed to traditional or hierarchical. It was also revivalistic, activistic, democratic, and republican.

The close of Lincoln's life—coinciding as it did with the close of the Civil War—marked the end of this religious era. Revivalistic evangelicalism would remain important in the country, but several new developments sharply reduced its dominance as a shaper of national culture. In the first instance, the Civil War spotlighted a glaring weakness in the religious norm that had guided the creation of antebellum civilization. The weakness was unresolved scriptural arguments over slavery, with the white South using the Bible to defend slavery, the abolitionist North using the same book to attack slavery, and much of the nonabolitionist white North vacillating on how to interpret the Scriptures. The uncertainty of the scriptural voice on the nation's greatest political controversy, followed soon thereafter by the rise of modern universities, with their more secular approaches to the ancient world, undercut the evangelical reliance on "the Bible alone" that had been such a major feature of American culture during Lincoln's lifetime.

In addition, demographic changes altered the nation's religious culture, with the rapid growth of Lutherans, Catholics, Jews, and nonbelievers undercutting the dominance of British-origin evangelicals. Furthermore, trust in science, reliance on industrial expansion, and the new civil religion sparked by efforts at reconciling North and South edged aside the nation's earlier, more evangelical understanding of Providence. In a word, after the Civil War most evangelicals remained revivalistic, democratic, and republican, but because the war and its aftermath reconstructed so much of American society, the meanings that evangelicals gave to democracy, republicanism, and social activism exerted reduced influence in the country as a whole. Abraham Lincoln's lifetime, in other words, defined a religious era. A sketch outlining how that era took shape makes it possible to see how Lincoln's religion related to his American times and places.

During the 1780s and 1790s, religion in the new United States existed in a state of confusing transition. The colonies' one total religious system, New England Puritanism, survived only in institutional fragments (especially the Congregational churches) and general intellectual influences (especially the moral significance ascribed to corporate national life). Puritanism's integrative force had been destroyed by the pietism of revival, which stressed personal faith over the corporate, and by the secularization of the Revolution, which stressed political action over divine commands. The main colonial alternative to Puritanism—church-state Anglicanism in the South—was even more thoroughly discredited through its association with the repudiated rule of king and parliament. In general, the War for Independence and the confusing years immediately after the war seriously disoriented or discredited the denominations that had been the main bearers of religion in the colonial era. To be sure, local religious revivals promoted by evangelical Protestants were taking place at many locations throughout the 1770s and 1780s, but these revivals were still marginal affairs. They were located on the frontiers, actively engaged African Americans, spread via Methodist itinerancy, and responded to Baptist lay preachers—in every case, that is, far from the new country's geographical or social centers of power.[13]

From this shaky situation there followed an explosion of religion, especially of evangelical Protestant religion. No other period of American history has ever witnessed such a dramatic rise in religious adherence as took place from 1800 to 1860. In no other period did main religious habits break so directly with what had gone before. In no other period has there been such a radical upsetting of the main assumptions about how to organize and practice religious faith.[14]

Between 1790 and 1860, the United States population increased eightfold; the number of Baptist churches, fourteenfold; the number of Methodist churches, twenty-eight-fold; and the change in the number of Disciples or Restorationist churches cannot be expressed as a ratio, since there were none of these churches in 1790 and more than two thousand in 1860. More generally, religion into the mid-nineteenth century remained overwhelmingly Protestant, and Protestant of British origin. The 1860 census reported that there were seventy-seven places of Jewish worship in the United States, which represented a doubling from only ten years earlier. The number of Roman Catholic places of worship had risen even faster, from about twelve hundred in 1850 to more than twenty-five hundred in 1860. But still the nation's formal religious life was dominated by Protestants: more than 83 percent of the value of church property, more than 92 percent of the seating accommodations in houses of worship, and more than 95 percent of the churches themselves (about fifty thousand of them). For an even sharper picture, the main families of Baptists, Congregationalists, Methodists, and Presbyterians—that is, the largest representation of evangelical, British-descended Protestantism—accounted for about 55 percent of the value of all church property, nearly 72 percent of all the seats available in churches, and almost 75 percent of the churches themselves.[15] Pluralism, both intra-Christian and among religions more generally, was definitely on the rise in 1860. But the reality on the ground in most regions of the country was still overwhelmingly Protestant, and Protestant of a readily identifiable, evangelical type.

Expectations in the early years of national history, and from some of the wisest Americans of that era, highlight how different the American religion that actually came into existence was from what had gone before. During the early days of the Continental Congress, the Baptist leader Isaac Backus came to Philadelphia to complain about the hypocrisy of Massachusetts in protesting against "enslavement" by Parliament when Massachusetts itself was persecuting Baptists and other Protestant Dissenters. In response to this complaint, John Adams told Backus that Massachusetts's establishment of religion was, in fact, very light; moreover, in Adams's view, it was more likely that the sun would not rise than that Massachusetts would ever give up the establishment of religion.[16]

Other expectations of what religion would look like in the new republic included the prediction, welcomed by Thomas Jefferson but decried as a catastrophe by Jefferson's religious opponents, that the United States would come to favor the rational, Enlightened, and ameliorative faith in Unitarianism. As late as 1822, Jefferson wrote a young friend that he expected some form of Unitarianism to be the dominant religion in the United States.[17] That prospect, which so encouraged Jefferson, was anathema to his foes, but many of them thought that it just might happen, as testified to by the religious militancy of their fierce opposition to Jefferson in the presidential election of 1800.[18]

For their part, many leaders of the Congregational and Presbyterian denominations expressed the confidence that some form of established or quasi-established Calvinist faith would continue to exert preeminent religious influence over the new republic. They were not entirely wrong, especially since American higher education continued to be conducted as primarily a Presbyterian or Congregational enterprise until the late nineteenth century. But the idea that the nation as a whole would be docilely led by Presbyterian Princeton, Congregationalist Yale, or Middlebury College, Union College, Transylvania University, the University of North Carolina, or the many other colleges founded more or less as Reformed Protestant academies—that idea was a fantasy.

What the creation of such colleges did reveal, however, was something very important about the nation's early intellectual history. The political ideology and religious tendencies that rejected the authority of inherited, assigned, or conferred status did not reject the authority of reason. The new colleges featured varieties of the era's Scottish and English moral philosophy in which a high value was placed on thought—but thought democratized and individualized. In this conception, each responsible white male adult shared God's gift of physical and moral perception that allowed him to grasp the basic character of scientific and ethical realities (in the new American polity, democratization had not yet extended to women or minority races). Belief in such "common sense" extended well beyond the colleges, however, and was in fact the common possession of almost all literate Americans. And on this key point, it is significant to note that the era of political and religious democratization was also the era of publishing democratization—with a vast expansion in the production of books, journals, and newspapers attending Lincoln's earlier years and beyond. This expansion, it is also important to realize, was led by a great outpouring of religious print.[19]

The American believers during the nation's early decades who expressed the fewest explicit plans for the religious future of the United States were those most consumed by the religious present. Methodists under the leadership of Francis Asbury, Baptists under the leadership (then as now) of no one person in particular, Disciples and Christians responding to the appeals of Thomas Campbell and Barton Stone were busy from the 1780s and became even busier after the turn of the new century. But they were busy in pursuit of specifically religious goals. Their concern was to preach the gospel, seek the salvation of souls, organize small groups and congregations, impress the need for discipline on families, recruit young men (and a few young women) willing to exhaust their lives as itinerants, and publish as much effective devotional literature as they could to inspire their loosely bound networks. For some Baptists and the Methodists, especially so long as Asbury was alive, there existed virtually no politics. For other Baptists and followers of Campbell and Stone, the Christian message was thoroughly mixed with a republican ideology jealous for liberty and hyper-alert to the corruptions of power. But for Methodists, Baptists, Disciples, Christians, and the many smaller varieties of Protestant sectarianism that came to flourish in the new republic, there were few specific predictions about the religious future of the United States. The sectarians were simply too busy. Their eyes were fixed too steadily on the battle for souls now and on the glorious prospects of millennial dawn.

Yet the path of the American future was being created much more by these sectarians than by the representatives of what had been the colonies' main churches. Against what almost anyone could have predicted as late as 1795 or even 1800, public religious life in the United States came to follow the upstart Methodists, Baptists, and Christians.

The American religion that flourished so luxuriantly in the first sixty years of the nineteenth century was intensely republican. It had internalized the fear of unchecked authority and the commitment to private virtue that drove the ideology of the first political founding. But it was also "Christian republican"—the virtue that the United States' energetic itinerants promoted was not classical manliness but humility in Christ. The religion that came to prevail was more antiformal than formal—it did not trust in ascribed authority or inherited bureaucracies but rather in achieved authority and ad hoc networking. It was populist or democratic—it championed the ability of any white man to assume leadership in any religious assembly. And it was biblicistic—it spoke of the Scriptures as a supreme authority that trumped or even revoked all other religious authorities.

Above all, the religion that came to prevail so vigorously in the nineteenth-century United States was voluntaristic. Voluntarism was a mind-set keyed to innovative leadership, proactive public advocacy, and entrepreneurial goal-setting. Voluntarism also became an extraordinarily influential practice that began with church organization and then mushroomed to inspire local and national mobilization on behalf of myriad social and political causes. Voluntarism also became a foundation for the strengths, and weaknesses, of American society as a whole. Local civilization would be built as local groups and individuals enlisted to address local needs. Not government, not an inherited church, not Big Business, but enterprising connections—forged voluntarily—built American civilization in the decades before the Civil War. But the Civil War brought out the great weakness of American voluntaristic civilization, since in the clash of principles and interests that led to the war there was no authority able to deflect the antagonistic energy generated by the Northern and Southern civil societies that emerged in the early history of the United States. One of the main reasons the Civil War marked the end of an era was its graphic demonstration of the limits of voluntary religious energy, which could not resolve the sectional crisis, and the potential of expanded governmental power, which did resolve that crisis.

A few small-scale voluntary societies had been formed in the United States before the turn of the nineteenth century, but as a self-created vehicle for preaching the Christian message, distributing Christian literature, encouraging Christian civilization, and networking philanthropic activity, the voluntary society came into its own after about 1810. Many of the new societies were formed within denominations, and a few were organized outside the evangelical boundaries, like the American Unitarian Association of 1825. But the most important were founded by interdenominational networks of evangelicals for evangelical purposes. The best-funded and most dynamic societies—like the American Board of Commissioners for Foreign Missions (1810), the American Bible Society (1816), or the American Education Society (1816)—were rivaled only by the Methodist Church in their shaping effects on national culture.

To the intimidating challenges posed by church disestablishment and the vigorous competition of a rapidly expanding market economy, the combination of sectarian denominational mobilization, revival, and the voluntary society offered a compelling response. Observers at the time took note of the innovation. Rufus Anderson, an early organizer of the American missions movement, wrote in 1837 that "The Protestant form of association—free, open, responsible, embracing all classes, both sexes, all ages, the masses of the people—is peculiar to modern times, and almost to our age."[20]

Under these impulses and with these new modes of organization, American religion was transformed in the first half of the nineteenth century. A period of tumultuous, energetic, contentious innovation first reversed the downward slide of religious adherence and then began to shape all of American society by the standards of voluntaristic evangelical religion. Most remarkably, evangelicals even conquered the South, where an honor-driven culture of manly self-assertion had presented a far less propitious field for recruiting than regions to the north where the Puritan leaven lingered. And in the border South, where Lincoln lived his early years, and central

Illinois, where he came to maturity, the imprint of the new religious culture was especially strong.

Lincoln's Religion and the Religion of Lincoln's America

The careful modern documentation of Lincoln's life makes it possible to realize how much a part he was of this new era of American religion, and yet also where he stood apart. Lincoln combined easily what later American experience found much harder to join up; he was distinctive for *how* his religious, political, and more generally intellectual commitments came together, not for any of the constituents as such.

First was his familiarity with the Bible, which he gained as a youth and which deepened as he read, reread, and quoted Scripture to the last. His first major public speech, the Lyceum Address of 1838, ended by quoting Matthew 16:18.[21] In the choice of metaphor for his critical "House divided against itself" speech from June 1858—as with Stephen Douglas in the great debates later that same year, at cabinet meetings during the war, in correcting others' misquotations, and in many private conversations—Lincoln regularly cited biblical phrases to make political or moral points. Often this quoting of the Bible was merely instrumental, as in the "House divided" speech. But in his last years, the quotations were not only integral to what he wanted to say but also made a distinctly religious contribution to his remarks, as illustrated most clearly in the incomparable words of the Second Inaugural that quote from Psalm 19:9: "Yet, if God wills that [slavery] continue, until all the wealth piled by the bond-man's two hundred and fifty years of unrequited toil shall be sunk, and until every drop of blood drawn with the lash, shall be paid by another drawn with the sword, as was said three thousand years ago, so still it must be said 'the judgments of the Lord, are true and righteous altogether.'"[22] On September 7, 1864, Lincoln responded to a group of African Americans who had presented him with a copy of the Bible with what appears to be his own mature judgment: "All the good the Saviour gave to the world was communicated through this book. But for it we could not know right from wrong."[23]

The Bible was, of course, a given in the history of Protestantism, including Protestant developments in early America. Yet after the decline of Puritanism and the rise of evangelical revivalism, Americans used Scripture much more often for personal and church admonition than for public purposes in society at large. The Bible continued to be a presence in the Revolutionary and Constitutional periods, but that presence was predominately rhetorical and ornamental. There are few biblical arguments in the Revolutionary era over public policy like the ones that began to proliferate after about 1800. From that time, however, the Bible figured large in public debates over the transport of mail on Sunday and more general questions of Sabbath observance, over goals and strategies of temperance advocates, over removal of the Cherokee, over the rights of women, and preeminently over the rights and wrongs of slavery.

The Bible became directly important for nineteenth-century public life because, in the great expansion of the evangelical churches, it was becoming so important for private life. The religious revivals that filled the churches, that generated such powerful ideals for domestic life, and that created a plethora of voluntary societies led also to a much more explicit deployment of Scripture in the public sphere.

Historian Joyce Appleby once observed that the United States Constitution "entered a culture already fully fitted out with symbolic systems and sacred texts." Among these, "the most important source of meaning for eighteenth-century Americans was the Bible."[24] Perry Miller had earlier claimed that "The Old Testament is truly so omnipresent in the American culture of 1800 or 1820 that historians have as much difficulty taking cognizance of it as of the air people breathed."[25] When, therefore, Lincoln read the Bible and then reproduced its phrases, rhythms, and ethos in his own public speaking, he was touching one of the most meaningful threads of the new nation's culture (whatever his own views were about the Scriptures he cited).

The striking contrast with Europe was that amid America's post-Revolutionary tide of antiformalism, antitraditionalism, democratization, and decentralization, trust in the Bible did not weaken but became immeasurably stronger. It was still "the Bible alone," as chief religious authority, that American Protestants trusted. But it was also "the Bible alone" of all traditional religious authorities that survived the antitraditional tide and then undergirded the remarkable evangelical expansion of the early nineteenth century. By undercutting trust in other traditional authorities, the power-suspicious republicans in the early United States had the ironic effect of scripturalizing the new country. Deference to the inherited authority of bishops and presbyters was largely gone, obeisance to received creeds was largely gone, willingness to heed the example of the past was largely gone. What remained was the power of intuitive reason, the authority of written documents that the people approved for themselves, and the Bible alone. Lincoln's Second Inaugural Address used the Bible much more directly than any previous inaugural in American history.[26] When he did so, this self-taught believer in "government of the people, by the people, and for the people" spoke to one of the most powerful motive agents in American society.

If Lincoln's knowledge of the Bible stood him in good stead with an American populace among whom the Bible was far and away the single best-known book, so also did his commitment to the powers of reason commend him to central values of antebellum religious culture. Lincoln's appeal to "Reason, cold, calculating, unimpassioned reason," which he made in one of his early public speeches, remained a principle theme all his life.[27] More romantic and affectional themes later modified this all-out rationalism, but Lincoln, along with most of the new nation's religious leaders, nonetheless remained committed to the need for reason to clarify conundrums, explicate problems, and convince open-minded listeners of the truth.

That commitment was firmly in place by the late eighteenth century, when the mistrust of intellectual authorities inherited from previous generations joined a belief that true knowledge arose from the use of one's own senses—whether the external senses for information about nature and society or the moral sense for ethical and aesthetic judgments. Most Americans of Lincoln's generation were thus united in the conviction that people had to think for themselves in order to know science, morality, economics, politics, and especially theology. For some Americans, this certainty was rooted in formal study guided by thinkers of the Scottish Enlightenment who developed formal theories concerning "common sense." For many more, including burgeoning numbers of sectarian Protestants and autodidacts, the certainty was the product of a strongly democratic process of epistemological self-assertion.[28]

Lincoln's relation to his Springfield minister, James Smith, illustrates the era's broad trust in the personal exercise of reason. Smith, a native Scot who had come into the Old School Presbyterian Church after service as a Cumberland Presbyterian, arrived as pastor of Springfield's First Presbyterian Church in 1849.[29] Like Lincoln, he was self-taught, yet an intense reader and reasoner. After conducting the funeral for young Eddie Lincoln in 1850, Smith continued to see the family. In 1852 Mary Todd Lincoln made a profession of faith and joined Smith's church, and the Lincolns regularly rented a pew thereafter.

As a demonstration of the era's confidence in rational argumentation, it is significant that Smith was the author of a substantial work of Christian apologetics, first published in 1843, that grew out of a public debate over several days with the "infidel" Charles G. Olmstead two years earlier. The book's title well explains its purpose: *The Christian's Defence, containing a fair statement, and impartial examination of the leading objections urged by infidels against the antiquity, genuineness, credibility and inspiration of the Holy Scriptures; enriched with copious extracts from learned authors.* It was a brickbat of a book, eventually available in two volumes and a densely packed, one-volume edition. The volume offered conventional, but closely argued, "proofs" for the reliability and authority of Scripture against David Hume, Tom Paine, Olmstead, and other skeptics. Multiple witnesses confirm that Lincoln read at least some of the book.[30] Its detailed arguments were painstakingly logical in the way that Lincoln himself, at least much of the time, pursued his own political and moral reasoning. In early 1867, Smith wrote a long letter to Herndon, which expressed his displeasure at Herndon's published account of the Lincolns' marital strife. That letter included brief comments about Lincoln's religion, including the claim that Lincoln had read and appreciated Smith's long book: "To the arguments [concerning Scripture] Mr. Lincoln gave a most patient, impartial and Searching investigation. To use his own language 'he examined the Arguments as a lawyer who is anxious to reach the truth investigates testimony.' The result was the announcement by himself that the argument in favor of the Divine Authority and inspiration of the Scripture was unanswerable."[31] In the margin of this letter, Herndon scribbled his opinion: "Foolish . . . Knows nothing of Lincoln. Smith gave Lincoln a book of his. Lincoln never condescended to write his name in it."[32] The truth about Lincoln's indebtedness to Rev. Smith's closely reasoned apologetics is probably somewhat closer to Smith's affirmation than to Herndon's denial, but only because Smith phrased so cautiously what it was that Lincoln actually affirmed.

The larger point illustrated by the Lincoln-Smith relationship concerns the deference of the era's religious leaders to the bar of reason. Smith joined many of the evangelical leaders of his day in adhering lightly to tradition while taking argumentation very seriously. Whether without formal education, like Smith, or as preceptors of the nation's colleges and seminaries, most of which were maintained by evangelical denominations, leading religious voices gave reason a very large role in supporting the faith, which in turn was a driving force in shaping the nation. Lincoln, though not an evangelical himself, showed that same commitment to logical demonstration.

Even more consistent than his rationalism, but just as reflective of the era's general trends, was Lincoln's belief that human affairs and the business of the world were ruled by higher powers. Belief in Providence was everywhere a mark of this evangelical age. How Lincoln defined those higher powers changed over time and was never orthodox, as defined by standard evangelicalism, but belief that they controlled the affairs of people and nations never wavered. The predestinarian Calvinism of the Separate Baptist preachers he heard as a young man, which may have been inculcated with gentle effect by his mother, his stepmother, and later the mother of his friend Joshua Speed, did give way to an Enlightenment fatalism during his New Salem years. Yet Lincoln's defensive handbill of 1846, where he fended off charges of infidelity, indicated how formally similar those systems of Calvinist and Enlightenment determinism were: "It is true that in early life I was inclined to believe in what I understand is called the 'Doctrine of Necessity'—that is, that the human mind is impelled to action, or held in rest by some power, over which the mind itself has no control; and I have sometimes (with one, two or three, but never publicly) tried to maintain this opinion in argument. The habit of arguing thus however, I have, entirely left off for more than five years. And I add here, I have always understood this same opinion to be held by several of the Christian denominations."[33]

Only once in his life did Lincoln seem to move beyond belief in an over-ruling general Providence to action based on a specific special Providence. That momentous occasion came in September 1862, when the battle of Antietam provided just enough good news for Lincoln to move against slavery in the Confederate states. The account that follows is from notes made at the time by Secretary of the Navy Gideon Welles: "he had made a vow, a covenant, that if God gave us the victory in the approaching battle, he would consider it an indication of divine will and that it was his duty to move forward in the cause of emancipation. It might be thought strange that he had in this way submitted the disposal of matters when the way was not clear to his mind what he should do. God had decided this question in favor of the slaves. He was satisfied it was right, was confirmed and strengthened in his action by the vow and the results."[34]

More typically, Lincoln's view of Providence did not lead him to identify specific actions with God's intentions (which, however, was the most common understanding of Providence in his day). Rather, Providence for Lincoln meant divine, but unfathomable, control of the universe, as he expressed in a private minute that was later labeled "a meditation on the divine will" from September 1862[35] and in the Second Inaugural Address from March 1865.[36]

In his general trust in Providence, if not in the shape of that trust, Lincoln was entirely typical for his age. A fine book from a generation ago by Lewis Saum, *The Popular Mood of Pre–Civil War America*, underscored how much like Lincoln were many of his ordinary peers. The book's extensive research into nonelite sources revealed a widespread American belief that a larger power—fate, destiny, or God—overruled the affairs of people and nations. Saum pointed out shrewdly that this general belief in an overarching Power, before which or whom individual choice often meant little, was very much in line with Lincoln's general perspective—though also greatly different from the well-publicized ego-optimism of Ralph Waldo Emerson.[37] In a new volume on American views of Providence, Nicholas Guyatt also shows that in several particulars Lincoln's providential view of the Civil War was also typical of his age. With many of his contemporaries, Lincoln believed that the war represented divine punishment for the national toleration of slavery, and that an end to the conflict depended on destroying this institution. Like many of his peers, Lincoln also held that abolishing slavery would allow the United States to fulfill its divinely appointed destiny of showing the entire world the benefits of democratic self-determination.[38] Saum, Guyatt, and other historians who have researched general American attitudes make an excellent point: it is just as important to see where Lincoln reflected the general thinking of his time as to note when he stood out distinctively.

As he came to the conclusion of the Second Inaugural, Lincoln returned to this theme of Providence, but again expressed in terms of mystery rather than in human understanding of God's designs. As he did so—and as a way of completing the circle of his own life's journey—he echoed opinions he had almost certainly read in *The Kentucky Preceptor* during his Indiana youth. That widely read handbook of Christian morality had affirmed, "Every occurrence in the universe is *Providential*. . . . But to select individual facts, as more directed by the hand of Providence than others, because we think we see a particular good purpose answered by them, is an infallible inlet to error and superstition."[39] Lincoln in the Second Inaugural said, more eloquently and more boldly, much the same thing: "The Almighty has his own purposes." If, by the time of the Civil War, more transparent understandings of Providence had come to prevail among his peers, Lincoln's own views remained closer to what he had been taught by the Calvinist Baptists of his youth.

The most important question about Lincoln's relation to the religious currents of his time asks why Lincoln, who displayed many of the common evangelical traits of his day and who as a politician so effectively appealed to Northern and border state evangelicals, never identified himself as an evangelical believer. The most convincing answer to this query almost certainly will be found in the realms of biography, which so many recent historians have probed with so much skill—if without being able to agree on a single, generally satisfying answer. But when examined from the public record, and setting aside the effort to understand Lincoln's psyche, a likely answer to the question can be found in the ordering of priorities. To put this suggestion directly: many of his era's most influential religious figures gravitated to the political views also held by Lincoln (first as Whigs and then Republicans) because they were evangelicals. Lincoln, by contrast, resonated with the views of a populace that was evangelical, or strongly influenced by evangelical values, because he was a Whig.

The Whig-evangelical nexus was first defined fully in a perceptive analysis by Daniel Walker Howe, which then was expanded in important books by Richard Carwardine, Allen Guelzo, and Stewart Winger.[40] In this interpretation, the key was the formal congruity that existed between Lincoln's passionate commitment to Whig political principles and Northern evangelical commitment to active religious voluntarism. Howe's masterful book shows how the United States' moderate Calvinism of the 1830s paralleled the main emphases of the Whig Party that emerged as the main opposition to Andrew Jackson and the Democrats during the nation's "second party system." In Howe's depiction, the ultimate goal of these evangelical Calvinists was "to win souls for Christ," but along the way their efforts also helped "to create a modern capitalist social order." What Howe accurately described was the mix of elements that went into much of the era's Calvinist theology as well as its Whig political ideology: self-realization linked to care for community, personal liberty coordinated with self-discipline, "moral responsibility" existing alongside "moral conditioning"—in a word, "the balancing of freedom and control."[41] Howe also showed how central to the Whig worldview were the instincts of republican political analysis and the intellectual tools of Scottish common sense philosophy. In general, the Whigs' objective was "to blend the activist, voluntaristic, ambitious, fluid attitudes of nineteenth-century America with the religious doctrines of the Reformation." In other words, "this meant formulating into a religious ideology the culture associated with Whiggery."[42]

To this convincing depiction, Stewart Winger has recently underscored the extent to which religious convictions were always part and parcel of Whig ideology and, thus, always part of Lincoln's basic political philosophy. Winger has been especially persuasive in arguing that the Whigs' commitment to "positive moral government" precisely mirrored the main features of Lincoln's mature political views. In this perspective, Whig commitment to capitalism, economic opportunity, and commercial expansion was analogous to the voluntary societies' mobilization for personal discipline, ethical progress, and general moral order—all under God. Significantly, the antebellum Whigs, with their evangelical allies, saw wage labor, not in the static, monopolistic terms that came to prevail in postbellum capitalism, but as only a temporary condition that the democratic United States opened up so that poor, but self-disciplined, individuals (like Lincoln) could rise to become self-sufficient citizens.

To this picture of Whig-evangelical congruence, there is an important qualification. Many Calvinist Baptists and some Southern Old School Presbyterians, such as Robert Dabney and J. H. Thornwell, remained fundamentally distrustful of aggressive personal striving in both theology and society; to them, activism of the Whig and voluntary kind meant a sinful replacement of dependency upon God with idolatrous reliance upon the self.[43] The result in politics was determined apoliticism or support for the Democrats. In theology, these apolitical or anti-Whig Calvinists held to convictions that resembled more the main currents of British evangelical thought at the same period, which tended toward a passive view of human agency, because they ascribed to God rather than to humans the motive power for social change.[44] Yet, for the main body of the United States' most active evangelicals in the antebellum period, their theology drew them toward the personal exertions, belief in progress, and drive toward public and private morality that also characterized Whigs' (and Lincoln's) political principles.

The critical elements that built this Whig-evangelical alliance flowed as directly from the unfolding of American history as from the historic resources of traditional Protestantism. Put positively, this stance affirmed that it was possible—indeed imperative—to take purposeful action in the face of personal need and social crisis in order to put oneself right with God and realize a healthier, more godly society. Put negatively, it took for granted that the social landscape contained no historic structures of authority that could be trusted, that no dictate of inherited learning, church tradition, or elite social status was as reliable as the precepts of Scripture and the truths of consciousness. America's main Calvinist streams, especially in the North, were never Whig to uniform or identical degrees, but they were nonetheless pushed decidedly in Whig directions. Significantly, the "ethnoreligious" political historians have found that most of the era's Northern Protestant constituencies voted either overwhelmingly or strongly Whig (and then Republican), while the religious constituencies that supported the Democrats were strongly Catholic, continental Protestant, and Southern.[45] Likewise, historians of the Civil War have shown that the things that mattered most to Lincoln also mattered most to his contemporaries (sometimes in agreement, sometimes in disagreement). In turn, the degree of religiouslike political commitment explains the religionlike fervor that caused and sustained the Civil War.[46] Lincoln provided effective leadership of the North, not just because he spoke the North's moral-religious-political language, but because he had built his life on many of the principles that gave expression to that language. He and the North were despised by the South not because their principles were so completely alien but because they contradicted only a few particulars in the South's similar set of moral, religious, and political precepts.

If this positioning of Lincoln in the religious world of his times is correct, it means that Lincoln was not extraordinary for his reference to the Bible, his reliance on reason, his convictions about Providence, or his commitment to the struggle for "positive moral government." Personally considered, he was distinctive in the shape of his belief in Providence. In historical terms, he was relatively unusual for grounding his public activity on Whig convictions, when more of his contemporaries were acting out of their commitment to voluntaristic evangelicalism. An explicit evangelical faith and membership in an evangelical church, which were supremely important to so many of Lincoln's contemporaries, seem to have remained less important than foundational Whig convictions to this (at once) very typical and very unusual American.

Notes

This chapter includes material adapted from some of my previous publications, where much fuller documentation can be found: "Lincoln's God," *Journal of Presbyterian History* 82 (Summer 2004): 77–88; *America's God: From Jonathan Edwards to Abraham Lincoln* (New York: Oxford University Press, 2002); and *The Civil War as a Theological Crisis* (Chapel Hill: University of North Carolina Press, 2006).

1. William Lee Miller, *Lincoln's Virtues: An Ethical Biography* (New York: Knopf, 2002), 85.

2. See William Barton, *The Soul of Abraham Lincoln* (New York: Doran, 1920); and David C. Hein, "Abraham Lincoln's Theological Outlook" (Ph.D. diss., University of Virginia, 1982), with the related essay by Hein, "The Calvinistic Tenor of Abraham Lincoln's Religious Thought," *Lincoln Herald* 85 (Winter 1983): 212–20. Also helpful, with much good information and movement toward a critical use of sources, is William J. Wolf, *The Almost Chosen People: A Study of the Religion of Abraham Lincoln* (Garden City, N.Y.: Doubleday, 1959).

3. Among the most important of these efforts have been Merrill D. Peterson, *Lincoln in American Memory* (New York: Oxford University Press, 1994); Don Fehrenbacher and Virginia Fehrenbacher, *Recollected Words of Abraham Lin-*

coln (Stanford, Calif.: Stanford University Press, 1996); Michael Burlingame, ed., *An Oral History of Abraham Lincoln: John G. Nicolay's Interviews and Essays* (Carbondale: Southern Illinois University Press, 1996); and Douglas Wilson and Rodney Davis, eds., *Herndon's Informants* (Urbana: University of Illinois Press, 1997). All of these fine efforts rely on Roy P. Basler, ed., *The Collected Works of Abraham Lincoln*, 9 vols., hereafter referred to as *Collected Works* (New Brunswick, N.J.: Rutgers University Press, 1953–55).

4. Especially important are the accounts in Allen C. Guelzo, *Abraham Lincoln: Redeemer President* (Grand Rapids, Mich.: Eerdmans, 1999); Stewart Winger, *Lincoln, Religion, and Romantic Cultural Politics* (DeKalb: Northern Illinois University Press, 2003); and Richard Carwardine, *Lincoln: A Life of Purpose and Power* (New York: Knopf, 2006). But there is also helpful material in Miller, *Lincoln's Virtues*; Lucas E. Morel, *Lincoln's Sacred Effort: Defining Religion's Role in American Self-Government* (Lanham, Md.: Lexington, 2000); Ronald C. White Jr., *Lincoln's Greatest Speech: The Second Inaugural* (New York: Simon and Schuster, 2002); and Joseph R. Fornieri, *Abraham Lincoln's Political Faith* (DeKalb: Northern Illinois University Press, 2003).

5. An excellent account of this early experience is provided in Louis A. Warren, *Lincoln's Youth: Indiana Years, 1816–1830* (Indianapolis: Indiana Historical Society, 1991), 112–24, 206–7.

6. *Collected Works*, 1:382.

7. For Lincoln and Smith, see Wilson and Davis, *Herndon's Informants*, 547–49; for Lincoln and Gurley, see Carwardine, *Lincoln*, 223.

8. Philipp Schaff, *Der Bürgerkrieg und das christliche Leben in Nord-Amerika* (Berlin: Wiegandt and Grieben, 1866), 67.

9. Peterson, *Lincoln in American Memory*, 98.

10. Guelzo, *Redeemer President*, 313–14. Guelzo's conclusion is shared by Douglas L. Wilson, *Honor's Voice: The Transformation of Abraham Lincoln* (New York: Knopf, 1998), 308–12.

11. Carwardine, *Lincoln*, 225. A variation on Carwardine's view is Stewart Winger's conclusion that Lincoln's early beliefs were never as antiorthodox as they appeared; see Winger, *Lincoln, Religion, and Romantic Cultural Politics*, 179–82.

12. Peterson, *Lincoln in American Memory*, 76.

13. I have been guided on this era by a work by Stephen A. Marini of Wellesley College,, "The Government of God: Religion in Revolutionary America, 1764–1792" (unpublished ms.).

14. A key interpretation is Nathan O. Hatch, *The Democratization of American Christianity* (New Haven: Yale University Press, 1989).

15. These figures, and much other interesting material, are found in *Statistical View of the United States . . . Being a Compendium of the Seventh Census* (Washington, D.C.: Bureau of the Census, 1854); and *Statistics of the United States . . . Being a Compendium from . . . the Eighth Census* (Washington, D.C.: Bureau of the Census, 1866).

16. See Thomas J. Curry, *The First Freedoms: Church and State in America to the Passage of the First Amendment* (New York: Oxford University Press, 1986), 131–32.

17. Jefferson to James Smith, Dec. 8, 1822, in *Jefferson's Extracts from the Gospels*, ed. Dickinson W. Adams, The Papers of Thomas Jefferson, 2nd ser. (Princeton, N.J.: Princeton University Press, 1983), 409.

18. See John J. Ferling, *Adams vs. Jefferson: The Tumultuous Election of 1800* (New York: Oxford University Press, 2005).

19. See David Paul Nord, *Faith in Reading: Religious Publishing and the Birth of Mass Media in America* (New York: Oxford University Press, 2004).

20. Rufus Anderson, "The Time for the World's Conversion Come" (1837–38), reprinted in *To Advance the Gospel: Selections from the Writings of Rufus Anderson*, ed. R. Pierce Beaver (Grand Rapids, Mich.: Eerdmans, 1967), 65.

21. *Collected Works*, 1:115.

22. Ibid., 8:333.

23. Ibid., 7:542.

24. Joyce Appleby, "The American Heritage: The Heirs and the Disinherited," *Journal of American History* 74 (Dec. 1987): 809.

25. Perry Miller, "The Garden of Eden and the Deacon's Meadow," *American Heritage*, Dec. 1955, 54.

26. For comparisons, see White, *Lincoln's Greatest Speech*, 101–2.

27. *Collected Works*, 1:115.

28. A fine survey is offered by Allen C. Guelzo, "'The Science of Duty': Moral Philosophy and the Epistemology of Science in Nineteenth-Century America," in *Evangelicals and Science in Historical Perspective*, ed. David N. Livingstone et al. (New York: Oxford University Press, 1999), 267–89.

29. There is some helpful information in Robert J. Havlik, "Abraham Lincoln and the Rev. Dr. James Smith: Lincoln's Presbyterian Experience of Springfield," *Journal of the Illinois State Historical Society* 92 (Autumn 1999): 222–37.

30. Fehrenbacher and Fehrenbacher, *Recollected Words*, 296.

31. Wilson and Davis, *Herndon's Informants*, 549.

32. Ibid., 547n1.

33. *Collected Works*, 1:382.

34. Fehrenbacher and Fehrenbacher, *Recollected Words*, 474.

35. *Collected Works*, 5:403–4.

36. Ibid., 8:333.

37. Lewis B. Saum, *The Popular Mood of Pre–Civil War America* (Westport, Conn.: Greenwood, 1980).

38. Nicholas Guyatt, *"The Peculiar Smiles of Heaven": Providence and the Invention of the United States, 1607–1865* (New York: Cambridge University Press, 2007).

39. Quoted from the 1812 edition in Winger, *Lincoln, Religion, and Romantic Cultural Politics*, 173.

40. Daniel Walker Howe, *The Political Culture of the American Whigs* (Chicago: University of Chicago Press, 1979), with expanded insights in *Making the American Self: Jonathan Edwards to Abraham Lincoln* (Cambridge: Harvard University Press, 1997), and *What Hath God Wrought: The Transformation of America, 1815–1848* (New York: Oxford University Press, 2007). See also Guelzo, *Redeemer President*; Winger, *Lincoln, Religion, and Romantic Cultural Politics*; Richard Carwardine, *Lincoln*; and *Evangelicals and Politics in Antebellum America* (New Haven: Yale University Press, 1993).

41. Howe, *Political Culture*, 158–61. Definitive treatment of the political phenomenon is found in Michael F. Holt, *The Rise and Fall of the American Whig Party: Jacksonian Politics and the Onset of the Civil War* (New York: Oxford University Press, 1999).

42. Howe, *Political Culture*, 159–60. For expansion, see Guelzo, *Redeemer President*, 63, 72, 138–40, 176, 456–63; and Carwardine, *Evangelicals and Politics*, 122–23, where it is noted that many of the era's Calvinist theologians—including Albert Barnes, Lyman Beecher, Nathan Beman, Charles Hodge, Moses Stuart, and N. W. Taylor—were active supporters of the Whig Party.

43. See Kenneth Moore Startup, *The Root of All Evil: The Protestant Clergy and the Economic Mind of the Old South* (Athens: University of Georgia Press, 1997), 90–95; James Oscar Farmer Jr., *The Metaphysical Confederacy: James Henley Thornwell and the Synthesis of Southern Values* (Macon, Ga.: Mercer University Press, 1986), 72–75; and Carwardine, *Evangelicals and Politics*, 124.

44. See, for example, the British evangelical reliance on Malthus's demographic determinism, which never was as important in America, as explained in Boyd Hilton, *The Age of Atonement: The Influence of Evangelicalism on Social and Economic Thought, 1785–1865* (New York: Oxford University Press, 1988), 64–76.

45. See Robert P. Swierenga, "Ethnoreligious Behavior in the Mid-Nineteenth Century: Voting, Values, Culture," in *Religion and American Politics: From the Colonial Period to the Present*, ed. Mark A. Noll and Luke Harlow, 2nd ed. (New York: Oxford University Press, 2007), 145–68.

46. On the quasi-religious character of the war, see Harry S. Stout, *Upon the Altar of the Nation: A Moral History of the Civil War* (New York: Viking, 2006).

5

The Middle-Class Marriage of Abraham and Mary Lincoln

Kenneth J. Winkle

On the night Abraham Lincoln was elected president, he walked to the telegraph office in Springfield, Illinois, to follow the election returns. Mary Lincoln stayed at home and in fact locked him out of the house. According to a reminiscence, Mary told Abraham "that if he wasn't at home by 10 o'clock she would lock him out. And she did so. But, Mr. Lincoln said that when she heard the music coming to serenade them she turned the key in a hurry." This story, like so many others depicting the Lincolns' sometimes-stormy marriage, casts both members of the couple in all-too-familiar roles. Mary is the headstrong, indeed shrewish, wife who resents her husband's absence from home even at this transformative moment in both their lives and the life of the nation. As on so many similar occasions during their marriage, Abraham turns to humor both to mollify his wife and to bear her reproach. Despite her demeanor, he remains "in fine spirits" and retails the anecdote the next day before a group of well-wishers. He makes the episode public, portraying himself as the victor in this domestic struggle, announcing that "he had a good joke on his wife." Indeed, Lincoln left for the telegraph office as a private citizen but returned as president-elect, followed by a crowd of well-wishers whom Mary had to let into her home. Mary, by contrast, is humorless, attempting to keep her transgression private, pointedly warning her husband, "Don't ever tell that again."[1]

On its face, this anecdote casts the Lincolns in stereotypical roles. Flighty and impetuous, Mary overlooks the possibility that Abraham might return with a crowd of celebrants, an honor guard of sorts, to bear witness to her pettiness. Abraham, by contrast, remains temperate, walking calmly up the front steps. A witness later recounted the scene as Lincoln walked home: "Across the street 10,000 crazy people were shouting, throwing up their hats, slapping and kicking one another." Through it all, "down the street walked Lincoln, without a sign of anything unusual."[2] As he so often did in life, Abraham Lincoln had the last laugh. Like most anecdotes that feature both Lincolns, this one portrays Mary negatively and Abraham favorably. Like some others, it may be apocryphal. Still, the story rings true, and the image of the locked door provides an apt metaphor for the kind of middle-class marriage the Lincolns—and many other nineteenth-century couples—led together.

Abraham Lincoln courted and married Mary Todd during an extraordinary period in American history. The early nineteenth century witnessed a dramatic transition within the institution of marriage, indeed within the American family itself. During the 1830s, a dynamic, new social class began to emerge in America's urbanizing Northeast. Practicing the growing range of nonmanual occupations increasingly available in commerce and the professions, a new middle class aspired to self-improvement and social reform, defined and defended sharp new gender roles, especially within marriage, and drew a rigid distinction between newly constructed public and private spheres, particularly home and work. To these ends, the new middle class glorified and romanticized family life. During the last several decades, beginning with the work of Burton Bledstein, historians have increasingly pointed to the emerging middle class as a driving force within nineteenth-century social and cultural development. As Stuart Blumin summed it up, "middle-class formation has now been offered, clearly and forcefully, as a central hypothesis for the study of the evolution of nineteenth-century American society." Part of that evolution was a dramatic transition to a new kind of family in America, motivated by middle-class values, or "Victorianism." The hallmark of the middle class was employment in nonmanual occupations, many of them new, others traditional but gaining in prominence—"head work" rather than "hand work," to borrow Blumin's distinction.[3]

In preindustrial America, families obeyed a traditional pattern that historians label *cooperative*. Cooperative families had a strong economic foundation in which all the members played a productive role. Most American men were farmers, 42 percent of them as late as 1900. A smaller minority of Americans practiced manual, nonfarm trades but usually in rural rather than urban areas. In this preindustrial era, most husbands and fathers worked at home, where they lived, usually on farms. Most food and goods were produced at home in an elaborate system of home manufacturing. Women played a crucial role in this subsistence economy, supervising dairy and poultry operations, making soap and candles, and above all producing cloth. Before the appearance of spinning and weaving mills after 1815, farm women made most of the clothing their families wore. They spun cotton and wool, wove cloth on looms, dyed the cloth with homemade dyes, and sewed it into clothing by hand, typically providing one set of clothing each season for every family member. As late as 1840, farm women produced more cloth at home than all American textile mills combined.[4]

Until he came of age in Illinois, this kind of traditional, subsistence family was all that Abraham Lincoln had ever known. During his youth, in both Kentucky and Indiana, the Lincoln family practiced classic subsistence agriculture. The Indiana farm in particular was isolated and self-contained, a literal wilderness without neighbors, roads, or towns. "An unbroken forest" was Lincoln's recollection. Indeed, the Lincoln family had to cut a road through the trees just to reach their claim. They arrived without "hogs—cows—chickens or such like domestic animals," according to cousin Dennis Hanks, who lived with the family, and initially they ate wild game, a staple of the frontier diet. "We always hunted," Hanks remembered; "it made no difference what came for we more or less depended on it for a living—nay for life." Even when the first crop of corn came in, the nearest mill was seventeen miles through the forest, on the Ohio River, and it ground only enough grain for home consumption rather than for sale. "It was a little bit of hand horse mill," as Hanks remembered, "the ground meal of which a hound could Eat as fast as it was ground. Yet this was a God Send."[5]

In Indiana, the Lincoln family practiced subsistence agriculture, trading only for tropical goods that they could not produce for themselves. According to Hanks, Thomas "Jest Raised a Nuf for his own use he Did Not Send any produce to any other place Mor than Bought his Shugar and Coffee and Such Like." Subsistence was the best guarantee of survival in a pioneer economy, and fortunately the Lincoln farm could meet most of the family's needs. "Lincoln's Little Farm was well Stocked with Hogs, Horses & cattle," another relative, A. H. Chapman, reminisced with apparent pride, as well as "a fine crop of wheat corn & vegetables." The Lincolns tanned their own leather, made their own shoes, wove their own cloth, and sewed their own clothing, all by hand. In this seasonal economy, Thomas supplemented farming by doing carpentry, cabinetmaking, and joinery for his neighbors "at odd times" during the winter. His wife, Sarah, ran the household and bartered with the neighbors. "Mr and Mrs Lincoln Each worked a head at their own business," Dennis Hanks remembered. "Thomas at farming—cabinet making—& hunting; She at cooking—washing—sewing—weaving, &c. &c." The frontier mother clothed her family in the traditional homespun and buckskin. According to Chapman, "There clothing was all made at home and the Material from which it was made was also made at home." As typical Southern settlers, the Lincolns raised cotton and flax, which they "picked carded & spun with their own hands." Early on, the men and boys wore buckskin pants and coonskin caps against the cold. Later, the family kept some sheep, and Sarah wove linsey-woolsey for the winter.[6]

Economic functions such as these shaped the "cooperative" family. Most household activities were devoted to two primary goals. First, families valued economic independence, achieved through home production. Farmers therefore practiced "safety-first farming," producing a wide variety of food and goods to feed and clothe their own families rather than purchasing necessities. In short, families practiced production rather than consumption. Second, families attempted *re*production, which meant not only bearing children but also reproducing their households, setting up their sons on farms of their own, preferably nearby, and "marrying off" their daughters in "good matches" to their neighbors' sons. In this system of subsistence agriculture, children were obligated to contribute to their families, working for their parents as youngsters and supporting them in old age. Parents therefore prized their children's economic contributions to the family quite apart from their emotional commitment to them. In short, children were expected to begin working for their families as soon as possible. At age seven, typically, boys joined their fathers to work in the fields and to learn farming while girls took their place beside their mothers to learn the household chores or "women's work" that constituted their lot. As a result, children were economic assets rather than liabilities, and farm couples were fertile, bearing as many children as possible to work for the family. Family relationships—between husbands and wives and between parents and children—therefore possessed a strong economic as well as emotional foundation. Above all, families worked together as a single economic unit.[7]

As a cooperative family, the Lincolns expected their son to fulfill his traditional economic obligation. As a friend of the family summed it up, the young Lincoln "devoted his time principally in assisting to clear a little farm and make a subsistence for the family." Lincoln put it more simply: "I was raised to farm work." According to his own testimony, Lincoln "though very young, was large of his age, and had an axe put into his hands at once." In fact, Lincoln was just seven, "and from that till within his twentythird year, he was almost constantly handling that most useful instrument." While growing up, the youth contributed fifteen years' worth of labor to his father's family, working at home between ages seven and twenty-two and hiring out to work for neighbors beginning at age thirteen.[8]

In Lincoln's Illinois, most families continued to work together in this way right up to the Civil War. In 1840, two years before Abraham and Mary were married, fully 80 percent of all men living in Sangamon County were farmers. Another 15 percent practiced manufacturing and trades, and most of those were self-employed. Only about 15 percent of the county's manufacturers and craftsmen worked in shops. The rest, presumably, worked in or near their homes. Overall, more than 95 percent of the county's adult males performed manual labor. Fewer than 5 percent engaged in commerce or a profession, as Lincoln did, and therefore qualified as members of the emerging middle class. In Springfield, the state capital, three-fourths of all workers performed manual labor, mostly in building, transportation, and skilled trades. Lincoln fit right into this familiar, family-based economy.[9]

The young Mary Todd, by contrast, experienced a dramatically different family life. A small minority of Americans lived an upper-class existence, usually in large, Eastern cities and the plantation South. The Todds were one of the most eminent families in Kentucky, founders of Lexington, at the heart of the lush Blue Grass country. Mary Todd's father was a lawyer, state assemblyman and senator, investor, land speculator, and slave owner. In their fourteen-room house on Lexington's Main Street, production was the work of domestic slaves rather than family members. Freed from the performance of household chores, Mary Todd spent a decade at private girls' academies to learn how to supervise an aristocratic home and family. In this upper-class enclave, girls' most important function was to serve their families by marrying well, not to produce but to reproduce. The Todds therefore educated Mary for a life of domestic ease and motherhood, what Jean Baker called a conspicuous "lack of any purposeful female activity." Emblematic of the social gulf that separated Mary Todd from Abraham Lincoln was his birth, in dramatically different circumstances, in a county named after one of her relatives.[10]

The economic boom of the 1830s, however, promoted rapid industrialization and urbanization and drew these two together within Springfield's emerging middle class. The budding factory system began calling men from farms to cities and drew them away from their homes as industrial workers, managers, merchants, clerks, and professionals. Traditional family patterns changed, and Western cities now hosted a nascent middle class of nonmanual workers. Farm families stopped producing most of the goods they consumed, growing cash crops for sale on a commercial market and, in turn, buying the necessities they had once made at home. Significantly, industrialization came first in the textile industry, freeing farm women from their endless rounds of spinning, weaving, dyeing, and eventually even sewing the fabric that clothed their families.[11]

As a Western state, Illinois was late in industrializing, but distinct middle and working classes began to emerge during the 1830s and 1840s, just as Abraham Lincoln and Mary Todd arrived, courted, and married. Most noticeably, agriculture declined as the mainstay of the state's economy. In 1840, farmers represented 85 percent of Illinois's workforce. By 1850, they had declined to 65 percent, and by 1860, they represented a minority, just 39 percent. At the same time, production shifted from farms and homes to factories and shops. Meanwhile, the middle class—practitioners of productive but nonmanual occupations, primarily merchants, professionals, and public officials—grew steadily in numbers. They represented a mere 4 percent in 1840 but increased to 5 percent in 1850 and nearly doubled to 9 percent of the state's employed men by 1860. At Lincoln's election to the presidency, about one-tenth of Illinois families were middle-class.[12]

Middle-class men left home to go to work every morning—a process that historians have labeled the "separation of home and work"—and therefore gained status as "breadwinners" in their families. Married women stayed home, and their primary role was to maintain the household for the benefit of their husbands and children. In short, they became "housewives." Housekeeping became a science, and middle-class women turned nervously to a spate of new publications—domestic manuals, as well as novels and magazines—to learn its arcane mysteries. Cooking, in particular, became the new standard by which husbands and the public now judged the quality of any woman's domestic skills. New standards of cleanliness occupied housewives during the long days while their husbands labored in factories, shops, and offices. Above all, housewives were expected to spend their husbands' salaries wisely. Families, and women in particular, became consumers rather than producers.[13]

In Illinois, factory goods gradually freed farm wives and daughters from the never-ending cycle of home production. The first manufactured goods appeared in general stores in Chicago and St. Louis during the 1830s, and farmers began trading for them on their twice-yearly trips to market. Years later, for example, one Illinois farmer's daughter remembered her father returning from Chicago with factory-made cloth and announcing triumphantly, "Wife and daughters, store away your loom, wheels, warping bars, spool rack, winding blades, all your utensils for weaving cloth up in the loft. The boys and I can make enough by increasing our herds and driving them to Chicago for sale." Freed forever from the constant drudgery of spinning and weaving, "The girls clapped their hands with delight." In short, textile production increasingly left the home for the factory. Emblematic of the shift from production to consumption was the growth of a local textile industry. In 1832, a mill opened eleven miles west of Springfield to card, spin, and weave wool. Families could now sheer their sheep, take their wool to Richland Creek to be carded, spun, and woven into cloth, and then sew it into clothing at home for their own use. Soon, John Hay Sr., father of Lincoln's future White House secretary, opened a cotton mill right in Springfield. He exchanged spun cotton for raw cotton for a fee payable in cash. Hay employed working-class boys age ten to twelve, along with blind horses, to run his mill. In this fashion, the work of textile production passed from middle-class girls to working-class boys, from homes to factories.[14]

As a result, middle-class children—like their mothers—lost their productive functions. Middle-class parents no longer passed on land to their children as future farmers but instead educated them for eventual middle-class careers of their own. As a result, children were no longer productive, reverting from economic assets into economic liabilities until they reached adulthood. As children lost their economic value within the family, middle-class couples began limiting their fertility. Around 1800, a dramatic "fertility transition" began. In traditional families, women typically bore seven children during their lives. By 1900, they were bearing only half as many. Limiting fertility allowed middle-class parents to devote more time, attention, and affection to each child as an individual, nurturing and educating their children to promote future success, rather than exacting immediate economic benefits. Within the household, middle-class women took on servants, usually adolescent girls and boys, to help them keep house while their own children went to school, studied at home, and played.[15]

The North underwent a "market revolution." During Springfield's formative years, families raised their own food in their backyards. Even as a flourishing lawyer, for example, Abraham Lincoln kept a backyard garden and milked his own cow. Soon, however, the town established a farmer's market to provide fresh produce from the countryside. A market master rented stalls to local farmers who sold their produce three days a week. Later, private markets appeared to supply middle-class housewives. The city's butchers, for example, reasoned that "their shops were more convenient for customers than the market house, located as they were in different parts of the city." Before long, only the working class continued to grow their own produce, laboring after-hours in what became the "poor man's garden." Middle-class women now fed their families through a daily round of "marketing." In 1851, ice deliveries began to supply middle-class families with refrigeration, and three years later the city began laying down gas lines for lighting and eventually cooking.[16]

By 1845, ready-made clothing was available in Springfield. Clothier E. R. Wiley advertised that "I have the most experienced Cutters and workmen constantly employed" and promised that "Those who favor me with a call, will be convinced that it is in their interest to buy their garments of me, rather than go to the trouble of having them made up, after the old fashion." By 1850, Wiley employed one hundred workers, ninety of them women, who manufactured 150 garments a day with the help of a steam engine. In the same year, other Springfield shops produced shoes, hats, gloves, soap, candles, furniture, flour, baked goods, candy, and twenty-five other necessities for local consumption. Freed from basic production, housewives now bemoaned a whole new set of middle-class inconveniences and modern problems. In 1855, for example, John Todd Stuart's wife complained that "We were expecting the gas men, to put the pipes in the house today, but they did not come." In short, Springfield housewives had stopped producing goods for their families and were now largely consumers.[17]

As a result, men and women were now said to inhabit "separate spheres." Men's sphere was the public world of work and politics. Women's sphere was the private world of home and family, where they toiled for the benefit of their husbands and children. Because women were not paid for their work, the work they did became a duty, the "domestic duty." The new ideology of separate spheres portrayed men and women as fundamentally different. Men were by nature supposed to be aggressive, competitive, and shrewd, to compete in the new ruthless world of work. Women, by contrast, were expected to be gentle, loving, and sensitive creatures, to nurture and succor their husbands and children. These gender differences complemented each other and bound husband and wife together in a new "companionate" marriage founded on emotional attachment. Industrialization therefore reshaped not only the family itself but also gender roles within the family. The home became a refuge for middle-class men who expected their wives to keep house and then nurture them when they came home from work. Middle-class men and women were now conceived to be exact opposites so that each could perform their complementary roles within the family.[18]

By the 1840s, Springfield hosted a burgeoning middle class that included the Lincolns. This study defines middle-class families as all households headed by white, adult males who practiced productive but nonmanual occupations—"head work" rather than "hand work"—primarily in commerce, the professions, services, and public office. The remaining families, whose heads engaged in manual occupations, such as manufacturing, building, labor, transportation, and agriculture, or were nonproductive, represent Springfield's working class. In 1840, one-fourth of all Springfield families belonged to the middle class, and this cohort remained stable until 1860. The midpoint of these two decades, 1850, provides a representative look at the middle class in Springfield.[19]

In 1850, middle-class men were, on average, older than their working-class neighbors, forty-one as compared to thirty-eight. After all, they had to invest considerable time and effort to climb the occupational ladder, as Lincoln did, and so were a few years older. Middle-class men were four-and-a-half times wealthier than manual workers, owning $3,478 on average in real property as compared to $758. Such wealth reflected the new rewards that attended nonmanual labor and funded a novel lifestyle characterized by consumption rather than production. Although industrialization was a largely Northern phenomenon, Southern birth by itself did not preclude upward mobility. Middle-class men hailed equally from the North and the South. They were, however, heavily native-born. Thirty percent of native-born couples were middle-class, as compared to only 20 percent of immigrants. This distinction affected all immigrant groups—Germans, Irish, and English—about equally.[20]

Middle-class status helped to shape private and public lives in Springfield. Victorian couples, for example, controlled their fertility and therefore limited the size of their families. Working-class couples exhibited a natural interval between births—2.7 years. Middle-class couples maintained a longer birth interval of 3.2 years, practicing some form of birth control and devoting more resources to fewer children. Education, rather than land, represented their primary legacy to their children.[21] Middle-class households also included more nonfamily members, 1.2 on average. They were more likely than working-class families to depend on a live-in servant within their home to help with both housekeeping and childrearing.[22]

Not surprisingly, middle-class men played a prominent political role in Springfield. More likely than working-class men to hold public office, they essentially ran the city. One in seven middle-class men held office, as compared to a mere one in twenty-five working-class men. Put differently, a majority of officeholders (57 percent) were middle-class. The Whig Party, and later the Republicans, championed the values that gave rise to industry, cities, commerce, and the middle class itself. As a result, Whigs were heavily Victorian. One-third of Whigs were middle-class, as compared to only one-fourth of Democrats. Put differently, two-thirds of the middle class were Whigs.[23]

Outwardly, the Lincolns were typically middle-class. Abraham Lincoln, of course, was a professional, a lawyer. He was exactly forty-one years old in 1850. The Lincolns were Southern and native-born. Further, the couple limited their fertility, bearing their four sons at intervals that averaged 3.2 years. Uncannily, they achieved precisely the average birth interval within Springfield's middle class.[24] The Lincolns also routinely kept servants to help maintain their household. In 1850, they employed one servant, which was average—an immigrant girl from Ireland. By 1860, they had two servants, a boy and a girl, both from Illinois. They were ardent Whigs, and Abraham Lincoln was a leading Whig officeholder. The most glaring deviation from the middle-class norm consists in their economic standing. The Lincolns reported no real property in the Census of 1850, reflecting the deep indebtedness that Abraham Lincoln incurred during his fledgling efforts to enter the middle class as a merchant in New Salem. By 1860, however, the Lincolns had rebounded, reporting enough real wealth to place them in the 90th percentile in Springfield. The real hallmark of the middle class, however, was not real property—land—but personal wealth, the physical trappings of genteel refinement. In 1860, the Lincolns reported enough personal wealth to put them in the 99th percentile among their peers. Indeed, Abraham Lincoln ranked 16th out of 2,225 white, adult males in terms of personal wealth.[25] Finally, most of the people Abraham Lincoln knew were also middle-class. Springfielders who can be linked with Lincoln in some way through surviving records were 51 percent middle-class, twice the proportion of the population at large. Of those who cannot be linked with him, only 20 percent were middle-class and therefore 80 percent were working-class.[26]

In many respects, the Lincolns observed typical middle-class values. Kathryn Kish Sklar, for example, has demonstrated that the Lincolns limited their fertility, as did other middle-class couples. Rodney Davis has scrutinized Abraham Lincoln's role as a middle-class husband and father. Daniel Walker Howe and Jean Baker have analyzed his personal and professional commitment to upward social mobility and Victorian values. Gabor Boritt has portrayed Lincoln as a thoroughly bourgeois economic thinker. And Jean Baker's biography of Mary Lincoln presents her as a typical middle-class wife and mother.[27] As such, Victorian values represented a positive influence within the Lincolns' public and private lives.

Less tangibly, however, their transition to Victorianism remained incomplete. The Lincolns often violated the very middle-class expectations that lay at the foundation of their marriage. Put simply, the new, middle-class values set an impossible standard that all too often the Lincolns failed to meet. In 1842, for example, just four months before the Lincolns married, a Springfield newspaper published an article entitled "The Happy Match," instructing middle-class husbands and wives in the new rules of married life. Clearly borrowed from an Eastern newspaper, the article depicted a middle-class husband, Harry Hemphill, introducing his new wife to the secrets of a happy marriage. "Now," Harry told his wife, "it's my business to bring money into the house, and yours to see that none goes foolishly out it." In this respect, they proved a perfect match. "He chose her, first because he loved her, and in the second place because he knew she was sensible, economical, and industrious—just the reason which influences a sensible man in his choice now." Significantly, "he thought it best that each should have a distinct sphere of action." In tune with the doctrine of separate spheres, "His business called for his whole attention; he wished, therefore, to pursue it undistracted by other cares." Meanwhile, "Her duties being all domestic, she was able to compass them better by turning her whole attention to them." Above all, their home was a reliable refuge from the turmoil of public life. "There he sought repose after the toil and weariness of the day, and there he found it. When perplexed and low spirited, he retired thither, and amid the soothing influence of its quiet and peaceful shades, he forgot the heartlessness of the world." In short, "While Harry was prospering in his business all went like clockwork at home."[28]

Of course, abundant evidence suggests that all did not "go like clockwork" in the Lincoln home, and historians have long debated the extent to which the couple enjoyed a "happy match."[29] For a variety of reasons, middle-class mores militated against a happy match—indeed happiness itself—within the Lincolns' marriage. As an emerging ethic of family life in America, Victorianism remained untested and ambiguous. Newly married couples, especially women, were unfamiliar with its demanding dictates, its arcane domestic duties, and its unnatural gender roles. For this reason, a flood of advice literature appeared, including etiquette books for women and success manuals for men, to prepare wives and husbands for the challenging gender roles they must now obey. On New Year's Eve, 1846, for example, Abraham Lincoln stopped at a general store in Springfield and bought Mary two domestic manuals, *Miss Leslie's Cookery* and *Miss Leslie's Housekeeper*. The timing suggests an attempt to improve Mary's housekeeping skills as part of a New Year's resolution. (Whether Abraham presented the books as a gift or bought them at Mary's direction is intriguing but moot.) Further, middle-class marriages were a minority. By 1860, the middle class included only one-tenth of Illinois families and only one-fourth of families in Springfield. Far too often, middle-class status was precarious. Between 1850 and 1860, three out of ten middle-class families in Springfield actually fell in status and slipped backward into the ranks of the working class. In short, maintaining a middle-class marriage, even in Springfield, was problematic.[30]

Above all, Abraham and Mary Lincoln approached their middle-class marriage from two opposing perspectives. When he married, Abraham Lincoln was just leaving the traditional, folk economy in which he had been raised. He found himself *rising* into the new middle class in Springfield, taking a definite step upward. When she married, by contrast, Mary Lincoln *fell* from her perch within the comfortable upper class of the Lexington Blue Grass, taking a definite step downward into Springfield's middle class. As one of Mary's relatives explained, "Mrs. Lincoln came from the best of stock, and was raised like a lady. Her husband was her opposite, in origins, in education, in breeding, in everything."[31] The middle class therefore proved a social and cultural gulf that separated the Lincolns from other families and from one another. Both Lincolns tried hard to lead a respectable middle-class life. This was, after all, the ideal for Americans of their age. But both often failed. Abraham Lincoln continually reverted to the traditional patterns of family life in which he had been raised. Mary Lincoln continually attempted to reproduce the upper-class lifestyle that she found so familiar. The middle class might have become a middle ground uniting this couple from such disparate backgrounds. Instead, it too often became a battleground, because neither partner ever successfully fulfilled the exacting strictures of the new middle class. Above all, Abraham Lincoln's vocation—law—and his avocation—politics—continually blurred the boundaries between public and private that were central to the new middle-class existence.

As a wife and mother, Mary Lincoln's foremost duty—as Harry Hemphill reiterated—was to keep a home for her husband. A lawyer who knew Lincoln made this point sympathetically: "At home he had at all times the watchful and efficient attention of Mrs. Lincoln to every detail of his daily life as regards those things she had learned were most essential to keep him at his constitutional best." As a result, "Mrs. Lincoln, by her attention, had much to do with preserving her husband's health. She was careful to see that he ate his meals regularly, and that he was well groomed. He was not naturally inclined to give much thought to his clothes, and if Mrs. Lincoln happened to be away from Springfield for a few days on a trip out of the city, we were pretty sure to be apprised of her absence by some slight disorder in Lincoln's apparel and his irregularity at meal-time." This positive contribution, however, could acquire a negative cast, as when an acquaintance heard Mary snap, "Why don't you dress up and try to look like somebody?" In short, middle-class status *empowered* Mary Lincoln but also *burdened* her with nearly complete supervision of the Lincoln family. Further, her authority ended at the front door at Eighth and Jackson. Like many middle-class couples, the Lincolns therefore led "divided lives." Abraham enjoyed tremendous prestige within the public sphere that diminished the moment he stepped inside his own home. Mary, by contrast, enjoyed a domestic authority that dissolved the moment she stepped outside her own front door.[32]

For his part, Abraham Lincoln understood, without fully accepting, this middle-class separation of spheres. Like other ambitious middle-class men, he felt more at ease in his office than in his own home. A colleague reminisced that "Lincoln, when in this little office, was more easy in manner and unrestrained in all respects than at any other place I ever saw him." Away from home, Lincoln—unlike Mary—had the run of the city: "He would leave to call at Diller's drug-store, or at one of the dry-goods stores, to meet a friendly group in the counting-room, or more often to meet friends at the State House, that was directly across the street from his law office, to visit the offices there, or spent an hour or two in the State Library." Like many men of his era, Lincoln clearly valued this public sphere over the private one. At one point, he conceded that "I myself manage all important matters. In little things I have got along through life by letting my wife run her end of the machine pretty much in her own way." This is a clear, indeed shrewd, assessment of the newly emerging gender roles. Still, Lincoln's "little things" were the family's domestic affairs. His "important matters" took place outside the home, in the masculine world of work and politics.[33]

All too often, Abraham Lincoln violated Victorian standards. As his law partner, William Herndon, pointed out, "Such want of social polish on the part of her husband of course gave Mrs. Lincoln great offence." Mary's role was precisely to enforce the very standards that her husband so frequently flaunted. "It is therefore quite natural that she should complain if he answered the door-bell himself instead of sending the servant to do so," one of her relatives explained, "neither is she to be condemned if, as you say, she raised 'merry war' because he persisted in using his own knife in the butter, instead of the silver-handled one intended for that purpose." To his credit, Lincoln was acutely aware of his own lack of polish and avoided awkward social situations. As Herndon put it, "For fashionable society he had a marked dislike, although he appreciated its value in promoting the welfare of a man ambitious to succeed in politics." In short, Lincoln valued middle-class mores but never mastered them. Indeed, "the consciousness of his shortcomings as a society man rendered him unusually diffident." He therefore masked his own awkwardness with a whimsical humor that seemed like indifference. One evening, for example, Lincoln answered the front door in his shirtsleeves and admitted two women, "notifying them in his open familiar way, that he would 'trot the women folks out.'" Of course, Mary's anger was "instantaneous." Still, Lincoln seemed to enjoy flaunting the genteel values that Mary cherished but that he could never master. For example, Mary once caught the president feeding a cat with a gold fork at a White House dinner party. In response, Lincoln reasoned that "If the gold fork was good enough for Buchanan I think it is good enough for Tabby."[34]

When his humor failed him, Lincoln's best recourse was to retreat, which the new separation of spheres facilitated. During social occasions at home, Lincoln drew on gender roles as a shield against unwonted gentility. According to Herndon, "at the very first opportunity he would have the men separated from their ladies and crowded close around him in one corner of the parlor," much to Mary's disgust. More often, he would simply leave home. Indeed, contemporaries attributed his long absences to Mary. During a domestic set-to, a neighbor noted, Abraham would "suddenly think of an engagement he had downtown, grasp his hat, and start for his office." During their worst episodes, Lincoln went to work early and came home late or never went home at all. His profession, of course, abetted these absences, and he spent weeks on end riding the circuit. In this fashion, Lincoln turned the Victorian separation of spheres to his own advantage. Christopher Lasch has argued that Victorians viewed the home as a "haven in a heartless world." Lincoln inverted this formula, seeking refuge away from home in the masculine public world. Work thus became a "haven from a heartless home." As Herndon stated more bluntly, "his home was *Hell*" and "absence from home was his *Heaven*." Still others put a positive face on these long absences. "The fact that Mary Todd, by her turbulent nature and unfortunate manner, prevented her husband from becoming a domestic man, operated largely in his favor," a sympathetic friend reminisced, "for he was thereby kept out in the world of business and politics."[35]

Often, however, Mary Lincoln drove her own husband from her home. A Lincoln neighbor, for example, reminisced that "she was seen frequently to drive him from the house with a broomstick." This unfortunate image conjures up the stereotype of a witch riding a broomstick but is in fact typically middle-class. The broom was the symbol of the Victorian housewife's commitment to domestic cleanliness, a quintessentially middle-class tool of housekeeping. Still, the contrast with Springfield's working class is striking. In 1855, for example, the *Springfield Journal* reported that "This forenoon, a German woman with a butcher knife in her hand, bare headed, in great excitement, was seen running up Sixth street, north from the square, in pursuit of a man." A proper, middle-class housewife, of course, would wield not a knife but a broom.[36]

And yet Mary Lincoln, too, violated middle-class standards. As Michael Burlingame has emphasized, she frequently attempted to reproduce the upper-class surroundings of her youth. Herndon found her "cold and repulsive to visitors that did not suit her cold aristocratic blood." A neighbor agreed that she "put on plenty [of] style." Like many Victorian housewives, Mary Lincoln had trouble finding, managing, and keeping servants. In fact, according to one neighbor, she "was quite disposed to make a servant girl of her husband." Abraham Lincoln would "get the breakfast and then dress the children" and finally "wash the dishes before going to his office," a pointed violation of Victorian gender roles. While performing routine housework, she once asked rhetorically, "What would my poor father say if he found me doing this kind of work." While attempting to live beyond her means, she still provoked charges of stinginess, facing the perpetual dilemma of the middle-class housewife—making her home comfortable for her husband while advancing his career, all on a middle-class budget.[37]

From this perspective, the Lincolns' greatest challenge lay ahead in Washington. Life in the White House would obliterate the already ambiguous line between public and private that plagued their lives in Springfield. In short, Abraham Lincoln's home would become his office and his public life merge ineluctably with the once private domain that Mary Lincoln dominated. Her extravagance would win national rather than merely local notoriety, her upper-class pretensions provoking more jealously than ever and her status as First Lady affording more opportunities for public displays of unbecoming ambition than ever before.

As Michael Burlingame has made clear, discord within the Lincoln family arose from personal and psychological as well as social and cultural influences.[38] Yet the rules of Victorian marriage surely contributed their share of problems. Above all, the semipublic life of a politician challenged the basic premises on which Victorian marriages rested, blurring the clear separation between public and private that lay at the heart of family life. Indeed, evidence suggests that marriages like the Lincolns' endured unusual stress during this period of cultural change. The overall divorce rate in Springfield was very low, just 1.3 percent between 1850 and 1860. But divorce rates varied dramatically across the city's occupational groups. Somewhat astoundingly, three groups—farmers, merchants, and professionals—enjoyed extremely stable marriages during the decade. Not a single household head who engaged in agriculture, commerce, or a profession divorced between 1850 and 1860. Overall, both middle-class and working-class couples experienced a thoroughly average divorce rate during the decade—1.3 percent. At the other extreme, however, one group—public officials—stood out. Officeholders suffered by far the highest divorce rate in Springfield. During the 1850s, nearly 9 percent of officeholders divorced, a stunning seven times the average. In fact, couples that Abraham Lincoln knew had a divorce rate three times higher than those he didn't know. Clearly, involvement in politics and public service put unusual stress upon otherwise typical marriages. By blurring the line between public and private life, politics, apparently, bred stormy marriages.[39]

This brings us back to the locked door on election night. The front door at Eighth and Jackson represented—figuratively and literally—the socially defined boundary between the Lincolns' separate spheres. It also represented the boundary between the public and private worlds that the couple struggled to reconcile. Mary Lincoln felt that she could lock the door through her socially prescribed authority within her private, domestic sphere, the home. But Abraham Lincoln's public life always took precedence over this private one. His resounding success in the public sphere opened the lock, so to speak, that guarded the Lincoln home. When he arrived at the door as president-elect, the socially delineated boundary broke down and the public world intruded, as it so frequently did during their married life together. Mary Lincoln now threw open the door and allowed the world to enter.[40]

Notes

1. Walter B. Stevens, *A Reporter's Lincoln* (St. Louis: Missouri Historical Society, 1916), 60.

2. Ibid., 48.

3. Stuart M. Blumin, "The Hypothesis of Middle-Class Formation in Nineteenth-Century America: A Critique and Some Proposals," *American Historical Review* 90 (April 1985): 299–338, and *The Emergence of the Middle Class: Social*

Experience in the American City, 1760–1900 (New York: Cambridge University Press, 1989); Burton J. Bledstein, *The Culture of Professionalism: The Middle Class and the Development of Higher Education in America* (New York: Norton, 1976); Paul E. Johnson, *A Shopkeeper's Millennium: Society and Revivals in Rochester, New York, 1815–1837* (New York: Hill and Wang, 1978); Mary P. Ryan, *Cradle of the Middle Class: The Family in Oneida County, New York, 1790–1865* (New York: Cambridge University Press, 1981); Steven Mintz, *Moralists and Modernizers: America's Pre–Civil War Reformers* (Baltimore: Johns Hopkins University Press, 1995).

4. U.S. Department of Commerce, *Historical Statistics of the United States: Colonial Times to 1970*, vol. 1 (Washington, D.C.: Bureau of the Census, 1975), 457. Excellent introductions to the household economy include Christopher Clark, *The Roots of Rural Capitalism: Western Massachusetts, 1780–1860* (Ithaca, N.Y.: Cornell University Press, 1990); Christopher Clark, "Household Economy, Market Exchange and the Rise of Capitalism in the Connecticut Valley, 1800–1860," *Journal of Social History* 13 (Winter 1979): 169–89; Bruce Laurie, *Artisans into Workers: Labor in Nineteenth-Century America* (New York: Noonday Press, 1989), 15–46; Mary Beth Norton, *Liberty's Daughters: The Revolutionary Experience of American Women, 1750–1800* (Glenview, Ill.: Scott, Foresman, 1980), 3–39; Jeanne Boydston, *Home and Work: Housework, Wages, and the Ideology of Labor in the Early Republic* (New York: Oxford University Press, 1990); Glenna Matthews, *"Just a Housewife": The Rise and Fall of Domesticity in America* (New York: Oxford University Press, 1987), 3–35; John Mack Faragher, *Women and Men on the Overland Trail* (New Haven, Conn.: Yale University Press, 1979), 40–65, and *Sugar Creek: Life on the Illinois Prairie* (New Haven, Conn.: Yale University Press, 1986).

5. Roy P. Basler, ed., *The Collected Works of Abraham Lincoln*, 9 vols., hereafter referred to as *Collected Works* (New Brunswick, N.J.: Rutgers University Press, 1953–55), 4:62; Statement of Dennis F. Hanks to William H. Herndon, June 13, 1865, Herndon-Weik Papers, Library of Congress, reprinted in Douglas L. Wilson and Rodney O. Davis, eds., *Herndon's Informants: Letters, Interviews, and Statements about Abraham Lincoln* (Urbana: University of Illinois Press, 1998), 39, 40.

6. Hanks to Herndon, January 26, 1866, Statement of Hanks to Herndon, June 13, 1865, and Statement of A. H. Chapman to Herndon, September 1865, in Wilson and Davis, *Herndon's Informants*, 176, 40, 41, 99–100.

7. See especially Clark, *Roots of Rural Capitalism*; and Joseph F. Kett, *Rites of Passage: Adolescence in America, 1790 to the Present* (New York: Basic Books, 1977), 11–108.

8. *Collected Works*, 3:511–12, 4:62; Mentor Graham to Herndon, July 15, 1865, in Wilson and Davis, *Herndon's Informants*, 76.

9. *Compendium of the Enumeration of the Inhabitants and Statistics of the United States Sixth Census* (Washington, D.C.: Thomas Allen, 1841), 87, 302–7; "U.S. Manuscript Census, Sangamon County, Illinois," 1840.

10. Jean H. Baker, *Mary Todd Lincoln: A Biography* (New York: Norton, 1987), 4, 6, 12, 32–34, 37, 40, 55, 62–63; Ruth Painter Randall, *Mary Lincoln: Biography of a Marriage* (Boston: Little, Brown, 1953), 23, 25. Hardin County was named after John Hardin, a general in the Kentucky militia; Joseph Nathan Kane, *The American Counties* (New York: Scarecrow Press, 1962), 129. General Hardin was the grandfather of John J. Hardin; Dumas Malone, ed., *The Dictionary of American Biography*, vol. 8 (New York: Charles Scribner's Sons, 1943), 245. John J. Hardin was Mary Todd's third cousin; Baker, *Mary Todd Lincoln*, 136. Richard C. Wade, *The Urban Frontier: The Rise of Western Cities, 1790–1830* (Cambridge, Mass.: Harvard University Press, 1959), offers a succinct examination of social and cultural life in Lexington and other early Western cities.

11. On the "Jacksonian boom" of the 1830s, see Peter Temin, *The Jacksonian Economy* (New York: Norton, 1969), 17–22, 68–69; and Douglass C. North, *The Economic Growth of the United States, 1790–1860* (New York: Norton, 1966), 136–37. Important studies of middle-class family formation include Nancy F. Cott, *The Bonds of Womanhood: "Woman's Sphere" in New England, 1780–1835* (New Haven, Conn.: Yale University Press, 1977); Carl N. Degler, *At Odds: Women and the Family in America from the Revolution to the Present* (New York: Oxford University Press, 1980); Steven Mintz and Susan Kellogg, *Domestic Revolutions: A Social History of American Family Life* (New York: Free Press, 1988), 43–65; Matthews, *"Just a Housewife,"* 35–65; Boydston, *Home and Work*; Ryan, *Cradle of the Middle Class*; Blumin, *Emergence of the Middle Class*; and William L. Barney, *The Passage of the Republic: An Interdisciplinary History of Nineteenth-Century America* (Lexington, Mass.: D. C. Heath, 1987), 73–115.

12. *Sixth Census*, 87; J. D. B. DeBow, *The Seventh Census of the United States, 1850* (Washington, D.C.: Robert Armstrong, 1853), 727–78; Joseph C. G. Kennedy, *Population of the United States in 1860* [Eighth Census] (Washington, D.C.: Government Printing Office, 1864), 105–6.

13. Matthews, *"Just a Housewife,"* 35–65; Richard L. Bushman and Claudia Bushman, "The Early History of Cleanliness in America," *Journal of American History* 74 (March 1988): 1213–38.

14. Elizabeth McDowell Hill, "Illinois Women: Stories of the Pioneer Mothers of Illinois," Women's Exposition Board, 1893, Illinois State Historical Library, Springfield, 24; *Sangamo Journal* (Springfield, Ill.), March 8, 1832, July 6, 1833.

15. Degler, *At Odds*, 178–248; Robert V. Wells, *Uncle Sam's Family: Issues in and Perspectives on American Demographic History* (Albany: SUNY Press, 1985), 28–56, and "Family History and Demographic Transition," *Journal of Social History* 9 (Fall 1975): 1–21.

16. *Sangamo Journal*, June 11, 1836; (Springfield) *Illinois Journal*, November 11, 1847, June 6, 1849, March 25, April 17, May 31, 1851, June 24, 1853, February 7, 1852, April 21, 1854; Statement of James Gourley to Herndon, 1865–66, in Wilson and Davis, *Herndon's Informants*, 453; Charles Sellers, *The Market Revolution: Jacksonian America, 1815–1846* (New York: Oxford University Press, 1991).

17. *Sangamo Journal*, November 20, 1845; *Illinois Journal*, May 10, 1850; Mrs. Stuart to daughter Elizabeth, May 14, 1855, Stuart-Hay Papers, Illinois State Historical Library.

18. Cott, *Bonds of Womanhood*; Mintz and Kellogg, *Domestic Revolutions*, 43–65; Matthews, *"Just a Housewife,"* 35–65; Ruth Bloch, "American Feminine Ideals in Transition: The Rise of the Moral Mother, 1785–1815," *Feminist Studies* 4 (June 1978): 100–126; Linda K. Kerber, "The Republican Mother: Women and the Enlightenment: An American Perspective," *American Quarterly* 28 (Summer 1976): 187–205.

19. Household heads practicing nonmanual but productive occupations in Springfield represented 28.4 percent of white, adult males in 1840, 26.5 percent in 1850, and 27.4 percent in 1860; "U.S. Manuscript Census, Sangamon County, Illinois," 1840, 1850, and 1860. It is possible but not particularly helpful to identify a small upper class in Springfield consisting of the top decile of wealthholders as reported in the U.S. Census. Such a quantitative definition, however, reveals only minor differences between the middle and upper classes. On average, upper-class men were three years older than middle-class men and employed two rather than one servant in their homes, and as a class, they were more heavily native-born—90 percent. A thorough examination of Springfield's upper class demands a qualitative rather than quantitative analysis.

20. Data compiled from "U.S. Manuscript Census, Sangamon County, Illinois," 1850. The analysis includes all 921 white, adult, male household heads living in Springfield in 1850. All differences reported in this study are significant at the .05 level.

21. The fertility data include all white, adult, male household heads living in Springfield in 1850 who could be linked with "Marriage Records, Sangamon County, Illinois, 1821–1850," Illinois Regional Archives Depository, University of Illinois–Springfield, along with an equal number living in Sangamon County in 1850 and drawn at random, for a total of 275.

22. "U.S. Manuscript Census, Sangamon County, Illinois," 1850.

23. Ibid., linked to "Manuscript Poll Books, Sangamon County, Illinois," 1848, Illinois State Historical Library, Springfield, 1848.

24. The Lincolns observed the following birth intervals: Robert to Eddie, 2.4 years; Eddie to Willie, 4.8 years; Willie to Thomas, 2.3 years; for an average of 3.2 years. Kathryn Kish Sklar, "Victorian Women and Domestic Life: Mary Todd Lincoln, Elizabeth Cady Stanton, and Harriet Beecher Stowe," in Cullom Davis, Charles B. Strozier, Rebecca Monroe Veach, and Geoffrey C. Ward, eds., *The Public and the Private Lincoln: Contemporary Perspectives* (Carbondale: Southern Illinois University Press, 1979), 20–37, analyzes the Lincolns' family limitation within the context of Victorian values.

25. "U.S. Manuscript Census, Sangamon County, Illinois," 1850 and 1860.

26. To determine the outlines of Lincoln's circle of acquaintances in Springfield, I matched the names of all voters who appeared in either the 1850 or 1860 manuscript census with the indexes in *Collected Works* and in Earl Schenck

Miers, ed., *Lincoln Day by Day: A Chronology, 1809–1865*, 3 vols. (Washington, D.C., 1960). By including only those acquaintances whose names appeared in written records, this analysis overlooks Lincoln's more casual acquaintances and focuses on those who were important enough to appear in Lincoln's correspondence and personal records.

27. Sklar, "Victorian Women and Domestic Life"; Rodney O. Davis, *Abraham Lincoln: Son and Father*, Edgar S. and Ruth W. Burkhardt Lecture Series (Galesburg, Ill.: Knox College, 1997); Daniel Walker Howe, *The Political Culture of the American Whigs* (Chicago: University of Chicago Press, 1979), 263–98, and *Making the American Self: Jonathan Edwards to Abraham Lincoln* (Cambridge, Mass: Harvard University Press, 1997); Jean Baker, *"Not Much of Me": Abraham Lincoln as a Typical American*, 11th annual R. Gerald McMurtry Lecture (Fort Wayne, Ind.: Louis A. Warren Lincoln Library and Museum, 1988), and *Mary Todd Lincoln*, 99–129; Gabor S. Boritt, *Lincoln and the Economics of the American Dream* (Memphis: Memphis State University Press, 1978), and "The Right to Rise," in Davis, Strozier, Veach, and Ward, *Public and Private Lincoln*, 57–70.

28. *Illinois State Register*, July 1, 1842.

29. Michael Burlingame, *The Inner World of Abraham Lincoln* (Urbana: University of Illinois Press, 1994), presents the most recent and comprehensive analysis of the Lincolns' private life.

30. Miers, *Lincoln Day by Day*, 1:281. Between 1850 and 1860, 28.7 percent of Springfield's middle-class males fell into the working class; "U.S. Manuscript Census, Sangamon County, Illinois," 1850 and 1860.

31. Paul Angle, ed., *Herndon's Life of Lincoln* (Cleveland: World, 1942), 345.

32. Henry B. Rankin, *Intimate Character Sketches of Abraham Lincoln* (Philadelphia: J. B. Lippincott, 1924), 117, 164; Burlingame, *Inner World of Abraham Lincoln*, 273; Davis, *Abraham Lincoln*, 13–14; Rosalind Rosenberg, *Divided Lives: American Women in the Twentieth Century* (New York: Hill and Wang, 1992).

33. Rankin, *Intimate Character Sketches*, 53, 58; Burlingame, *Inner World of Abraham Lincoln*, 321; Robert H. Wiebe, "Lincoln's Fraternal Democracy," in John L. Thomas, ed., *Abraham Lincoln and the American Political Tradition* (Amherst: University of Massachusetts Press, 1986), 11–30.

34. Angle, *Herndon's Life of Lincoln*, 342–43, 345; Burlingame, *Inner World of Abraham Lincoln*, 274.

35. Angle, *Herndon's Life of Lincoln*, 343, 349; Burlingame, *Inner World of Abraham Lincoln*, 271–72, 274, 320; Christopher Lasch, *Haven in a Heartless World: The Family Besieged* (New York: Basic Books, 1977).

36. *Illinois State Journal*, September 18, 1855; Burlingame, *Inner World of Abraham Lincoln*, 277.

37. Burlingame, *Inner World of Abraham Lincoln*, 274–75, 276, 279; Davis, *Abraham Lincoln*, 14–16, esp. 14.

38. Burlingame, *Inner World of Abraham Lincoln*, 268–355.

39. These data include white, adult household heads who lived in Springfield in 1850 and divorced between 1850 and 1860; "U.S. Manuscript Census, Sangamon

County, Illinois," 1850, linked to "Divorce Index, Sangamon County, Illinois, 1850–1860," Illinois Regional Archives Depository, University of Illinois–Springfield. For the circle of Lincoln's acquaintances, see note 26. As a lawyer, Lincoln represented many couples in divorce proceedings, which undoubtedly increased the proportion of his acquaintances who divorced during the 1850s.

40. Karen Halttunen, *Confidence Men and Painted Women: A Study of Middle-Class Culture in America, 1830–1870* (New Haven, Conn.: Yale University Press, 1982), analyzes the symbolism inherent in Victorian domestic architecture.

Abraham Lincoln: The Making
of the Attorney-in-Chief

Frank J. Williams

*A*merica's sixteenth president is best known for his political career, but his quarter-century practice of the law prepared him for his ultimate role as the attorney-in-chief in the executive mansion. His political skills were honed in his training as a lawyer and the practice of the law in Illinois. In many ways, the issues of slavery and secession were legal issues, and he was prepared to tackle them based on his training and the practice of the law that took place within the context of his emerging political career. As a result, he was sharper than John C. Calhoun in understanding the foundation of democratic political theory, he could more than hold his own in the series of debates with the political Little Giant, Stephen A. Douglas, and he similarly was more than a match for the aging chief justice of the United States Supreme Court, Roger B. Taney.

In order to put Abraham Lincoln into the context of his time, we must focus on his life not only as a lawyer but, more specifically, as a circuit-riding lawyer in central Illinois. The time and the place both contributed to his development as a man—and as a lawyer. This chapter explores Lincoln's legal education and training; his relationship with colleagues; his law practice; and the effect these men and these experiences had on his life, not only in Illinois but, eventually, in the White House.

Becoming a Lawyer and a Local Politician

Unlike most people then and now, Abraham Lincoln virtually became a lawyer and a politician at the same time. No one knows precisely when he first toyed with the notion of becoming a lawyer. Legend has it that he read his first law book, *The Revised Laws of Indiana*, while still a youth living in that state, and he is believed to have hung around the tobacco-splattered log courthouses at Rockport and Booneville, watching and listening as country lawyers harangued juries, cross-examined witnesses, and bantered with the judge.[1]

Most of the cases Lincoln witnessed might seem mundane to us—quarrels over missing livestock, suits for slander, disputes over land, bad debts, and the like. But in Lincoln's time, the courtroom offered the onlooker both entertainment and edification—qualities otherwise in short supply in the Indiana backwoods. And, for all their bluster and strut, country lawyers were, by and large, bright and resourceful men, among the first Lincoln ever saw who prospered on their wits rather than by hard physical labor.

Lincoln may have been impressed by the lawyers he saw and heard, but he did not immediately seek to emulate them. With less than a year's formal schooling, he evidently did not think himself up to the rigors of studying law, and over the next few years—first in Indiana, then in New Salem, Illinois—he seems to have tried almost everything else. While at New Salem, he held at least ten different jobs—from store owner to tender of a whiskey still.

Through it all, however, he retained his interest in law: he served on juries, appeared as a witness, wrote out complaints, mortgages, deeds, and other legal instruments for his neighbors, even argued a few cases for free before his friend Bowling Green, the local justice of the peace.

Nonetheless, Lincoln was a victorious politician before he seriously began the study of law. While serving in the Illinois militia during the Black Hawk War and when campaigning for the state legislature in 1834, Lincoln became acquainted with John T. Stuart, a shrewd Springfield attorney who was soon to become the Whig floor leader. It was apparently Stuart who finally persuaded Lincoln that he could master the law, that knowledge of it would make him a better legislator and an abler politician. It is believed that the first law book he actually studied was Sir William Blackstone's *Commentaries on the Laws of England*.[2]

In the 1830s, most American lawyers did not attend law school; indeed, there were only six law schools in the entire country, and all but one were east of the Appalachians. Instead, most would-be attorneys "read law" in a more or less supervised way in the office of a practicing lawyer. Lincoln, however, did it all on his own, poring over books borrowed from Stuart or bought at auction, reading long passages aloud to commit them to memory. The process took him three years—ironically, the same number of years as a law school education today.

Lincoln was understandably proud of his achievement and years later took time out to write to a young law student who was worried, as Lincoln once had been, that learning the law would prove an impossible task. He responded to the young man: "If you are resolutely determined to make a lawyer of yourself, the thing is more than half done already. It is but a small matter whether you read with anybody or not . . . get the books, and read and study them until you understand them and their principal features; and that is the main thing."[3]

Nowhere were law and politics more closely linked than in antebellum Illinois. Lincoln had three law partners over the years: John T. Stuart, Stephen T. Logan, and William H. Herndon. All three were sometime politicians. Lincoln also had scores of part-time "partners," country lawyers scattered across the state with whom he worked when in their neighborhoods; many, perhaps most, of them dabbled in politics as well. His chief political rival, Stephen A. Douglas, was a lawyer and a former judge. Portly David Davis, the circuit judge before whom Lincoln practiced for twelve years, later acted as his presidential campaign manager and became a Lincoln appointee to a seat on the Supreme Court of the United States.

From 1834 to 1837, in addition to the support of fellow veteran and Whig John T. Stuart, Lincoln borrowed books from the Springfield office of Stuart and Dummer. Henry E. Dummer, an erudite Easterner, a graduate of Bowdoin and Harvard, called him "the most uncouth looking young man" he had ever seen.[4] Lincoln did not read law with this firm, however; he read by himself in New Salem. Later in his career, when prospective lawyers applied to read with him, Lincoln invariably suggested that they try his solitary method.

No examination was needed for admission to the Illinois bar until 1841. All that was required was a "certificate of good moral character." Obtaining this, Lincoln received a license from the Illinois Supreme Court on September 9, 1836. On March 1, 1837, he formally enrolled as counsel and was permitted to practice in all Illinois courts.[5]

On April 15, 1837, Lincoln packed his belongings, borrowed a horse, and moved to Springfield, where the *Sangamo Journal* announced that he would practice "conjointly" with John T. Stuart in Office No. 4, Hoffman's Row upstairs. Since the senior partner soon thereafter left to take his seat in Congress, Lincoln inherited the sole management of one of the leading firms in what was to be the capital of Illinois. As junior partner, he chopped wood for the office stove and did the clerical work, a task singularly uncongenial, for he found preparation tedious and office routine drudgery. When he became

junior partner of Stephen Trigg Logan in 1841, the judge showed little toler-
ance for Lincoln's disorderly ways, and he taught Lincoln the fine points of
drafting legal pleadings. The association lasted only three years—in part,
because Logan wanted to make room for his son. "The intellectual self-
discipline acquired through association with the Spartan-like Logan was
to stand Lincoln in good stead through many a trying period in the years
ahead," wrote John J. Duff in *A. Lincoln: Prairie Lawyer*.[6] Lincoln hoped to
function primarily as a trial lawyer, and when he left Judge Logan in 1844,
he entered a partnership with William H. Herndon, a junior who apparently
did "most of the legal research and briefing," a claim that no doubt has been
encouraged by Herndon's own exaggerated accounts of his stewardship.[7]

According to Mark E. Steiner, "Abraham Lincoln was not a diligent student of the law, but when pressed by necessity, he was a sophisticated user
of the available sources of legal information. His early legal training and the
rapid changes in antebellum law ensured that his legal education continued
throughout his law career. Although Lincoln advised would-be lawyers to
'still keep reading' after becoming licensed, Lincoln's reading instead was
directed toward the case before him."[8]

Lincoln had nothing but contempt for the sort of lawyer we now call an
ambulance chaser. "Never stir up litigation," he said. "A worse man can
scarcely be found than one who does this."[9] For Lincoln the practice of law
was more than a means to a comfortable living: it permitted an attorney
to be a useful citizen. "Discourage litigation," he advised young lawyers.
"Persuade your neighbors to compromise whenever you can. Point out to
them how the nominal winner is often a real loser—in fees, expenses, and
waste of time. As a peace-maker, the lawyer has superior opportunity of
being a good man. There will still be business enough."[10]

At the same time, Lincoln was eminently practical. "The matter of fees
is important," he wrote. Not only did they provide the lawyer's "bread and
butter" but also insured his best effort in presenting his client's case. An
attorney should never agree to be paid in advance, Lincoln argued, for once
he was paid he would have to be "more than a common mortal if he [could]
feel the same interest in the case as if something [were] still in prospect."
On the other hand, a fee should always be agreed upon in advance and paid
in full when the time came.[11]

By such methods, Lincoln earned a good living that peaked at about
$5,000 a year during the late 1850s. It was volume, not high fees, that permit-
ted him to do so well. He and his partners handled hundreds of cases each
year. Lincoln was notorious among his fellow lawyers for charging overly

modest fees: $100 was always a large fee for him; many clients paid as little as $5 or $10. The largest bill he ever presented was for $5,000 to the Illinois Central Railroad—and he had to sue to collect.[12]

Brian Dirck notes that "Lincoln was at his best and most comfortable on the [Eighth Judicial] circuit: more so than in his office or the pressure cooker of a courtroom. This was true to the extent that, when he was offered a lucrative Chicago partnership in 1852, he turned it down. He begged off by claiming that 'the close application required of him and the confinement in the office would soon kill him.' Herndon then remembered him adding that 'he preferred going around on the circuit, and even if he earned smaller fees he felt much happier.'"[13]

One of the legends arising out of Lincoln's law practice insists that he only took cases in which he was convinced that right was on his client's side; that he helped only the innocent and the otherwise unprotected. The facts are different. Like most able lawyers, before and since, Lincoln took cases as they came. So long as he presented his client's case in the best possible light and the opposing attorney did the same, he believed, justice would be served. That was and is how the American adversary system is supposed to work.

Mark E. Steiner, in his excellent study, *An Honest Calling: The Law Practice of Abraham Lincoln*, points out that lawyers took cases from every part of the legal spectrum. Lincoln and his colleagues argued both sides of every legal issue, defending capitalists and defending their victims. Lincoln especially defended railroads and was on retainer by the Illinois Central Railroad for a while, but he also sued railroads. Steiner notes that some free-market rules favored capitalists in Lincoln's Illinois. Lawyers in the state adopted the fellow-servant doctrine that limited the social costs of railroading.

Looking at the practice of law on a daily basis in the state, Steiner notes that it would have been difficult for lawyers like Lincoln to hire their guns out only on one side of any issue. They needed cases to pay their rent, and they charged relatively low or competitive fees to get all the business they could as plaintiffs' or defendants' lawyers. On at least five occasions, Lincoln sued for his fees in cases involving less than $10.

Despite the need for many cases to survive economically, Lincoln followed the Whig social philosophy that said, "Settle, mediate disputes in the interest of community order." This was especially true of slander and libel cases, which Lincoln urged clients not to take into the public arena of the courthouse.

No case seems to have been too large—or too insignificant—for Lincoln to take on. Like most Western lawyers of his time, he was a general practitioner, capable of handling the entire range of legal challenges presented to him. A random sampling of the thousands of cases Lincoln argued over twenty-five years hints at the diversity of his practice. At one time or another, he represented a black man suing for his freedom and a slave master seeking the return of runaways; a Revolutionary War widow seeking her pension and the son of an old friend accused of murder; businessmen declaring bankruptcy and banks seeking to foreclose on farmers' mortgages; powerful corporations and the owner of a vagrant pig; an acting troupe seeking to stage a play that the city fathers thought was immoral and a band of temperance women trying to close down a local saloon.

Steiner provides an especially helpful discussion of the *Matson* case. In *Matson*, Lincoln defended the right of a slave owner to take his slaves back into Kentucky, out of Illinois where they might be free. Legions of Lincoln defenders have tried to explain away Lincoln's actions here, so contrary to his widely known hostility to slavery. Steiner notes that Lincoln was here guided by the morality of his role as a lawyer.[14]

As another writer has recognized, Brian Dirck is convincing when he illustrates that accounts of Lincoln's career as a "fiery, folksy fighter against injustice" were overdrawn.[15] As Dirck brings to light, the bulk of Lincoln's legal work consisted of ordinary legal matters commonly handled by small-town lawyers with a general practice. "[P]roperty disputes, petty criminal cases, family arguments over money, neighbor at war with neighbor, bankruptcies, and, oddly, libel suits where local women defended themselves against charges of prostitution," were among the matters that fueled Lincoln's law practice.[16] One commentator described his practice as the "legal equivalent of a small-town doctor's, treating head colds, lice, scarlet fever, and a rare case or two of venereal disease."[17]

While practicing law, Lincoln learned one lesson that would prove immensely important during his presidency. Lincoln learned to detach himself from the issues and, like every good lawyer and negotiator, to seek out a middle ground between adversaries, a technique that would prove far more effective than persistent battle. In this vein, Dirck says, "we can see Lincoln the President trying hard to apply a lawyer's grease to the shrill machinery of war."[18] Dirck observes that Lincoln's "magnanimity was also a function of his lawyerly sense of distance from other people's motives, and his appreciation—honed by decades of witnessing nearly every imaginable form of strife in Illinois's courtrooms—of the value of reducing friction as much as possible."[19] It was virtually a necessity for small-town lawyers to learn to detach themselves from the issues that plagued their clients. It comes as no surprise that one of Lincoln's favorite expressions, his secretary John Hay explained, was "I am in favor of short statutes of limitation in politics."[20] Make no mistake; Lincoln's ardent negotiating and great compromises were nothing short of strategic.

But if Lincoln had few opportunities to demonstrate greatness in the courtroom, he was undeniably a great lawyer-in-politics. Lessons learned in the courtrooms of Illinois stood in good stead throughout his political career. To begin with, the practice of law taught Lincoln to think on his feet. Without a lifetime of courtroom give and take, he could never have dared meet and match Stephen A. Douglas in debate.

The law taught him, too, the precise meaning and weight of words. He once gave his verbose young partner, William Herndon, some shrewd advice about political rhetoric. "Billy, don't shoot too high," he said, "shoot low down, and the common people will understand you. . . . If you shoot too high, your bullets will go over the heads of the mass and only hit those who need no hitting."[21] Years spent trying to persuade juries of skeptical Illinois farmers of the rightness of his clients' causes had taught him that.

And the law taught him how to deal with all kinds of people. A tired Herndon once described the tedious routine of the partners' daily practice. "A law office," he said, "is a dry place for incident of a pleasing kind. If you love stories of murder, rape, fraud, etc., a law office is a good place, but, Lord, let me forget all about a law office."[22] Yet Lincoln never seems to have complained: he enjoyed the diverse parade of would-be clients who climbed the stairs to his Springfield offices to seek his help. From weighing their tales of woe, he learned how to put anxious callers at their ease, how to calm their anger, offer mediation, swiftly see to the heart of the matter. Later, the demands of jealous politicians, timorous generals, and temperamental cabinet members held few terrors for him. Finally, his practice instilled in him a love for the law as an abstract ideal that approached religious faith. He first made these feelings known in a speech titled "The Perpetuation of Our Political Institutions," delivered before the Young Men's Lyceum of Springfield on January 27, 1838. He was not yet twenty-nine years old. Lincoln had been horrified by news reports of mob lawlessness across the land—lynchings, riots, the death of abolitionist editor Elijah Lovejoy at the hands of an Alton, Illinois, crowd. Such events threatened the survival of the republic, he believed.

Passion had been crucial to the Revolution, Lincoln told the lyceum; without violent emotion, the United States could never have been created. But calm and consolidation were needed now. Passion should be replaced by "reason, cold, calculating, unimpassioned reason." How could the republic be rescued from the rising tide of lawlessness? "The answer is simple. Let every American . . . swear by the blood of the Revolution, never to violate in the least particular, the laws of the country; and never to tolerate their violation by others. . . . [L]et reverence for the laws, be breathed by every American mother to the lisping babe, that prattles on her lap—let it be taught in schools, in seminaries, and in colleges;—let it be written in primers, spelling books, and in Almanacs;—let it be preached from the pulpit, proclaimed in legislative halls, and enforced in courts of justice. And, in short, let it become the political religion of the nation."[23]

The overblown language of this youthful address might have embarrassed the mature Lincoln, whose public utterances remain unmatched for their power and simplicity. But the sentiments expressed remain constant throughout his life: he was uncompromisingly committed to the application of "cold, calculating, unimpassioned reason" to the great issues of his time.

The bulk of this documentary heritage of the prairie years is, in terms of quantity at least, a dreary catalog of frontier business transactions. On the surface, Lincoln's voluminous legal correspondence is singularly dull and uninteresting. Few, if any, of the business letters give evidence that their author was a celebrated humorist; but an analysis of their content reveals the motivations, the weaknesses, and the pervasive troubles of our pioneer forefathers. They give, in effect, a bird's-eye view of frontier society.

The first extant legal document in Lincoln's hand is the appraisal of a stray mare. His phrasing forecasts his later stylistic genius: "a bright bay 14 hands high—a Small blaze and a Snip in her face."[24] Lincoln's first bill in the Illinois legislature concerned the disposition of stray horses, a nostalgic item reminiscent of the place the horse once had in American life.[25] Carl Sandburg called Illinois a "horsy country of horsy men" who "brushed horse hair from their clothes after a drive."[26]

From the date of his appraisal of the mare on December 16, 1830, Lincoln regularly performed legal chores for his New Salem neighbors. As one of the few literate members of the community, he drew up petitions, certificates, bills of sale, mortgages, deeds, promissory notes, and election returns long before his formal admittance to the bar. In a melancholy transaction on February 9, 1833, Lincoln and twenty-seven neighbors petitioned the Sangamon County Commissioners to consider the case of one Benjamin Elmore, claiming him "to be insane and wholly unable to earn a livelihood either by labour or any other employment." The petition and all but six of the twenty-eight signatures are in Lincoln's hand, a statistical commentary on frontier literacy. A later document in Lincoln's hand shows that his stepmother, who taught him to read, signed the deed to her property with an X.[27]

Lincoln's well-advertised carelessness about office procedure can be easily documented. Henry C. Whitney, a circuit-riding contemporary, recalled that he "had no method, system or order in his exterior affairs; he had no library, no clerk, . . . no *index rerum*, no diary." When he "wanted to preserve a memorandum, he noted it down on a card and stuck it in a drawer or in his vest pocket."[28] There is, of course, in the *Collected Works* a copy of the apology to a client for losing a letter: After he bought a new hat, Lincoln explained, "the old one was set aside, and so the letter lost sight of for a time." On another occasion, he failed to acknowledge a bond sent by a New York firm. "When I received the bond, I was dabbling in politics; and, of course, neglecting business," the prairie lawyer frankly confessed. "Having since been beaten out, I have gone to work again."[29] Papers often seemed to elude him, and then there was his legendary envelope marked "When you can't find it anywhere else, look here."

Lincoln's casual procedures were hardly different from those of his colleagues. Frontier courts and lawyers amazed sophisticated visitors who found courthouses crude, accommodations miserable, and lawyers and judges slovenly. Courtroom situations were sometimes indeed such as "to make Dame Justice smile."[30] One Eastern lawyer, for example, could hardly "repress a burst of laughter" at the Sangamon County Court in the 1830s: "Judge Logan was on the bench, and Mr. Douglas . . . on the floor. . . . the judge, with his chair tilted back and his heels as high as his head, and in his mouth a veritable corn-cob pipe; his hair standing nine ways for Sunday, while his clothing was more like that worn by a woodchopper than anybody else. There was a railing that divided the audience; outside of which smoking and chewing and spitting tobacco seemed to be the principal enjoyment."[31]

Riding Circuit and Practicing Politics

Cynics have argued that Lincoln rode circuit to get away from his spouse; gay activists have more recently asserted—without historical evidence—that it was due to what they allege was his homosexual orientation. There may be something to the first charge, but it is equally likely that he was trying to support his growing family and Southern belle spouse. It is also fairly clear that he enjoyed himself on circuit because he could practice politics over a larger area than Springfield. But there is no reason to believe it had anything to do with sex, gay or straight. His Springfield legal practice was humdrum, while riding circuit allowed him to exercise his unique political skills, which at that time consisted mostly of entertaining others, while still practicing the law.

Lincoln shone first on the Eighth Judicial Circuit, a vast, shifting area that at one time encompassed fourteen counties—more than one-fifth of the state, or about the size of Maryland. Twice a year the presiding judge made a pilgrimage around the circuit, holding court for a week or so in each county seat. Lincoln and a genial caravan of lawyers went with him.

Riding the circuit was an exhausting grind. Away from home for weeks at a time, the lawyers endured hours of bone-jarring travel, bad food, and worse lodging. The justice dispensed was often hasty and usually informal: lawyers frequently only had moments to confer with their clients in the courthouse square before going to trial; and decisions were often made more on the apparent right and wrong of the thing than on the statutes or legal precedents.

But the circuit had its compensations, and by all accounts, Lincoln thrived on it. He formed lifelong friendships with clients and fellow lawyers and loved to swap stories with them around the tavern fire after court was adjourned for the day. Above all, perhaps, circuit riding got him out among the voters. His courtroom skills, his ready wit—and his political successes— helped win him an enthusiastic following wherever he went and a host of "partisans" all across central Illinois. Such celebrity was good for his law practice, of course, but it was even better for his political career.

Each spring and fall, often from February to June and from September to Christmas, Lincoln jogged about the Eighth Judicial Circuit, first on horse-back, later in a one-seated gig behind "Old Buck," a nag described as "an indifferent, raw-boned specimen."[32] Roads were quagmires in the spring; dusty in the summer and fall. Rivers and streams often had to be forded. "Don't you remember a long black fellow who rode on horseback with you from Tremont to Springfield nearly ten years ago, swimming your horses over the Mackinaw?" Lincoln asked a chance acquaintance while in Congress. "Well, I am that same one fellow yet."[33]

Sleeping accommodations at the vermin-infested inns were primitive, if not intolerable. Often as many as eight guests shared a single room, sometimes three in a bed. One circuit-riding companion described the prevailing fashion in bedroom attire. Lincoln slept in "a home made yellow flannel undershirt" which reached "halfway between his knees and ankles." This particular observer recalled the night-shirted Lincoln as "the ungodliest figure" he had ever seen.[34]

Lincoln's friend Judge Davis has provided a graphic description of the woes of traveling his backwoods judicial circuit. The judge assured his wife that "fleas . . . don't trouble me as much," but he complained that he was being "eaten up by bed bugs and mosquitoes." The food, he said, was "hardly fit for the stomach of a horse." Davis must nevertheless have thrived on this disagreeable diet; his weight was variously recorded as 250 to 300 pounds. Here is his description of one of the most disreputable county-seat taverns: "The tavern at Pulaski is *perhaps* the hardest place you ever saw," he once wrote his wife, ". . . every thing dirty & the eating *Horrible*. . . . The old woman looked as we would suppose the witch of Endor looked. She had a grown daughter, who waited on the table—table greasy—table cloth greasy—floor greasy. . . . The girl was dressed in red calico . . . with a wreath of artificial flowers . . . around her head. . . . I guess the dirt must be half an inch thick all over her."[35]

In the *only* biography of Judge Davis to date, Willard King notes that Lincoln uttered no complaint about miserable accommodations.[36] When the other lawyers escaped for weekends with their families, Lincoln would remain in the dreary county-seat towns, sometimes the center of attention as a storyteller at the local grocery, sometimes as a recluse in some obscure corner. His contemporaries apparently understood his melancholy, and no one disturbed his brooding. Horace White of the *Chicago Tribune* recalled that on some occasions he was "overspread with sadness."[37]

But there were happy times, too: songs by Ward H. Lamon, stories by Lincoln, and uproarious kangaroo courts conducted by the portly Judge Davis.[38] Once at Shelbyville, a leading citizen staged an elegant party for the court, with a supper featuring "Roast Pig, Ham, Turkeys, Custard, Coffee, Tea & a variety of Cakes & Pies" plus "Wines & liquors on the side board." "Lincoln was happy," Davis insisted, "as happy as *he* could be, when on the circuit—and happy in no other place."[39] Circuit riding of course made life difficult for the lawyers' wives. Lincoln married Mary Todd on November 4, 1842. "Nothing new here," he wrote to a friend, "except my marrying, which to me, is a matter of profound wonder." The bride and groom moved into quarters at the Globe Tavern, where, as he explained, room and board for two cost only four dollars a week.[40] Later, they moved to the house on Eighth Street, where Mary endured many lonely days. "I hope," she once wrote in confidence, "you may never feel as lonely as I sometimes do."[41] Judge Davis's wife agreed. "I trust you will never be a politician . . . ," she advised her son at Beloit College. "Life seems too valuable to be wasted in the turmoil of politics."[42]

Court trials on the frontier provided a major form of entertainment as well as the dispensation of justice. Murder trials, particularly, excited intense interest; and hangings gave a sadistic amusement to the thousands who invariably attended. The size of crowds at the largest political meetings, for example, were always compared to those at the most recent execution. After one spectacular murder sensation, the victim unexpectedly turned up alive. The local drayman confided to Mary Lincoln that "it was too *damned* bad to have so much trouble, and no hanging at all."[43]

Trial lawyers were the popular stars of the day. In the days before mass media like radio or television, citizens idolized the traveling lawyers of Judge Davis's court. Lincoln's unique style and manner, to say nothing of his humor, made him a widely acclaimed personality. When he appeared at court in Danville in May 1850, the local paper offered its readers a character sketch. Lincoln, said the editor, was

> rough, uncouth, and unattractive . . . stern . . . and unfamiliar . . . slow and guarded . . . [yet] profound in the depth of his musings. . . . He lives but to ponder, reflect and cogitate. . . . In his examination of witnesses, he displays a masterly ingenuity . . . that baffles concealment and defies deceit. And in addressing a jury, there is no false glitter, no sickly sentimentalism to be discovered. In vain we look for rhetorical display. . . . Seizing upon the minutest points, he weaves them into his argument with an ingenuity really astonishing. . . . Bold, forcible and energetic, he forces conviction upon the mind, and by his clearness and conciseness, stamps it there not to be erased. . . . Such are some of the qualities that place Mr. L. at the head of the profession in this state.[44]

Fellow lawyer Leonard Swett put it this way:

> As he entered the trial, where most lawyers would object he would say he "reckoned" it would be fair to let this in, or that; and sometimes, when his adversary could not quite prove what Lincoln knew to be so-and-so. When he did object to the court, and when he heard his objections answered, he would often say, "Well, I reckon I must be wrong." . . . When the whole thing was unraveled, the adversary would begin to see that what he was so blandly giving away was simply what he couldn't get and keep. By giving away six points and carrying the seventh he carried his case, and the whole case hanging on the seventh, he traded away everything which would give him the least aid in carrying that. Any man who took Lincoln for a simple-minded man would very soon wake up with his back in a ditch.[45]

While on the circuit, Lincoln took up the study of the six books of Euclid, proving theorems amid the chaos and revelry of the county taverns. Sometimes for amusement, he would attempt to force a complicated political issue into a rigid formula of geometry, thus deriving from the cold logic of mathematics a more lucid oral style. Fragments resembling these geometrical exercises sometimes appear in his most eloquent public statements.[46]

Lincoln's study of geometry may have contributed to his orderly arrangement of ideas. "His was," says John Frank, "an inquiring but not a wandering mind." Frank lauds his "natural flair for good tight organization . . . one of the most valuable attributes for a lawyer." In spite of his excellent memory, Lincoln nevertheless relied on carefully prepared notes, one set of which concluded with the line, "Skin the defendant."[47] He was especially meticulous in clarifying the complicated facts of scene and situation. In the Rock Island Bridge case, for example, he visited the scene of the disaster and carefully scrutinized the river currents and all the circumstances that contributed to the collision of the steamboat *Effie Afton*. Once he thoroughly understood the situation, the prairie lawyer had no difficulty in marshaling his evidence before a jury, though Herndon sometimes thought he spent too much time "reasoning out his positions."[48]

Since no one took the trouble to make a verbatim record of frontier trials, scholars must rely upon the hazy reminiscences of participants to reconstruct courtroom arguments. Lincoln's dramatic defense of Duff Armstrong and his ingenious use of an almanac to prove the unreliability of an opposing witness are well known. In that case, the prosecution's star witness adamantly testified that although it was 11:00 P.M., by the moonlight he saw Lincoln's client strike the deceased with a sling shot. When Lincoln questioned the witness, he confronted him with an almanac for 1857 that showed that at 11:00 P.M. that night the moon was low in the sky and could not have illuminated the area, as the witness contended. The witness searched for an answer but had none. The case became so famous that it has been called "The Almanac Trial" ever since. Less well-heralded is Lincoln's precise phrasing, an attribute that contributed to the stereotype of "Honest Abe" and that helps to account for his powerful influence with juries and voters. "I do not state a thing and say I know it, when I do not," he explained in one of his debates with Douglas. ". . . I mean to put a case no stronger than the truth will allow."[49] The naked precision, the blunt truth of his legal phrasing still shines through 150 years later.

Lincoln's colleague, James C. Conkling, recalled, "No man was stronger than he when on the right side, and no man weaker when on the opposite. Knowledge of this fact gave him additional strength before the court or a jury, when he chose to insist that he was right. He indulged in no rhetorical flourishes or mere sentimental ideas, but could illustrate a point by one of his inimitable stories, so as to carry conviction to the most common intellect."[50]

Judge David Davis said:

> The framework of his mental and moral being was honesty and the wrong was poorly defended by him. The ability which some eminent lawyers possess of explaining away the bad points of a cause by ingenious sophistry, was denied him. In order to bring into full activity his great powers, it was necessary that he should be convinced, of the right and justice of the matter which he advocated. When so convinced, whether the cause was great or small, he was usually successful. He read law books but little, except when the case in hand made it necessary; yet he was usually self-reliant, depending on his own resources, and rarely consulting his brother lawyers, either on the management of his case or on the legal questions involved.[51]

Abraham Lincoln believed in alternative dispute resolution before that term was ever coined. Judge Davis recalled that "he was not fond of controversy, and would compromise a lawsuit whenever practicable."[52] As Steiner has noted, "Lincoln always seemed comfortable with the lawyering style demanded by purely local lawsuits. Like most lawyers in small communities, he was keenly aware that the community orientation of those disputes favored mediation and compromise, and he thus tried to serve as a mediator or peacemaker."[53] And Lincoln was, at the same time, collegial. "Mr. Lincoln was the fairest and most accommodating of practitioners, granting all favors which he could do consistently with his duty to his client, and rarely availing himself with any unwary oversight of his adversary."[54]

Fellow Illinois attorney Abram Bergen wrote about Lincoln's defense of "a very wealthy, aristocratic Democrat . . . colonel Dunlap, in an action for ten thousand dollars damage brought against him by the editor of the opposition, or as many then called it, the abolition paper, on account of a deliberate, carefully planned, cowhiding administered by the colonel to the editor on a bright Saturday afternoon in the public square of the town, in the presence of hundreds of the town and country people whom the colonel desired to witness that degrading performance. The editor's attorney, Benjamin Edwards, brought the jury to tears, with his description of the wounds to the editor's body." But Bergen described what happened next:

> Before all eyes were dry, it came Lincoln's turn to speak. He dragged his huge feet off the table on the top of which they had been calmly resting, set them on the floor; gradually lifted up and partly straightened out his great length of legs and body and took off his coat. While he was removing his coat, I, and all others noticed his eyes were intently fixed upon something

on the table before him. He picked up the object, a paper, from the table. Scrutinizing it closely and without having uttered a word, he broke out into a long loud, peculiar laugh, accompanied by his most wonderfully funny facial expression—there never was anything like the laugh or the expression. A comedian might well pay thousands of dollars to learn them—it was magnetic. The whole audience grinned. He laid the paper down slowly, took off his cravat; again picked up the paper, looked at it again, and repeated the laugh. It was contagious. By that time all in the packed courtroom were tittering or trying to hold in their cachinnations. He then deliberately took off his vest, showing his one yarn suspender, took up the paper, again looked at it and again indulged in his own loud peculiar laugh. Its effect was absolutely irrepressible. The usually solemn and dignified Judge Woodson, the jury and the whole audience could hold themselves no longer, and broke out into a long, loud continued roar; all this before Lincoln had ever uttered a word. I call this acting. The occasion for his merriment was not very funny, but it was to the point. He apologized to the court for his seemingly rude behavior and explained that the damages as claimed was at first written $1,000. He supposed the plaintiff afterwards had taken a second look at the colonel's pile and had thereupon concluded that the wounds to his honor were worth $10,000. The result was to at once destroy the effect of Edwards' tears, pathos, towering indignation, and high wrought eloquence and to render improbable a verdict for more than $1,000. Lincoln immediately and fully admitted that the plaintiff was entitled to a verdict for some amount, argued in mitigation of damages, told a funny story applicable, and specially urged the jury to agree upon some amount. The verdict was for a few hundred dollars and was entirely satisfactory to Lincoln's clinet [*sic*].[55]

As Dirck has pointed out, "Lincoln knew that people judge cases as much by their hearts as by their heads . . . in the courtroom, he understood how to manipulate emotions in the name of [legal] reason."[56]

At times, Lincoln served as judge, as recounted by William H. Somers, who had been clerk of the Circuit Court of Champaign County. "Judge Davis frequently called Mr. Lincoln to take the bench while he went out for exercise, a courtesy which I do not remember of seeing him extend to any other attorney of the twenty or more in attendance."[57]

Attorney-in-Chief

When Abraham Lincoln took his oath as the sixteenth president of the United States on March 4, 1861, he had less experience in public office than any previous president with the exception of Zachary Taylor and perhaps William Henry Harrison. He had held no position of executive responsibility. He had

had no formal education worthy of the name. He had served four terms in a frontier state legislature and only one term in Congress. His principal training had been acquired in the dingy courtrooms of the Eighth Circuit—in remote places like Bloomington, Danville, Decatur, and Metamora. His companions on the circuit, particularly David Davis, Leonard Swett, and Ward H. Lamon, were largely responsible for his nomination at the Wigwam in Chicago. The friends he had made during his legal travels provided the popular support he needed in his home state. In preparing to face frontier juries, the unassuming backwoods pleader had readied himself to influence the behavior of editors, politicians, and diplomats. "Nobody," said Horace White of the *Chicago Tribune*, "knew better than he what was passing in the minds of the people."[58] Dumas Malone, the biographer of Thomas Jefferson, admits that "not even in the Declaration of Independence" did the Sage of Monticello "ever attain the stark grandeur of Lincoln's most famous passages." Lincoln's intimate association with the people made him "a conscious craftsman, an artist in the use of words—spoken words."[59]

It is the accepted version of practically all his biographers that Lincoln concluded the practice of law on the day when he last visited his office to wind up some cases that were then pending. He talked of old times with his partner, Herndon, and they exchanged reminiscences. As Lincoln gathered a bundle of papers and stood ready to leave, he told Herndon that their law partnership would go on, that their shingle would stay up. We are led to believe that, since this was his last visit to his law office, and since he never returned to it, he concluded the practice of law in all its phases on that date. Nothing could be farther from the truth. It would be more accurate to say that the most important part of his career as a lawyer was just beginning; that he was about to put to the highest use all that he had learned since his admission to the bar.

The fruition of that training was displayed in his grappling with the grave constitutional questions that he was called upon to solve from the very moment of his inauguration; for the emissaries of the South were upon him with their proposals for adjusting the withdrawal of the Confederate states. The problems of Lincoln's presidency were largely legal problems, and Lincoln was the legal expert who had to deal with them.

He analyzed and decided the numerous novel, important, and difficult questions of constitutional interpretation and law that came with the war—questions relating to the president's war powers, conscription, treason, suspension of the writ of habeas corpus, military rule and arbitrary arrest, martial law and military commissions, ordinances applicable to a regime of conquest and occupied districts of the South, confiscation, emancipation, compensation to slaveholders, the partition of Virginia, and creation of the new state of West Virginia; and questions concerning the relations between federal and state governments that had not arisen since the adoption of the Constitution.[60] These were some of the grave problems Lincoln had to solve. Consider, for example, his justification for suspension of habeas corpus in his July 4, 1861, message to Congress: "To state the question more directly, are all the laws, *but one,* to go unexecuted and the government itself go to pieces, lest that one be violated? Even in such a case, would not the official oath be broken, if the government should be overthrown, when it was believed that disregarding the single law would tend to preserve it?"[61]

There was, of course, an attorney general, Edward Bates, who did his best in advising the president, but practically every novel question was brought to Lincoln for final decision. It is certain that none of his predecessors, nor any president who has followed him, has had to solve such novel and grave constitutional and legal problems as Lincoln faced, and there had been none who was so completely his own legal adviser.

Conclusions

John P. Frank has written that Lincoln

> may not have brought great learning to the practice of law, but Lincoln did have five qualities which were either inherent or highly developed, and these qualities together are so invaluable that the best lawyer in America might well trade all his books for them:
>
>> A personality which attracted clients and instilled confidence in juries.
>> A striking capacity in the organization of material to come clearly to the heart of a matter.
>> Coupled with this was his brevity.
>> Restrained and effective verbal expression.
>> A peculiarly retentive mind.
>> He worked.[62]

To be sure, Lincoln's place in history derives not from his career as a lawyer but from his qualities as a human being and his seminal achievements as president. Still, the law nurtured his rhetoric and analysis, honed his skills of advocacy and debate, and developed his style in the public arena. In the practice of law, he gained professional and public recognition, became involved in public affairs, and forged friendships and alliances that lasted a lifetime. He was part of the evolution of American common law on the frontier of his day and left an imprint on it. And the imprint the law left on him is reflected in his writings and in his actions as president.

Notes

The author acknowledges his appreciation to Nicole Dulude and Martha L. Agapay for their research and assistance.

1. Brian Dirck, *Lincoln the Lawyer* (Urbana: University of Illinois Press, 2007), 15.

2. Ibid., 16.

3. Roy P. Basler, ed., *The Collected Works of Abraham Lincoln,* 9 vols., hereafter referred to as *Collected Works* (New Brunswick, N.J.: Rutgers University Press, 1953–55), 2:327.

4. Douglas L. Wilson and Rodney O. Davis, eds., *Herndon's Informants: Letters, Interviews, and Statements about Abraham Lincoln* (Urbana: University of Illinois Press, 1997), 442–43.

5. Wayne C. Temple, "Lincoln's First Step to Becoming a Lawyer," *Lincoln Herald* 70 (Winter 1968): 207.

6. John J. Duff, *A. Lincoln: Prairie Lawyer* (New York: Rinehart, 1960), 94.

7. Ibid., 79.

8. Mark E. Steiner, *An Honest Calling: The Law Practice of Abraham Lincoln* (DeKalb: Northern Illinois University Press, 2006), 56.

9. Notes for a Law Lecture [July 1850], *Collected Works,* 2:81–82.

10. Ibid.

11. Ibid.

12. William H. Herndon, *Herndon's Life of Lincoln: The History and Personal Recollections of Abraham Lincoln* (New York: Da Capo, 1983), 284.

13. Dirck, *Lincoln the Lawyer,* 53.

14. Steiner, *Honest Calling,* 136.

15. Adam Gopnik, "Angels and Ages: Lincoln's Language and Its Legacy," *New Yorker,* May 28, 2007.

16. Ibid.

17. Ibid.

18. Dirck, *Lincoln the Lawyer,* 169.

19. Ibid.

20. Tyler Dennett, ed., *Lincoln and the Civil War in the Diaries of John Hay* (New York: Dodd, Mead, 1939), 239.

21. Don E. Fehrenbacher and Virginia Fehrenbacher, eds., *Recollected Words of Abraham Lincoln* (Stanford: Stanford University Press, 1996), 252.

22. Emanuel Hertz, ed., *The Hidden Lincoln: From the Letters and Papers of William H. Herndon* (New York: Viking Press, 1938), 177.

23. *Collected Works,* 1:108–15.

24. Ibid., 1:3.

25. Ibid., 1:27.

26. Carl Sandburg, *Abraham Lincoln: The Prairie Years*, 2 vols. (New York: Harcourt, Brace, 1926), 1:298.

27. *Collected Works*, 1:17, 263.

28. Henry C. Whitney, *Life on the Circuit with Lincoln* (Caldwell, Idaho: Caxton, 1940), 122.

29. *Collected Works*, 2:80–81, 139.

30. Frances McCurdy, "Courtroom Oratory of the Pioneer Period," *Missouri Historical Review* 54 (October 1961): 2.

31. Albert A. Woldman, *Lawyer Lincoln* (Boston: Houghton Mifflin, 1936), 28.

32. Albert J. Beveridge, *Abraham Lincoln, 1809–1858*, 2 vols. (Boston: Houghton Mifflin, 1928), 1:501.

33. *Collected Works*, 1:450.

34. Beveridge, *Abraham Lincoln*, 1:504.

35. Willard L. King, *Lincoln's Manager, David Davis* (Cambridge: Harvard University Press, 1960), 75, 77, 83.

36. Ibid., 77.

37. David C. Mearns, ed., *The Lincoln Papers*, 2 vols. (Garden City: Doubleday, 1948), 1:190.

38. Whitney, *Life on the Circuit*, 61–88.

39. King, *Lincoln's Manager*, 71, 85.

40. *Collected Works*, 1:305, 325.

41. Reinhard Luthin, *The Real Abraham Lincoln* (Englewood Cliffs, N.J.: Prentice Hall, 1960), 133.

42. King, *Lincoln's Manager*, 142.

43. Paul M. Angle and Earl Schenck Miers, eds., *The Living Lincoln: The Man, His Mind, His Times, and the War He Fought, Reconstructed from His Own Writings* (New Brunswick, N.J.: Rutgers University Press, 1955), 40–41.

44. Willard L. King, "Riding the Circuit with Lincoln," *American Heritage*, February 1955, 106.

45. Herndon, *Life of Lincoln*, 269–70.

46. William H. Herndon and Jesse W. Weik, *Abraham Lincoln: The True Story of a Great Life*, 2 vols. (New York: D. Appleton, 1909), 1:308–9, 319.

47. John P. Frank, *Lincoln as a Lawyer* (Urbana: University of Illinois Press, 1961), 67–68, 78.

48. Beveridge, *Abraham Lincoln*, 1:600; Joseph F. Newton, *Lincoln and Herndon* (Cedar Rapids: Torch, 1910), 252–53.

49. *Collected Works*, 3:126.

50. Rufus Rockwell Wilson, *Lincoln among His Friends: A Sheaf of Intimate Memories* (Caldwell, Idaho: Caxton, 1942), 105–12.

51. Ibid., 466.

52. Rufus Rockwell Wilson, *Intimate Memories of Lincoln* (Caldwell, Idaho: Caxton, 1942), 70.

53. Steiner, *Honest Calling*, 75.

54. Wilson, *Intimate Memories of Lincoln*, 69.

55. Ibid., 76–77.

56. Dirck, *Lincoln the Lawyer*, 102–3.

57. Wilson, *Intimate Memories of Lincoln*, 101.

58. Herndon and Weik, *Abraham Lincoln*, 1:xxi.

59. Dumas Malone, "Jefferson and Lincoln," *Abraham Lincoln Quarterly* 5 (June 1949): 341–42.

60. Frank J. Williams, *Judging Lincoln* (Carbondale and Edwardsville: Southern Illinois University Press, 2002), 34–79.

61. *Collected Works*, 4:430.

62. Frank, *Lincoln as a Lawyer*, 97–98.

"No Such Right": The Origins of Lincoln's Rejection of the Right of Property in Slaves

James Oakes

"*I* can express all my views on the slavery question," Lincoln declared in August 1858, "by quotations from Henry Clay." One month earlier he said that he had "always hated slavery, I think as much as any Abolitionist," adding—as if this explained everything—"I have been an Old Line Whig."[1] What did Lincoln mean by this? Which of his "views on the slavery question" did he trace back to Clay, the most prominent Whig politician of the age? In the quotation Lincoln cited most often, Clay had looked back to the nation's founding principles, to the ideal of fundamental human equality, as a solemn commitment to bring slavery to an end in America. It goes against the grain of most scholarship to trace the promise of human equality back to the Whig Party, yet Lincoln made matters worse when he sat down a year later to "hail" Thomas Jefferson not for his proposition that "all men are created equal" but for a very different legacy, one more reasonably derived from the Whigs. The "Jefferson party," Lincoln explained, was marked by its "superior devotion to the personal rights of men, holding the rights of property to be secondary only, and greatly inferior" (*Collected Works*, 3:375). This precept—the superiority of personal over property rights—is not the same as fundamental human equality, and it is almost certain that Lincoln did not get it from Thomas Jefferson. He was putting Jefferson's egalitarianism into Henry Clay's mouth, and Whig idealism into Jefferson's.

The tangled pathways along which Lincoln traced the origins of his own antislavery politics have been uncovered in recent scholarship.[2] Some of the old orthodoxies still stand: There is no reason to reject the commonplace view that at some point—probably in the 1820s—Jeffersonian republicanism fused with populist racism to produce the proslavery Democratic Party.[3] But the story has lately become more complicated. It now seems misleading to draw one straight line from Andrew Jackson to Jefferson Davis and another from Henry Clay to Abraham Lincoln.[4] From the very beginning, the politics of slavery was messier than that. After the Revolution, for example, the abolition of slavery in the North was accomplished not by a handful of prominent Federalists but by broader blocs of Jeffersonian Republicans leading the charge within the various state legislatures.[5] In Congress as well, it was Northern Jeffersonians who struggled without success to restrict the expansion of slavery into Mississippi Territory, the Louisiana Purchase, Kentucky, and Missouri. In Ohio, Indiana, and Illinois, Northern Republicans again took the lead in thwarting the slaveholders who tried to overturn the Northwest Ordinance's ban on the importation of slaves into those areas. During the Missouri crisis, the congressional vote split along sectional lines, with Northern Jeffersonians staunchly supporting slavery's restriction.[6] Scholars have recently traced the ideological lineage from Jacksonian attacks on the "money power" in the 1830s to Republican Party attacks on the "slave power" in the 1850s. Thus the well-known critique of the slave power derived as much from Jacksonian anticapitalism as from free-labor ideology. If proslavery Democrats could trace their roots to Jeffersonian republicanism, so could a large number of Free-Soilers.[7]

But Lincoln came out of a different tradition.[8] Whigs had never attacked the money power, and perhaps for that reason the concept of the slave power played a minor role in his critique of slavery.[9] Still, he and his party had their own concerns about the market revolution, concerns that would later reverberate through Lincoln's antislavery politics. Above all, Whigs were disturbed by the sheer disorder, even anarchy, that seemed to spread as capitalism developed. They recoiled from the apparent loosening of social and political restraints and so resisted the extreme individualism and unfettered self-interest unleashed by "the great transformation" of their day. Whigs devoted much of their energy to restricting and channeling the otherwise disruptive forces of the market. They would close down businesses on Sunday. They would regulate the banks. They would protect debtors from the ruinous effects of bankruptcy and shield domestic manufacturers from foreign competition. They imagined the family as a "haven in a heartless world," a place where human values prevailed over the values of the marketplace. Whigs wanted children to go to school rather than to work. They denounced greed, speculation, and hedonistic consumerism. In all of this, the Whigs developed a critique of unrestrained capitalism that has remained a fixture of American political culture to this day.[10]

What the Whigs feared was not capitalism as such but capitalism *without restraints.* Markets and individuals alike tended to be selfish; they could not be counted on to act in the interest of society as a whole. And just as individuals needed to be socialized by the guiding hand of institutions—families, churches, schools, prisons, asylums, and governments—so too did the economy require the guidance of centralized banks, protective tariffs, and state-sponsored internal improvements. Markets, like individuals, were dangerous if left entirely to themselves. Banks had to be regulated, usurers suppressed, and insolvent debtors relieved. Even westward expansion had to be controlled; restrained but not stopped. "Opposed to the instinct of boundless acquisition," Horace Greeley explained in 1851, "stands that of Internal Improvement."[11]

Lincoln embodied this tradition. The first speech we have of his, dating from 1832, argued for "the public utility of internal improvements"—he was especially keen on dredging the Sangamon River—thus making it easier for farmers to get their surpluses to market. Yet in the same speech, Lincoln proposed a law against "the baneful and corroding" practice of usury. It should be a strict law, he said, tough enough to prevent lenders from evading the ban on exorbitant rates of interest. Here was a characteristically Whig stance: Lincoln would encourage the development of capitalism while at the same time legally restraining its excesses. Similarly, he would establish a system of universal public education, "and by its means, morality, sobriety, enterprise and industry, shall become much more general than at present." For Lincoln, as for many Whigs, the weak institutions of early America were simply inadequate. It would take the firm hand of the state, acting through its schools, to cultivate a generation of sober, industrious, and enterprising young citizens. Whatever else Whigs stood for, it was not laissez faire (*Collected Works*, 1:5–9).

There had to be some clamping down on the unfettered market. Lincoln was particularly clear about this in an address he delivered to the Washington Temperance Society in Springfield, Illinois, on February 22, 1842. It was a peculiar speech—a lengthy critique of the temperance movement by a lifelong advocate of temperance. For too long, Lincoln said, the movement's leaders had tended to be moralistic and heavy-handed, condemning drinkers as dissolute, dismissing them as hopeless. Now things were beginning to change, and the movement was enjoying greater success. Lincoln sensed a more humane attitude toward the "dram drinker," but he also detected a new appreciation of the evils of "dram selling." If reformers had once been too harsh on those who bought and consumed alcohol, Lincoln argued, they had also been too easy on those who manufactured and sold it. In those bad old days, he said, liquor was treated as if it were "a respectable article of manufacture and of merchandize. The making of it was regarded as an honorable livelihood; and he who could make most, was the most enterprising and respectable. Large and small manufactories of it were every where erected, in which all the earthly goods of their owners were invested. Wagons drew it from town to town—boats bore it from clime to clime, and the winds wafted it from nation to nation; and merchants bought and sold it, by wholesale and by retail, with precisely the same feelings, on their part of the seller, buyer, and bystander, as are felt at the selling and buying of flour, beef, bacon, or any other of the real necessaries of life" (*Collected Works*, 1:274). Until recently, he went on to argue, it had been the "universal public opinion" that alcohol could be manufactured, distributed, and sold, no differently than any other commodity—flour, beef, or bacon. But it was no such thing, Lincoln insisted. Liquor was not one of the basic groceries that people bought and consumed each day, and it should not be treated as such.

Twelve years later, Lincoln would begin talking about slavery in almost the same way. He would no more denounce slaveholders as sinners in the 1850s than he had condemned drunkards as dissolute in the 1840s. He would gauge the progress of antislavery by the same standard he had used to measure the progress of temperance—how far it advanced the principle of self-government (*Collected Works*, 1:278). If intemperance undermined the alcoholic's ability to govern himself, how much greater was the affront slavery represented to the right of all humans to govern themselves. But there was another theme in the temperance address, reflected in the longer passage quoted above, that echoed in Lincoln's later antislavery argument. There were limits to the reach of the marketplace, Lincoln declared; there were some things that should not be bought and sold. In the 1840s, it was alcohol. In the 1850s, it was human beings.

Lincoln thought most people agreed that when it came to slavery the forces of the market had to be restrained. As evidence, he pointed repeatedly to the various ways in which Americans had placed limits on the trade in slaves. The Founders themselves had denounced the Atlantic slave trade, made provision for the nation's eventual withdrawal from it, and impatiently outlawed it at the earliest possible date. When that time came, even most Southerners in Congress supported the withdrawal. Twelve years later, in 1820, most Southern congressmen once again joined a unanimous North in declaring participation in the international slave trade a capital offense. "Have not all civilized nations," Lincoln asked, "our own among them, made the slave trade capital, and classed it with piracy and murder?" (*Collected Works*, 2:245). As part of the compromise measures passed in 1850, Congress had acquiesced in the North's demand for the abolition of the slave trade in Washington, D.C. And didn't Southerners themselves stigmatize the "SLAVE DEALER" as a disreputable lowlife, someone to be shunned in decent society (2:264)? All of this suggested to Lincoln a wide acceptance, even a consensus, that some forms of commerce were simply unacceptable.

At the same time, Lincoln began to warn that the consensus was breaking down. The slaveholders claimed a constitutional right to bring their slaves into the Western territories, but if that were true, Lincoln argued, they must also have the right to bring slaves from Africa to the United States. "[I]f it is a sacred right for the people of Nebraska to take and hold slaves there," Lincoln reasoned, "it is equally their sacred right to buy them where they can buy them cheapest; and that undoubtedly will be on the coast of Africa" (*Collected Works*, 2:267). Lincoln used this argument as a scare tactic, repeating it over and over in the late 1850s, warning that if the slaveholders were not stopped the time would surely come when the Atlantic slave trade would be reopened. Here, too, he was assuming that few Northerners—not even Stephen Douglas—were prepared to tolerate an unregulated market in African slaves.

The roots of this argument are buried deep within the political culture from which Lincoln sprang, although they have been obscured by a long tradition that sees Whig ideology as an uncomplicated defense of the emerging capitalist system.[12] In fact, Lincoln was uttering basic Whig orthodoxy when he insisted that the forces of the market had to be restrained, whether this involved matters as relatively insignificant as the manufacture and sale of alcoholic beverages or as large and disruptive as the sale of human beings.

But if Lincoln thought it was immoral to treat a human being like property, he would have to translate that moral precept into a legal principle that carried political conviction. For in antebellum politics, as Jonathan Bingham recalled, "everything was reduced to a Constitutional question."[13] The more Lincoln thought about it, the closer he came to the proposition that there was no such thing as a "right of property" in human beings. When he first took up antislavery politics in 1854, Lincoln had nothing to say about the right of property in slaves. It took time for his argument to emerge; it grew out of his reactions to the shocking events of the decade, in particular to the *Dred Scott* decision of 1857. Even so, Lincoln's ultimate denial of a right to property in slaves rested on two deeply held convictions that were already in place when he gave his first major antislavery speech: that slavery dehumanized its victims, and that it was sustained by an all-too-human selfishness.

From his earliest years in public life, Lincoln associated the treatment of slaves with the treatment of animals. In 1840, while still in the Illinois legislature, he wrote a letter to Mary Speed, commenting on a group of slaves he had seen while on a trip down the Mississippi River. "They were chained six and six together . . . ," Lincoln wrote, "strung together precisely like so many fish upon a trot-line" (*Collected Works*, 1:260). That sort of language became habitual with Lincoln after he took up antislavery politics in 1854. At Peoria he spoke of the slave trade in the nation's capital as "a sort of negro-livery stable, where droves of negroes were collected, temporarily kept, and finally taken to Southern markets, precisely like droves of horses" (2:249). Yet Americans were being taught to believe that such treatment was perfectly acceptable, and the chief architect in this project of dehumanization, Lincoln claimed, was Stephen Douglas, the leading voice of the Democratic Party in the North. Through their relentless race-baiting, their demagogic insistence that blacks were not entitled to the fundamental rights enumerated in the Declaration of Independence, Douglas and his fellow Democrats had brought about a "significant change" in public opinion—"no less than changing the negro, in your estimation, from the rank of a man to that of a brute. They are taking him down," Lincoln concluded, "and placing him, when spoken of, among reptiles and crocodiles" (3:424).

This inexorable dehumanization of blacks was compounded, even motivated, by a selfish disposition that left all too many people blind to the moral disgrace of slavery. "Slavery," Lincoln said, "is founded in the selfishness of man's nature" (*Collected Works*, 2:271). He loaded his speeches with blunt assaults on insatiable greed, naked self-interest, and the relentless pursuit of mammon. He likened the slaveholders, with their avaricious thirst for ever more land, to one of two starving men who had agreed to divide their last loaf of bread. But "the one," presumably the slaveholder, "hastily swallowed his half, and then grabbed the other half just as he was putting it to his mouth!" (2:262). The true principle of self government was fundamentally incompatible with slavery, Lincoln insisted. "They are as opposite as God and mammon" (2:275).The position of the black man was declining in part, Lincoln claimed, because "Mammon is after him" (2:404). The Southerners were at an advantage in the debate over slavery's extension because they were united "as one man" by an "immense, palpable pecuniary interest," whereas "moral principle is all, or nearly all, that unites us in the North" (2:351).

Lincoln attacked Northern greed as well as Southern, claiming repeatedly that selfish motives had not only robbed the slaves of their freedom but were now threatening to destroy the liberties of free men and women as well. In his Peoria speech, Lincoln warned that "In our greedy chase to make profit of the negro, let us beware, lest we 'cancel and tear to pieces' even the white man's charter of freedom" (*Collected Works*, 2:276). In a private letter written the following year, he complained of the blind self-interest that was leading Americans to abandon the maxim that all men are created equal. Now that "we have grown fat," Lincoln wrote, "we have become so greedy to be *masters* that we call the same maxim 'a self-evident lie'" (2:318). The "selfishness" at the heart of slavery, Lincoln warned, threatened to undermine the founding principle of fundamental human equality. Left undisturbed, this selfishness diminished people's "love of justice" and undermined the liberties even of free men and women. The "WHOLE PEOPLE," he cautioned, were in danger of losing their freedom "to a mere hand-full of men, bent only on temporary self-interest" (2:270).

In Lincoln's mind, avarice and the dehumanization of blacks were inseparable. And once again, the archvillain in Lincoln's story, the person who brought selfishness and dehumanization together, was Stephen Douglas. By arguing that slavery should be allowed to go wherever it proved to be efficient, Lincoln complained, Douglas "favors the idea, that if you can make more money by flogging niggers than by flogging oxen, there is no moral consideration which should interfere or prevent your doing so" (*Collected Works*, 2:545). As early as 1856, Lincoln complained that slavery "is looked upon by men in the light of dollars and cents" (2:365). By 1859, he declared, repeatedly, that Douglas was responsible for spreading this self-interested cast of mind. To him, "it is simply a question of dollars and cents" (3:349). Lincoln used the same phrase, made the identical accusation, twice in a single speech in Chicago in March of 1859 and twice again in another speech at Columbus, Ohio, in September (3:367, 368, 423, 425). In the latter speech, he offered a stinging summation that brought together the phrasing of Henry Clay, the ideals of Thomas Jefferson, the attack on dehumanization, and the condemnation of greed: Stephen Douglas and his supporters were busily at work, Lincoln said, "blowing out the moral lights around us; teaching that the negro is no longer a man but a brute; that the Declaration has nothing to do with him; that he ranks with the crocodile and the reptile; that man, with body and soul, is a matter of dollars and cents" (3:425).

Although he had been denouncing the dehumanization and selfishness of slavery since 1854, it was not until 1857 that Lincoln began to question the

existence of a right of property in slaves, and it was the *Dred Scott* decision
that forced him to do it. Before then, Lincoln had focused his criticism on Stephen Douglas's "deceitful" doctrine of popular sovereignty. But the Supreme
Court undermined both Lincoln *and* Douglas by asserting in its majority
decision, written by Chief Justice Roger Taney, that "the right of property
in a slave is distinctly and expressly affirmed in the Constitution." This was
a remarkable claim in view of the well-established fact that the delegates in
Philadelphia had gone out of their way *not* to include any express affirma-
tions of slavery in the Constitution. In fact, Taney deduced a specific right
of property in slaves from the fact that the Constitution "makes no distinction between that description of property [slaves] and other property owned
by a citizen." Congress could no more deprive a citizen in the territories of
the right of property—whether in slaves or horses—than it could establish
religion, obliterate due process, or upend the right to bear arms.[14]

The Court thereby gave constitutional sanction to the position the slaveholders had maintained ever since the eighteenth century. As soon as some
Americans began questioning the existence of slavery in a nation founded
on the principle of universal rights, slaveholders began to insist that among
the most sacred and inviolable of all rights was that of property in slaves.
Inspired by Revolutionary principles, for example, the Virginia legislature
in the 1780s made it much easier for individual masters to free individual
slaves. But any move that even hinted at emancipation provoked a backlash
among Virginia masters, and in 1784 more than a thousand citizens signed
a petition objecting to one such proposal. "We were put in Possession of our
Rights of Liberty and Property" by the recent Revolution, the petitioners
noted. "But notwithstanding this, we understand a very subtle and daring
Attempt is made to dispossess us of a very important Part of our Property."[15]
Charles Cotesworth Pinckney, who had fought tenaciously to protect slavery
at the Philadelphia convention in 1787, urged his fellow South Carolinians
to ratify the Constitution because it "provided the best terms for the security of this species of property it was in our power to make."[16] A decade
later, a Virginia slaveholder objected to recent moves to make manumis-
sion more difficult on the ground that the right to property included "the
right to dispose of property freely." The argument endured into the 1820s,
when Benjamin Watkins Leigh invoked the legacy of the Revolution to claim
that the "power over our property" in slaves "belonged, of right and exclusively, to us the owners." It erupted again a few years later when Virginians
debated slavery for the last time. James Gholson protested a proposal for
the very gradual elimination of slavery from Virginia as "*monstrous and*

unconstitutional." The right to property in slaves, he said, was as "perfect and inviolable as that to any other property we possess." John Thompson Brown agreed. The "right of property in slaves," he insisted, "is found in nature."[17] It was from this tradition that Taney drew when he proclaimed the existence of a constitutional right to property in slaves. Even Stephen Douglas agreed that the "point upon which Chief Justice Taney expresses his opinion is simply this: that slaves being property, stand on an equal footing with other property, and consequently that the owner has the same right to carry that property into a territory that he has any other, subject to the same conditions" (*Collected Works*, 3:324).

Almost immediately, Lincoln began to fit Taney's reasoning into his long-standing critique of the selfishness and dehumanization of slavery. He denied that the slaveholder had the same political "right to take his negroes to Kansas that a freeman has to take his hogs or his horses" (*Collected Works*, 2:245). He questioned the premises of the justices who "tell us that the negro is property anywhere in the light that horses are property" (3:78). For Lincoln, the *Dred Scott* decision was the latest in a string of policy decisions, begun with the opening of Kansas to slavery in 1854, all of which "succeeded in dehumanizing the negro" and making it "forever impossible to be but as the beasts of the field" (3:95). Although the Court had openly rejected Douglas's version of popular sovereignty, Lincoln nevertheless held Douglas responsible for the *Dred Scott* decision. It was Douglas, after all, who "has done all in his power to reduce the whole question of slavery to one of a mere *right of property*" (2:468).

Notwithstanding Lincoln's readiness to attack the *Dred Scott* decision, the Court's reasoning presented him with a serious intellectual and constitutional challenge. All of his antislavery politics revolved around the proposition that Congress should continue to restrict slavery's expansion into the territories, as it had done since the nation's founding. But Taney's decision explicitly denied that Congress had such power, since that would involve infringing on the right of property in slaves. Lincoln struggled for months trying to get around the Court's central ruling. At first, he claimed that because the Constitution allows the government to confiscate property by the "due process of law," Congress could pass a law banning slaves from the territories—and if any slaveholders chose to violate it, they would forfeit their property in a presumably legal manner (*Collected Works*, 3:101). Such specious reasoning could not hope to pass constitutional muster, and it is hardly surprising that Lincoln abandoned it almost as soon as he mentioned it. Instead, along with many other Republicans, Lincoln moved to dismiss most of the *Dred Scott* decision as mere *obiter dicta,* judicial opinions that carry no legal weight. Once the majority decided that Scott was not a citizen and so had no legal standing to bring his suit, everything else the Court said—including its assertion of a right to property in slaves—was extraneous verbiage. But in the end, Lincoln was not satisfied with this argument either. Instead he spent two years piecing together a much more sweeping, not to say radical, position.

His first move was to reassert the constitutional distinction between slaves and other forms of property, a distinction Taney denied. He made two points, the first of which concerned the wording of the Constitution itself. Lincoln argued that the fugitive slave clause could not have been written to prevent horses and sheep from escaping their owners; it singled out slaves and thereby differentiated slaves from other forms of property. More tellingly, in only one instance did the Constitution single out a specific commodity—slaves—and endow Congress with the power to prohibit its importation. Lincoln's second point was that what counted as property in a state did not necessarily count as property that was constitutionally protected. Lincoln never denied that slaves were technically classified as "property" under the laws of the states in which slavery existed, but he did deny that those state laws placed slavery under the constitutional protection of fundamental property rights. The "right of property in negroes," he insisted, is "confined to those states where it is established by local law," and he denounced the attempt to elevate that local institution by cloaking it in the constitutional right of property (*Collected Works,* 3:80).

Lincoln was not the first person to talk this way. Ever since the American Revolution, opponents of slavery had denied that humans could be property. Rhode Island's gradual emancipation act of 1784 reasserted the principle of fundamental human equality before declaring that "holding mankind in a state of slavery, as private property . . . , is repugnant to this principle."[18] But the tradition of antislavery constitutionalism that developed in the nineteenth century developed not from a denial of the right of property in slaves but from the principle that freedom prevailed except where slavery was created by "positive law." For a radical antislavery constitutionalist like William Goodell, the "right of property in man" was a "premise" from which flowed a long train of proslavery policies. But rather than demonstrate why there was no such right, Goodell instead posited an alternative premise, universal rights, from which he derived his antislavery reading of the Constitution.[19] It was not until the Supreme Court forced the issue in 1857 that Lincoln developed one of the most radical implications of antislavery constitutionalism into a full-fledged argument against a right of property in slaves.

Before that time, Lincoln subscribed to another basic precept of moderate antislavery constitutionalism: that whereas freedom was national, slavery was merely local. Lincoln always insisted that the Founders had written a Constitution that recognized slavery in the Southern states out of *necessity*, even as they stigmatized it as a *wrong*. From this fact, Lincoln drew a critical distinction between those forms of property that were constitutionally protected and those that were not. He spelled this out during his sixth debate with Douglas, at Quincy. When Douglas says "that slave property and horse and hog property are alike to be allowed to go into the Territories, upon principles of equality, he is reasoning truly as if there is no difference between them as property." But if there is a difference, "if the one is property, held rightfully, and the other is wrong, then there is no equality between right and wrong" (*Collected Works*, 3:257). In effect, the Supreme Court had turned a wrong into a right.

Lincoln spun out the shocking implications of Taney's decision: If the fundamental rights of property prevented the territories from excluding slaves, Lincoln argued, it logically prevented states from doing the same thing—even more so, as the Constitution explicitly enjoined the states from interfering with such rights. What was to stop the slaveholders in Georgia from asserting their right to buy slaves in Africa? What right did Ohio have to deprive masters of their rights by abolishing slavery? If the right of property in slaves was so inviolate that the territorial governments could not interfere with it, neither could state governments. "Once admit that a man rightfully holds another man as property on one side of a line," Lincoln argued, "and you must, when it suits his convenience to come to the other side, admit that he has the same right to hold his property there" (*Collected Works*, 3:369). Taken to its logical conclusion, Lincoln argued, a constitutional right of property in slaves would spread slavery across the nation and make it forever untouchable.

It was in the spring of 1859, at the very moment when Lincoln was struggling to formulate a coherent argument against Taney's decision, that he praised Thomas Jefferson for having elevated the "rights of persons" over the "rights of property." The same phrasing began to seep into his speeches. He supported the rights of property, he said, but whenever they came into conflict with the rights of persons, he would not hesitate to favor persons over property. He was groping for an escape from the insidious logic of the *Dred Scott* decision, and the solution he came to was to declare that the Supreme

Court was simply wrong, that "the right of property in a slave is *not* distinctly and expressly affirmed in the Constitution" (*Collected Works*, 3:231).

But it was not enough to say it; Lincoln had to show it. He went back to the library later that year, and when he finished his research, he organized his evidence, wrote up his report, and traveled to New York City to present his results. This was the great burden of the Cooper Union Address: to prove that there was no such thing as a constitutional right of property in slaves. Ever since his Peoria speech in 1854, Lincoln had relied on the history of the founding era to buttress his antislavery politics. But not until Cooper Union, in February of 1860, did he focus his historical analysis on the specific question of whether the Founders had written a right of property in slaves directly into the Constitution. His answer was a resounding "no." The Cooper Union Address was billed as a "political lecture" rather than a campaign speech, and though it effectively functioned as both, it had many of the hallmarks of a carefully crafted historical essay that built its argument step by step.[20]

Lincoln began with a plausible demonstration that the Founders had deliberately excised from the Constitution any wording that might have suggested that human beings could be property. In his footnotes, he quoted extensively from James Madison's notes on the debates within the constitutional convention to show that several delegates in Philadelphia were adamant that nothing in their proposed charter should leave a suggestion that humans could rightfully be property. Roger Sherman had objected to a clause that would have taxed immigration because it could be read "as acknowledging men to be property." Madison's own notes quoted him agreeing. It would be "wrong to admit in the Constitution the idea that there could be property in men," Madison had told his fellow delegates (*Collected Works*, 3:545). Next, Lincoln produced a detailed historical narrative showing how many of the same men who wrote the Constitution went on to support various laws aimed at restricting slavery's expansion.

And finally, in another lengthy footnote, Lincoln quoted a host of contemporary Southerners who claimed that any attempt to restrict slavery's expansion amounted to an assault on their fundamental right to property in slaves. The antislavery platform of the Republican Party, one Georgia congressman had warned, offered "death and destruction to the rights of my people." The governor of Mississippi said he would sooner have his state leave the Union "in preference to the loss of constitutional rights." A prominent South Carolinian likewise threatened that his state would secede unless it got "higher guarantees for the protection of our rights and property" (*Collected*

Works, 3:542, note 31). With that, the history lesson was over; it was time for Lincoln to start arguing.

Addressing Southerners directly, Lincoln said, "[when you] make these declarations, you have a specific and well-understood allusion to an assumed Constitutional right of yours." By that presumed right, he went on, Southerners would carry their slaves into the Western territories and keep them there as property. "But no such right is specifically written into the Constitution," Lincoln declared. "The instrument is literally silent about any such right." Speaking for the Republican Party as a whole, Lincoln then articulated the position he had been struggling to develop for nearly two years. "We," Lincoln said, "deny that such a right has any existence in the Constitution, even by implication." The words *slave* and *slavery* appear nowhere in the document, he pointed out. The word *property* appears nowhere in connection to slavery. And "wherever in that instrument the slave is alluded to, he is called a 'person'" (*Collected Works*, 3:543–45). No matter how loudly or how often the Southerners assert their constitutional right to property in slaves, Lincoln told his New York audience, do not believe it. There is no such right.

The significance of Lincoln's claim can scarcely be underestimated. It was possible to argue, as a few proslavery intellectuals did, that there was nothing wrong with enslaving human beings, that the defense of slavery did not necessarily entail a denial of the slave's humanity. But there was no escaping the fact that Southern slaves were defined at law and treated in practice as property—bought and sold, bequeathed and inherited, traded, bartered, conveyed, and auctioned. And when it came time to defend their system, the slaveholders turned first, instinctively and overwhelmingly, to their inviolable rights of property. They said it to themselves in their diaries. They wrote it to family and friends in their private letters. They repeated it on the stump and in the pulpits, in speeches and editorials, from Montgomery, Alabama, to Washington, D.C. And in every secession convention in every Southern state, they proclaimed that the South must leave the Union because the man who had just been elected president denied the existence of their sacred right to property in slaves. Once Roger Taney wrote the slaveholders' defense into the Constitution, once Lincoln responded by denying the very existence of a right of property in slaves, the dispute over slavery had become irreconcilable. Take away the debate over the right of property in slaves, and the Civil War is almost unimaginable.

So is emancipation. The legality of emancipation would have been much harder to demonstrate had there been no debate over the right of property in slaves, had Lincoln and the Republicans not already worked out the difference between those forms of property that were protected by the Constitution and those that were not. From the earliest months of the war, lawmakers in Congress were impeded by the fact that the Constitution restricted the confiscation of property to persons duly convicted of treason. How could slaves be confiscated in the face of such a prohibition? Lincoln's answer was simple: slave property is not protected by the Constitution's ban on bills of attainder. "I may remark that this provision of the constitution," Lincoln blithely told Congress, "applies only in this country, as I understand, to real, or landed estate" (*Collected Works*, 5:331). He had been there before. Having worked his way past the *Dred Scott* decision, Lincoln had long since concluded that slaves were property only insofar as states and localities made them so, not because the Constitution recognized them as such. Emancipation was legal, because there was no such thing as a right of property in slaves.

Lincoln's antislavery arguments rested on a series of cascading premises that are not easily disentangled. They owed as much to Jeffersonian egalitarianism as to Hamiltonian statism, as much to Andrew Jackson's populism as to Henry Clay's humanitarianism. But at the core of Lincoln's argument was a profound conviction that the market had to be restrained, that the rights of property could not trump the rights of humanity. Lincoln's resistance to the dehumanization of slaves was inseparable from his resistance to the unfettered marketplace. There had to be limits. Some things should not be bought and sold, among them human beings.

Notes

1. Roy P. Basler, ed., *The Collected Works of Abraham Lincoln*, 9 vols. (New Brunswick, N.J.: Rutgers University Press, 1953–55), 2:492; 3:79. Hereafter cited in text and notes as *Collected Works*.

2. There are several excellent studies of antislavery politics: Richard Sewell, *Ballots for Freedom: Antislavery Politics in the United States, 1837–1860* (New York: Oxford University Press, 1976); Frederick J. Blue, *No Taint of Compromise: Crusaders in Antislavery Politics* (Baton Rouge: Louisiana State University Press, 2005); and Bruce Laurie, *Beyond Garrison: Antislavery and Social Reform* (New York: Cambridge University Press, 2005).

3. Robert Pierce Forbes, *The Missouri Compromise and Its Aftermath: Slavery and the Meaning of America* (Chapel Hill: University of North Carolina Press, 2007).

4. Daniel Walker Howe, *The Political Culture of the American Whigs* (Chicago: University of Chicago Press, 1979), 290, observes that Lincoln "transcended Old Whiggery by synthesizing it with elements from Jacksonian political

thought," while Alexander Stephens, the vice president of the Confederacy, "also synthesized Whiggery with Democratic beliefs, but he took over the worst side of Jacksonianism, the commitment to white supremacy." More recently, Sean Wilentz, *The Rise of American Democracy: Jefferson to Lincoln* (New York: Norton, 2005), has demonstrated that a popular antislavery politics could not emerge until the Old Whigs abandoned their habitual elitism and wed their antislavery convictions to the commitment to human equality that went back through Andrew Jackson to Thomas Jefferson.

5. On Federalist antislavery, see Paul Finkelman, *Slavery and the Founders: Race and Liberty in the Age of Jefferson*, 2d ed. (Armonk, N.Y.: Sharpe, 2001); Garry Wills, *Negro President: Jefferson and the Slave Power* (New York: Houghton Mifflin, 2003). Wilentz, *Rise of American Democracy*, 163, sharply disputes the Federalists' antislavery credentials: "Rarely has any group of Americans done so little to deserve such praise." But see Wills's rejoinder in the introduction to the paperback edition of *Negro President*.

6. John Craig Hammond, *Slavery, Freedom, and Expansion in the Early American West*, Jeffersonian American Series (Charlottesville: University of Virginia Press, December 2007).

7. Jonathan H. Earle, *Jacksonian Antislavery and the Politics of Free Soil, 1824–1854* (Chapel Hill: University of North Carolina Press, 2004). See also Frederick J. Blue, *The Free Soilers: Third Party Politics, 1848–1854* (Urbana: University of Illinois Press, 1973).

8. The importance of Lincoln's Whig background is a classic theme in the Lincoln literature. See David Donald, "Abraham Lincoln: Whig in the White House," in *Lincoln Reconsidered*, 2d ed. (New York: Vintage Books, 1961); Kenneth M. Stampp, "Abraham Lincoln: The Politics of the Practical Whig," in *The Era of Reconstruction* (New York: Knopf, 1975); and more recently, Michael Vorenberg, "Slavery Reparations in Theory and Practice: Lincoln's Approach," in Brian R. Dirck, ed., *Lincoln Emancipated: The President and the Politics of Race* (DeKalb: Northern Illinois University Press, 2007), 117–29.

9. Lincoln made almost no use of the concept of the slave power in his various antislavery speeches. In late 1858, during the weeks right after he lost his race for a seat in the U.S. Senate to Stephen Douglas, Lincoln wrote a series of short notes to various supporters in which he referred to the temporary victory of the "slave power." These were, of course, private notes, and as they were very brief, they developed no sustained argument against it. See the letters to Henry Asbury (November 19, 1858), Anson S. Miller (November 19, 1858), Charles H. Ray (November 20, 1858), and B. Clarke Lundy (November 26, 1858), in *Collected Works*, 3:339–42.

10. Michael F. Holt, *The Rise and Fall of the American Whig Party: Jacksonian Politics and the Onset of the Civil War* (New York: Oxford University Press, 1999), is comprehensive, although not concerned primarily with political thought. The standard study of Whig political culture is still Howe, *Political Culture of the American Whigs*. But see also Lawrence Frederick Kohl,

The Politics of Individualism (New York: Oxford University Press, 1989); John Ashworth, *"Agrarians and Aristocrats": Party Political Ideology in the United States, 1837–1846* (New York: Cambridge University Press, 1987), which is sympathetic to the Jacksonians; and Daniel Feller, *The Jacksonian Promise: America, 1815–1840* (Baltimore: Johns Hopkins University Press, 1995), which has a more Whiggish bias. Virtually all the major surveys of the period are written from an underlying sympathy with the Democrats, but even those scholars who are partial to the Whigs accept the premise that the party unambiguously favored capitalist development.

11. Quoted in Howe, *Political Culture of the American Whigs*, 21.

12. "If the Democrats' attitude toward commerce was complex," John Ashworth writes, "that of the Whigs was not"; *Slavery, Capitalism, and Politics in the Antebellum Republic*, vol. 1, *Commerce and Compromise, 1820–1860* (New York: Cambridge University Press, 1995), 315. See also note 9, above.

13. Quoted in Eric Foner, *Free Soil, Free Labor, Free Men: The Ideology of the Republican Party before the Civil War* (New York: Oxford University Press, 1970 and 1995), 85. This "constitutionalism" is one of the central themes of Wilentz, *Rise of American Democracy*, xxi: "For Americans of the early republic, politics, government, and constitutional order, not economics, were primary to interpreting the world and who ran it." Lincoln's particular devotion to constitutionalism is the theme of Phillip Shaw Paludan, *The Presidency of Abraham Lincoln* (Lawrence: University Press of Kansas, 1994).

14. *Dred Scott v. Sanford.* 60 U.S. 393 (How.). The definitive study of the case is Don E. Fehrenbacher, *The Dred Scott Case: Its Significance in American Law and Politics* (New York: Oxford University Press, 1978). See also Kenneth M. Stampp, *America in 1857: A Nation on the Brink* (New York: Oxford University Press, 1990), 68–109.

15. Quoted in James Oakes, *The Ruling Race: A History of American Slaveholders* (New York: Knopf, 1982), 32.

16. Quoted in Wilentz, *Rise of American Democracy*, 34.

17. Quoted in Eva Sheppard Wolf, *Race and Liberty in the New Nation: Emancipation in Virginia from the Revolution to Nat Turner's Rebellion* (Baton Rouge: Louisiana State University Press, 2006), 124, 192, 214, 215.

18. William M. Wiecek, *The Sources of Antislavery Constitutionalism in America* (Ithaca: Cornell University Press, 1977), 50.

19. William Goodell, *Views of American Constitutional Law, in Its Bearing upon American Slavery* (Utica: Jackson and Chaplin, 1845), 14.

20. For the background and significance of the speech, see Harold Holzer, *Lincoln at Cooper Union: The Speech That Made Abraham Lincoln President* (New York: Simon and Schuster, 2004).

$$8$$

Abraham Lincoln and the Antislavery Movement

Richard Striner

$\mathcal{W}$hat was it in the leadership of Abraham Lincoln that set him apart from all the others who strove to end slavery?

The first of the important distinctions that elevates Lincoln above the rank and file of America's antislavery leaders is obvious enough: Lincoln was the leader who occupied the White House and meted out a series of blows to the institution of slavery that cumulatively killed it. But this preeminent distinction of the sixteenth president was part of a larger distinctiveness in overall strategy and tactics that put him in a class by himself—as the Great Emancipator.

To be sure, the uniqueness of Lincoln's contribution was based upon some long-term antislavery traditions that the Founding Fathers pioneered. The achievement of the founding generation in preventing the spread of American slavery above the Ohio River—an achievement that began with the Northwest Ordinance of 1787—laid the groundwork for a program of incremental phaseout, a program that Lincoln endorsed well beyond the Emancipation Proclamation.

As Lincoln put it in his "House divided" speech, Americans needed to "arrest the further spread" of slavery and "place it where the public mind shall rest in the belief that it is in course of ultimate extinction."[1] Lincoln made it clear that he belonged to a "gradualist" school of American antislavery leadership—and he proudly acknowledged his debt to the antislavery Founders. In 1859, he told supporters of slavery that "we mean to treat you as near as we possibly can, like Washington, Jefferson, and Madison treated you."[2] But he usually reminded his listeners that many of the Founding Fathers had hoped to see the institution of slavery reduced until it vanished from the nation altogether. In 1860, Lincoln noted that Washington expressed "his hope that we should at some time have a confederacy of free states."[3]

The phaseout of slavery depended on reviving the Founders' preliminary step: a quarantine to seal off the evil. And the logic of a gradual phaseout was heightened by the time that Lincoln launched his political career by two important, subsequent developments: the founding in 1816 of the American Colonization Society, which aimed to facilitate the slow repatriation of emancipated slaves to Africa, and the influence of Great Britain's antislavery program, which approached its culmination in 1833—when Parliament began the final phaseout of slavery with compensation to the owners. Compensation had also been employed by the American Colonization Society.

The programmatic package that Lincoln espoused until late in the game comprised all of these elements, arrayed in the following sequence: (1) the revival of the Founders' attempt to contain the institution of slavery, a program that developed a massive support base via the "Free-Soil movement" in both major parties by the 1840s; (2) the defusing of the vexing racial issue through the concept of colonization, which could make the lurid fear (and the aggressive racial hatred) of American white supremacists moot by allowing the races to go their separate ways in peace; and (3) the phaseout of slavery by means of the British method: compensation.

Lincoln's vision is easy to grasp through the picturesque devices that he used to portray it at the time. In 1854 he likened slavery to a disease—"a wen or a cancer" that could not be "cut to the bone at once," lest the patient bleed to death. Nonetheless, "the cutting may begin at the end of a given time."[4] Lincoln's antislavery prescription was therefore to isolate the illness by preventing it from spreading any further in the body politic. Then the illness would be slowly purged away: removed from the system through the wise applications of statecraft.

The partial British inspiration for the antislavery vision of Lincoln was apparent in a private memorandum that he wrote shortly after he delivered his "House divided" speech in the summer of 1858. "I have not allowed myself to forget," he wrote, "that the abolition of the Slave-Trade by Great Brittain [*sic*], was agitated a hundred years before it was a final success.... School-boys know that [William] Wilbe[r]force, and Granville Sharpe [Sharp], helped that cause forward; but who can now name a single man who labored to retard it?"[5] Though he never chose to broadcast the fact that the British achievement played a role in his thinking on the slavery issue, the influence is obvious enough. The act of Parliament that ended British slavery in 1833 paid twenty million pounds in compensation to the owners of slaves in the

British West Indies. And it created an apprenticeship system to provide for a gradual transition from slavery to freedom over a time span of seven years. Black children under six were freed at once.[6] These provisions bear a close resemblance to measures that Lincoln supported in the White House.

Overall, Lincoln took the long view on the subject of slavery for several reasons. One of them was in part humanitarian; as he later told a correspondent, his initial "preference for *gradual* over *immediate* emancipation" had been "misunderstood" by certain antislavery critics. It was no lack of zeal for the objective, Lincoln protested. It was rather a preference for proper supervision and support as opposed to the mischievous effects of cruel anarchy. Lincoln explained that he had dreaded the effects of upheaval because of the *suffering* the slaves would endure: "I had thought that *gradual* would produce less confusion and destitution," he wrote.[7]

Another reason for Lincoln's belief that emancipation would take a long time was the *power* that American supporters of slavery had been able to gather through ruthless machination. In most of the slave states, the mere expression of an antislavery opinion was prohibited under the slave codes. The slave-owning class had created a police state, where the slavery issue was concerned, in most of the South.

Furthermore, the slave-state leaders had been able to control (or at least to manipulate) the nation's presidential politics as often as not. Especially since 1852, the Democratic presidents Franklin Pierce and James Buchanan had relentlessly striven to placate the slaveholding South by supporting some aggressive attempts to expand the institution of slavery. And as the *Dred Scott* decision made clear, proslavery advocates controlled the Supreme Court as well.

Proslavery leaders were assertive, imperious, and arrogant; as Lincoln noted in his Cooper Union speech of 1860, they had managed to silence the deep force of conscience in themselves, and they refused to listen to anything that challenged their dogmas. "The whole atmosphere must be disinfected from all taint of opposition to slavery, before they will cease to believe that all their troubles proceed from us," Lincoln ruefully observed.[8]

Furthermore, the force of racial prejudice in many of the free states (including the state of Illinois, as Lincoln knew very well from experience) formed a powerful base of opposition to emancipation measures. As Lincoln made haste to admit to a delegation of blacks at the White House in 1862, "on this broad continent, not a single man of your race is made the equal of a single man of ours." Lincoln declared that this was "a fact about which we all think and feel alike, I and you." Yet it was "a fact with which we have to deal, for I cannot alter it."[9] So he urged them to reflect upon the benefits of colonization.

The colonization idea looks vile by contemporary standards. Indeed, significant numbers of blacks found the concept insulting in the antebellum years. A month after the American Colonization Society was founded in December 1816, for example, a group of black leaders met at Philadelphia's Bethel Church to condemn the organization.[10] The free black leader Simeon Jocelyn of Connecticut was deeply contemptuous of colonization at the time, as were many other black Americans.

On the other hand, the "back to Africa" theme has resurfaced among African American radicals perennially. The idea possessed biblical resonance: as the Hebrews of old had been led from the house of bondage to the promised land of the patriarchs, so the latter-day African "Israel" would be repatriated. Lincoln invoked this comparison in 1852:

> Pharaoh's country was cursed with plagues, and his hosts were drowned in the Red Sea for striving to retain a captive people who had already served them more than four hundred years. May like disasters never befall us! If as the friends of colonization hope, the present and coming generations of our countrymen shall . . . succeed in freeing our land from the dangerous presence of slavery; and, at the same time, in restoring a captive people to their long-lost father-land, with bright prospects for the future; and this too, so gradually, that neither races nor individuals shall have suffered by the change, it will indeed be a glorious consummation.[11]

Lincoln made this statement in a eulogy for Henry Clay, who had served for a number of years as the president of the American Colonization Society. Lincoln was an ardent admirer of Clay.

There were blacks who found the prospect of colonization compelling. As historian Ira Berlin has observed, "emigration found an increasingly large following" among blacks "in the decade before the Civil War. . . . Reluctantly, some free Negroes looked for a new home where they might find a modicum of freedom, new opportunities, and a taste of manhood. '[I] cannot be a man heare and . . . I an ready to go if i live on bread and warter or die the never day i get there,' declared a Liberia-bound black." Indeed, as Berlin has affirmed, "emigration drew support from a broad spectrum of free Negro society. Many elite free Negroes who had previously shown little interest in Africa now had second thoughts."[12] It bears noting that when Lincoln began his experiment with colonization in the middle of the Civil War, hundreds of blacks took him up on the deal and embarked for an island off the coast of Haiti. No one coerced them into going.

It was not to be, of course. And the colonization idea is now central to the anti-Lincoln critiques that rate him a wishy-washy antislavery leader compared with such forthright firebrands as William Lloyd Garrison, Wendell Phillips, and Frederick Douglass. It is true, however, that even the fiery Garrison had toyed awhile with the concept of colonization. In an 1828 issue of the *Journal of the Times*, which Garrison edited, he suggested the payment of federal funds for the gradual liberation of slaves, to be followed by "the transportation of such liberated slaves and free colored people as are desirous of emigrating to a more genial clime."[13] A few years later, he abandoned such views and became an "immediatist"—a radical. He attacked the American Colonization Society, accusing it of being "steeped in sin [and] deep in pollution" (Nye, 68).

Garrison's case is instructive. It reveals the many deep disagreements that developed in the ranks of the antislavery movement in the years before Lincoln rose to power. Garrison's search for a morally "pure" form of antislavery agitation divided the antislavery movement profoundly. And his radicalism kept increasing. He gradually renounced the use of force in all human affairs. From his early opposition to war, he approached the brink of anarchism—a renunciation of government—by the end of the 1830s.

In 1833 (in a "Declaration of Sentiments" that he wrote to accompany the founding of the American Anti-Slavery Society), Garrison had called for the removal of slavery "by moral law and political action" (Nye, 72). But a few years later, all political action was anathema to him and his followers. Abolitionists had to "voluntarily exclude themselves from every legislative and judicial body, and repudiate all human politics, worldly honors, and stations of authority," he proclaimed (115).

By the 1830s, two programmatic issues were dividing the American antislavery movement. The first was the issue of "gradual versus immediate" emancipation. The other was the issue of political versus nonpolitical agitation. Significantly, the first of these issues led to hybrid solutions that combined the "immediate" and "gradual." For example, some antislavery students at the Lane Seminary in Cincinnati, Ohio—after organizing a famous series of debates in 1834 between "Immediatism versus Gradualism"—formed a group that endorsed emancipation, "not by rebellion, war, or congressional interference," but rather through a moral and spiritual reawakening, which had to begin "immediately" (Nye, 81). But the "immediatism" of these antislavery students was tempered by prudential qualifications. "By immediate emancipation," they explained, "we do not mean that the slaves shall be turned loose on the nation." Rather, the goal was "gradual emancipation, immediately begun" (95). The gap between this "radical" position and the later statecraft of Lincoln is not very large.

Pragmatic calculations assumed an ever-greater degree of importance for the abolitionist movement as the antipolitical bias of Garrison and his circle was challenged by politicized activists. By 1840, such activists had founded the Liberty Party, with James G. Birney, a former owner of slaves whom the abolitionist Theodore Dwight Weld had converted to the antislavery movement, as its presidential candidate. And with the growth in the 1840s of an antislavery bloc in Congress (John Quincy Adams was its leader in the House of Representatives), along with the rise of the Free-Soil movement in both of the major political parties, questions of political strategy and calculation became more urgent for antislavery activists. At last, as the newly founded Republican Party put the slavery issue at the center of its national agenda, political strategy became paramount. As historian Russel B. Nye pointed out long ago, "more and more abolitionists believed after 1840 that success lay in politics, in the Liberty Party, in the Free-Soil Party, and eventually in the Republican Party" (131).

Conventional wisdom views "Lincoln the gradualist"—or "Lincoln the moderate"—as fundamentally at odds with abolitionist militants. There is an element of truth in this notion. The black abolitionist Frederick Douglass was a critic of Lincoln at least until 1863. And the famous abolitionist Wendell Phillips was vituperative in his attacks upon Lincoln—whom he viewed as a tepid equivocator—down to the end.

But even Phillips acknowledged that the antislavery movement in America was broad enough to encompass (and indeed to require) a division of labor, making use of the skills of very different sorts of antislavery activists. As historian Eric Foner has observed, "it is important to remember that despite their criticisms of the Republican Party, leading abolitionists maintained close personal relations with Republican leaders. . . . [They] recognized the complex interrelationship between abolitionist attempts to create a public sentiment hostile to slavery, and the political anti-slavery espoused by the Republicans. 'Our agitation, you know, helps keep yours alive in the rank and file,' was the way Wendell Phillips expressed it to [Charles] Sumner."[14]

Lincoln in the White House was constantly engaged in an "insider/outsider" orchestration with the abolitionist militants. Their relationship was synergistic, though the fact was concealed from the public by Lincoln as much as possible. A memorable instance was recorded by the abolitionist Moncure Daniel Conway, who called upon Lincoln at the White House (together with William Ellery Channing, a nephew of the famous Unitarian clergyman of the same name) in January 1862. The account is worth quoting at length.

Channing opened the discussion by suggesting to Lincoln that "the opportunity of the nation to rid itself of slavery had arrived." Lincoln asked, "how he thought they might avail themselves of it. . . . Channing suggested emancipation with compensation for the slaves," and Lincoln said, "he had for years been in favour of that plan."

Conway continued: "When the President turned to me, I asked whether we might not look to him as the coming Deliverer of the Nation from its one great evil. . . . He said, 'Perhaps we may be better able to do something in that direction after a while than we are now.'" Conway pressed him; he asked Lincoln whether "the masses of the American people would hail you as their deliverer if, at the end of this war, the Union should be surviving and slavery still in it." Yes, said Lincoln, "if they were to see that slavery was on the downhill."

The give-and-take continued awhile, but then Lincoln made a stunning declaration to Conway and Channing. Though leavened with a dose of Lincoln humor, its point was unmistakable: "I think the country grows in this direction daily, and I am not without hope that something of the desire of you and your friends may be accomplished. Perhaps it may be in the way suggested by a thirsty soul in Maine who found he could only get liquor from a druggist; as his robust appearance forebade the plea of sickness, he called for a soda, and whispered, 'Couldn't you put a drop o' the creeter into it unbeknownst to yourself?'" In other words, Lincoln would expand his antislavery agenda by degrees, while maintaining what political observers today would call "deniability."

At the end of the interview, the president made a suggestion that was even more remarkable and cunning. Conway recalled it as follows: "We had, I think, risen to leave and had thanked him for his friendly reception when he said, 'We shall need all the anti-slavery feeling in the country, and more; you can go home and try to bring the people to your views; and you may say anything you like about me, if that will help. Don't spare me!'"[15] In other words, Lincoln was encouraging these militants to go and *pick a fight* with him in public—to *exaggerate* their differences with him to the point of abusing him and calling him names—in order to create the kind of pressure that he secretly wanted and intended to exploit.

Just two months later, Lincoln said the same thing to Wendell Phillips when he called at the White House. As historian LaWanda Cox has paraphrased Phillips's account of the meeting (which he recounted in a private letter), Lincoln told a funny story of "an Irishman in legally dry Maine who asked for a glass of soda with a 'drop of the crathur [put] into it *unbeknown to myself.*'"[16]

In these contemporaneous accounts, we have a vivid demonstration of the qualities—of the gifts—that put Lincoln in a class by himself within the antislavery movement. It was Lincoln's great achievement to gather and orchestrate power through Machiavellian methods—and then to *use* that power in the cause of liberation, just as fast as the contingencies permitted. As I have argued elsewhere at length, Lincoln's genius as a moral strategist is quite unsurpassed in American history.[17]

Here is how the work played out as the events unfolded. Lincoln's paramount goal in the 1850s was to stop the expansion of slavery. "Phase One" of his long-term plan—containment, as a prelude to gradual phaseout—could never be accomplished if the evil of slavery expanded. And the leaders of the South were playing every clever angle to increase the number of the slave states—with vigorous help from the White House.

American success in the Mexican War had expanded the United States enormously. Concurrently, the issue of how the new Western lands—the "Mexican Cession"—would be handled in regard to slavery led to growing sectional tension. Lincoln, in the course of a one-term stint in Congress, voted "free-soil": he opposed any further spread of slavery.

After California's admission as a free state pursuant to the Compromise of 1850—which included a tough new Fugitive Slave Law intended to placate the slaveholding South—proslavery leaders were incensed and increasingly militant. To appease them further, the Kansas-Nebraska Act was pushed through Congress in 1854. Lincoln's outrage at this legislation made him challenge its author, Stephen A. Douglas.

Douglas had convinced the members of Congress to repeal the old dividing line (as established in the 1820–21 Missouri Compromise) that kept slavery out of the northern and most of the central parts of the Louisiana Purchase. As soon as the Kansas-Nebraska Act was signed into law by Franklin Pierce, the supporters of slavery had begun to groom the new territory of Kansas to be the very next slave state.

Simultaneously, proslavery leaders were attempting to coerce the Spanish into parting with Cuba—which would then become another new slave state. Indeed, a secret proslavery organization called the "Knights of the Golden Circle" was plotting to foment a second Mexican War to take all of Central and upper South America—and turn the new lands into slave states.[18]

Senator Albert Gallatin Brown of Mississippi proclaimed that he wanted Southern forces to conquer "Cuba . . . and one or two other Mexican States; and I want them all for the same reason—for the planting and spreading of slavery."[19] (It bears noting that in 1861 some Confederate forces invaded New Mexico as part of a projected scheme of Central American conquest.)[20] A Tennessean named William Walker invaded Nicaragua with a band of his followers in 1855 and instituted slavery.

As this brutal campaign of proslavery aggression unfolded, the Republican Party was created by "Free-Soil" leaders. The Republicans intended to legislate the free-soil agenda into federal law and thus contain or roll back slavery. But then the *Dred Scott* decision ruled it unconstitutional to stop the spread of slavery, at least within the federal lands. The Democratic Party closed ranks around the *Dred Scott* decision very quickly.

Only one step remained, thought Lincoln and a great many others, to defeat the abolitionists completely: a second *Dred Scott* decision that permitted the owners of slaves to take their slaves anywhere in the country they wished—even into the free states. The political economy of slavery would thus become a nationally legal institution. "We shall *lie down* pleasantly dreaming that the people of *Mississippi* are on the verge of making their state *free*," Lincoln warned, and then "we shall *awake* to the *reality*, instead, that the *Supreme* Court has made *Illinois* a *slave State*."[21] Slave labor would become the new norm, both North and South.

Perhaps the whole western hemisphere, at least below Canada, would start to take its social cues from Dixie. Southern slaves could be used to break industrial strikes in the North, Southern slaves could be used to furnish vast new supplies of raw materials from Latin American sources. Dixie would reign supreme right across the equator. And that was how Alexander Stephens viewed the matter just a few years later, when he started out his term as the Confederates' first vice president: the slaveholding states, he proclaimed, comprised "the nucleus of a growing power, which, if we are true to ourselves, our destiny, and high mission, will become the controlling power on this continent."[22]

This was the scenario that Abraham Lincoln meant to stop.

Democrats like Stephen Douglas told the voters that the "slave power" plot was unreal. He said the fears of the Free-Soil leaders were hallucinations, or worse. He said that Southerners were all fellow patriots. He urged the voters to shrug the whole matter off and to come together around the great principle that unified the North and the South: white supremacy. Nothing really mattered where the fate of black people was concerned, said Douglas, for "inferior races" deserved pretty much what they got. It was nothing that the whites should really care about.

From 1854 onward, Lincoln made it his single-minded business to oppose Stephen Douglas and to throw him out of office if he could. For if Douglas should succeed in seducing the Northern electorate, the game was truly over for the antislavery movement. Douglas was counting on the ideology of white supremacy to unify the North and the South. And he intended to occupy the White House.

In Lincoln's 1858 bid to remove Stephen Douglas from the Senate, he attacked the latter's racist views as much as he could. But many Illinois voters were bigots. And so Lincoln had to walk a fine line. Consider this passage from a charismatic speech that Lincoln gave at a torchlight rally in Chicago at the start of his 1858 campaign. His abhorrence of slavery is obvious. (Note—Lincoln never referred to Stephen Douglas as "Senator Douglas" but tagged him "Judge Douglas" for some earlier service on the Illinois Supreme Court):

> Those arguments that are made, that the inferior race are to be treated with as much allowance as they are capable of enjoying; that as much is to be done for them as their condition will allow. What are these arguments? They are the arguments that kings have made for enslaving the people in all ages of the world. You will find that all the arguments in favor of king-craft were of this class; they always bestrode the necks of the people, not that they wanted to do it, but because the people were better off for being ridden. That is their argument, and this argument of the Judge is the same old serpent that says you work and I eat, you toil and I will enjoy the fruit of it. Turn in whatever way you will—whether it come from the mouth of a King, an excuse for enslaving the people of his country, or from the mouth of men of one race as a reason for enslaving the men of another race, it is all the same old serpent, and I hold if that course of argumentation that is made for the purpose of convincing the public mind that we should not care about this, should be granted, it does not stop with the negro. I should like to know if taking this old Declaration of Independence, which declares that all men are equal upon principle and making exceptions to it where will it stop. If one man says it does not mean a negro, why not another say it does not mean some other man? If that declaration is not the truth, let us get the Statute book, in which we find it and tear it out! Who is so bold to do it! [Voices—"me" "no one," &c.] If it is not true let us tear it out![23]

Douglas's answer was simple: Lincoln was a "negro-lover," and he meant to start a war between the states. Here is a sample of the racist abuse that Douglas spouted in the Lincoln-Douglas debates:

I ask you, are you in favor of conferring upon the negro the rights and privileges of citizenship? ("No, no.") Do you desire to strike out of our State Constitution that clause which keeps slaves and free negroes out of the State, and allow the free negroes to flow in ("never") and cover your prairies with black settlements? Do you desire to turn this beautiful State into a free negro colony, ("no, no") in order that when Missouri abolishes slavery she can send one hundred thousand emancipated slaves into Illinois, to become citizens and voters, on an equality with yourselves? ("Never," "no.") If you desire negro citizenship . . . then support Mr. Lincoln and the Black Republican party.[24]

Lincoln had to counter such abuse. No doubt it would have been very tempting for him—all too tempting—to have told the hoi polloi who were cheering on Douglas that they were fools and could go to the devil. But he would never get elected that way. And it was *public office* that he wanted—to get the *power* he would need to strike at slavery.

And so he temporized whenever he had to. He denied that he had ever espoused extending civil rights to blacks—while carefully avoiding a discussion of his possible actions in the future. Such disclaimers were slippery enough (for Lincoln was a clever attorney, after all) to cause Douglas to complain in the course of their debates that Lincoln had "a fertile genius in devising language to conceal his thoughts."[25]

Lincoln's tactics were sufficiently impressive to make him a presidential contender a few years later. His pitch to the voters was exactly what Republicans needed in a national contest. For them to capture the White House in 1860, the Republicans would have to carry all of the states in the lower Northern tier—the *swing states*, where bigotry was strong—to achieve an electoral majority.

Lincoln was perfectly positioned to attract the kind of votes that were needed. Compared to the other major presidential aspirants, like William H. Seward and Salmon P. Chase, who sought to carry the Republican banner in 1860, Lincoln was "centrist" enough to attract all the mainstream swing votes. And yet his moral fundamentals were strong. He attacked the institution of slavery in fervent moral terms and made a charismatic stand for free soil. But compared to the others, he seemed to be "moderate," and therefore "electable."

It was clever politics. And it did the trick for the Republicans. Lincoln led them to a landslide victory in 1860: they captured both the White House and Congress. And this unleashed all the slave-state secessions.

But Lincoln would not allow secession. He shot down a compromise in Congress that aimed to placate the slaveholding South: a compromise permitting the extension of slavery. "Hold firm, as with a chain of steel," he told his fellow Republicans.[26] In a confidential letter, he laid down the following edict: "Entertain no proposition for a compromise in regard to the *extension* of slavery. The instant you do, they have us under again; all our labor is lost, and sooner or later must be done over. . . . Have none of it. The tug has to come & better now than later."[27]

Thanks to Lincoln's implacable stand, the Republicans' agenda prevailed in the first Civil War Congress. In defiance of the *Dred Scott* decision, the Republicans enacted a measure to prohibit the extension of slavery. In the meantime, the Civil War raged—and Lincoln strove to crush the Southern rebellion with overwhelming force.

He also launched the second phase of his antislavery plan—the gradual phaseout—using wartime logic as his pretext. On March 6, 1862, he sent to Congress a message recommending "a Joint Resolution . . . as follows: 'Resolved that the United States ought to co-operate with any state which may adopt gradual abolishment of slavery, giving to such state pecuniary aid . . .'"[28] Lincoln argued that the offer might shorten the war by removing the incentive for rebellion. Republicans approved this measure on a party-line vote, while the Democrats decried it as a waste of the taxpayer's money.

"No taxes to buy Negroes" was one of the new Democratic slogans as they denounced the Republicans for goading the South into rebellion. And they condemned Lincoln's rationalization for the antislavery buyout plan: they denied it was a necessary measure that would shorten the war. The antiwar section of the Democratic Party (the "Copperheads," as their antagonists called them) urged a simpler approach to reunion: open peace negotiations with the South and reestablish the Union on distinctly pro-Southern terms.

Some of the radical members of Lincoln's party were unhappy for reasons of their own. In their view, Lincoln's antislavery plans were too "mild." They wanted outright emancipation. But at least one of the Radical Republicans in Congress was impressed by the incremental strategy of Lincoln. Speaking about the Lincoln plan to compensate the owners of slaves, Senator Charles Sumner of Massachusetts pointed out that no president had ever espoused such a sweeping antislavery measure before. "Proceeding from the President," Sumner wrote, Lincoln's plan "must take its place among the great events of history." And even if the plan should prove a failure, he continued, the momentum and direction of the Lincoln policies were perfectly obvious. Sumner urged a Republican critic of Lincoln to be mindful of everything the president had done "in a brief period," and then, "from the past . . . discern the sure promise of the future."[29]

Significantly, the old abolitionist William Lloyd Garrison was also impressed by Lincoln's measures. Garrison, who had become such a purist by the 1850s that his simple solution to the slavery question was to urge the free states of the North to secede from the South ("No Union with Slaveholders"), became converted to political action and incremental tactics by Lincoln's example. "There is no mistake about it in regard to Mr. Lincoln's desire to do all he can . . . to uproot slavery," Garrison wrote to his wife (Nye, 184).

Lincoln's buyout plan was indeed a failure: despite his repeated attempts to persuade delegations of leaders from the border slave states loyal to the Union, such as Kentucky (where Lincoln was born), not a single state rallied to the president. So Lincoln made his stupendous decision in the summer of 1862: he would free all the slaves of the *rebels*. He would institute a midcourse correction in his antislavery strategy.

The result was the Emancipation Proclamation, which Lincoln issued in preliminary form on September 22, 1862, and in final form on January 1, 1863. To avert a white supremacist backlash, and also to establish the necessary legal basis for the action, Lincoln strove to make the case that it was purely a Union-saving measure. To soften up public opinion, he stated in a famous open letter to the Republican editor Horace Greeley that "my paramount object in this struggle *is* to save the Union, and is *not* either to save or destroy slavery." He elaborated in some lines that would soon become canonical: "If I could save the Union without freeing *any* slave I would do it, and if I could save it by freeing *all* the slaves I would do it; and if I could save it by freeing some and leaving others alone I would also do that."[30]

Nonsense. There were many other ways in which the president could have saved the Union. The truth of the matter was this: Lincoln strove to save the Union *his way*—with slavery on course toward "extinction," as he stated in his "House divided" speech. He neglected to mention all the things that he *refused* to do—like allowing the extension of slavery—in his battle to save the Union. He was engaged in a justified deception.

Look at it this way: If Lincoln's only goal had been preserving the Union, then why did he oppose the congressional attempts to preempt the Civil War by allowing the extension of slavery? It was Lincoln's own *refusal* to permit the spread of slavery that precipitated the crisis of the Union—the wave of secessions by the slave states—in the first place.

In Lincoln's letter to Greeley was a consummate demonstration of Machiavellian tactics. It was a virtuosic way of making good upon his promise to Conway, to Channing, and to Phillips: his promise to extend his antislavery goals in a manner that possessed deniability, like a "thirsty soul" who connived to spike a soda "unbeknownst to himself."

It was a masterpiece of cunning. Frederick Douglass caught on to Lincoln's ways by the time the proclamation was issued. He saw in the document nothing less than "the entire abolition of slavery, wherever the evil could be reached by the Federal arm."[31]

In places that could not be "reached by the Federal arm," Lincoln kept his compensation offer open. Since the proclamation was a *military* measure that was only justifiable (as such) in Confederate states where rebellion was active, the president continued to dangle his offer of federal funding in front of the border slave states. Meanwhile, he encouraged the emancipated slaves to don the uniform of the United States and to confront their former masters in battle. And he backed away from colonization.

Lincoln knew that the proclamation would probably release a white supremacist backlash, and so it did. This is not the time or place to discuss at great length the many gambits that Lincoln used to protect his proclamation from political or legal reversal in the event that a racist electorate should throw the Republicans out—or if appeals should reach the highest court in the land, where his old foe Roger Taney, of *Dred Scott* infamy, continued to sit as chief justice.

Suffice it to say that Lincoln tried everything he could: he recommended to Congress a package of constitutional amendments in December 1862 that would write his antislavery plans into the Constitution itself; and he used his famous (and supposedly "lenient") Reconstruction plan of December 1863—what we know as the "ten-percent plan"—to turn occupied Confederate states into newly minted free states before the next election. (Antislavery minorities as small as only 10 percent could, according to Lincoln's plan, overturn the wishes of a 90 percent proslavery majority, since only those Southerners who swore to uphold emancipation were allowed to cast votes in this Reconstruction plan). "Give us a free-state reorganization of Louisiana, in the shortest possible time," Lincoln secretly instructed General Nathaniel Banks in December 1863.[32] In the meantime, Lincoln fought total war—a war to the death—against Confederate troops, as he urged his squeamish generals to smash and annihilate the armies of the rebels (or force their surrender).

When it looked as if a backlash from advocates of white supremacy and sheer war weariness would put a racist, proslavery Democrat into the White House in 1864, Lincoln called a secret meeting with the black abolitionist Frederick Douglass. He told Douglass to organize "a band of scouts, composed of colored men, whose business should be . . . to go into the rebel

States, beyond the lines of our armies, and carry the news of emancipation, and urge the slaves to come within our boundaries."[33]

The battlefield victories of Sherman and Sheridan (star performers in the cadre of "total war" generals whom Lincoln had encouraged and promoted) in the weeks just before the election turned everything back Lincoln's way, and he led the Republicans to yet another landslide victory. Then he worked with the Radical Republicans to force through the Thirteenth Amendment to the Constitution, abolishing slavery everywhere. He signed the Radical Republicans' daring new bill to establish a federal agency, the Freedmen's Bureau, to extend humanitarian, legal, and educational assistance to former slaves. He let stand an extraordinary military order by Sherman transferring a vast tract of seized plantation lands to former slaves (this order was rescinded by Andrew Johnson after Lincoln's death). And in the very last speech of his life, Lincoln gave the nod to black voting rights—to be extended on an incremental basis. To avert this liberating future, Lincoln's killer struck a final, savage blow on behalf of "death and Hell," as old William Lloyd Garrison had called the Southern slavery system.

Though John Wilkes Booth made certain that the ultimate benefits of Lincoln's political genius were kept from the nation for another hundred years—had Lincoln lived, a true civil rights revolution might have started shortly after Appomattox—Lincoln prevented the kind of future that John Wilkes Booth would have welcomed. Specifically, Lincoln stopped the extension of the slavery system to the North—and beyond. Moreover, he stopped the Confederate states from projecting their system through the western hemisphere—and beyond.

As Harry V. Jaffa once wrote,

> there is no reason to suppose that, should slavery in the mines, foundries, factories, and fields of the free states have proved advantageous to powerful groups therein, new systems of discipline might not have been invented to make the exploitation of slave labor highly profitable. The totalitarian regimes of the twentieth century provide us with ample evidence of the variety of ways that this might have been done. . . . It is simply unhistorical to say that such a thing *couldn't* happen because it *didn't* happen. It didn't happen because Lincoln was resolved that it *shouldn't* happen. And nothing but his implacable resolve made it impossible.[34]

By opposing Stephen Douglas, and by opposing the extension of slavery, Lincoln found his own effective ways to make certain that the slave-labor system would be kept far away from the North. And by opposing the Confederates' bid for independence, he made certain of a great deal more. Historian

Roger L. Ransom has recently published a "counterfactual" book about the possible course of historical events if the Confederates had won their independence. He projected a Confederate phaseout of slavery beginning in the 1880s. Ransom brought his account to the brink of the First World War and then stopped with the confession that he had "pushed" his "counterfactual recipe" as far as it could go.[35]

Perhaps not. Here's a different counterfactual analysis. If the Confederates had won their independence, almost certainly their "golden circle" of white supremacist rule—the tropical empire for slavery—would have spread throughout much of our hemisphere. And if a powerful Confederate slaveholding empire had been launched into the twentieth century, a horrid scenario suggests itself. Is it too far-fetched to imagine for a moment that the next generations of Confederates, armed with their master-race theory and their program of conquest, would have fit right in with the Axis-pact nations in the 1930s and 1940s? Is it too far-fetched to imagine that a power formation such as theirs might have kept United States forces contained, while the Confederates went on to ship massive amounts of raw materials—along with slave labor both from here and from Africa itself—to the war machines of Hitler and Japan? Perhaps a formula for global Axis victory?

Thanks to Lincoln, the world will never know. As he once told the membership of Congress, they were fighting "for a vast future also."[36] Lincoln was a consummate wielder of power in the service of freedom. America was close to moral ruin in the Civil War years—but Lincoln saved the situation in time. He did more, much more, than "save the Union." He saved America . . . for the world.

Notes

1. Abraham Lincoln, "'A House Divided,' Speech at Springfield, Illinois," June 16, 1858, in Roy Basler, ed., *The Collected Works of Abraham Lincoln*, 9 vols., hereafter referred to as *Collected Works* (New Brunswick, NJ: Rutgers University Press, 1953–1955), 2:461.

2. Abraham Lincoln, "Speech at Cincinnati, Ohio," September 17, 1859, ibid., 3:453.

3. Abraham Lincoln, "Address at Cooper Institute, New York City," February 27, 1860, ibid., 3:536–37.

4. Abraham Lincoln, "Speech at Peoria, Illinois," October 16, 1854, ibid., 2:274.

5. Abraham Lincoln, "Fragment on the Struggle against Slavery," ca. July 1858, ibid., 2:482.

6. R. K. Webb, *Modern England: From the Eighteenth Century to the Present* (New York: Dodd, Mead, 1968), 219.

7. Lincoln to John A. J. Creswell, March 7, 1864, *Collected Works*, 7:226.

8. Lincoln, "Address at Cooper Institute, New York City," February 27, 1860, ibid., 3:547–48.

9. Abraham Lincoln, "Address on Colonization to a Deputation of Negroes," August 14, 1862, ibid., 5:370–75.

10. See Benjamin Quarles, *Black Abolitionists* (New York: Oxford University Press, 1969), 3–4.

11. Abraham Lincoln, "Eulogy on Henry Clay," July 6, 1852, *Collected Works*, 2:129–32.

12. Ira Berlin, *Slaves without Masters: The Free Negro in the Antebellum South* (New York: Oxford University Press, 1974), 356–57.

13. William Lloyd Garrison, quoted in Russel B. Nye, *William Lloyd Garrison and the Humanitarian Reformers* (Boston: Little, Brown, 1955), 22. Hereafter cited in text as Nye.

14. Eric Foner, *Free Soil, Free Labor, Free Men: The Ideology of the Republican Party before the Civil War* (New York: Oxford University Press, 1970), 302–3.

15. Moncure Daniel Conway, *Autobiography, Memories and Experiences*, vol. 1 (New York: Houghton Mifflin, 1904), 345–46.

16. LaWanda Cox, *Lincoln and Black Freedom: A Study in Presidential Leadership* (Columbia: University of South Carolina Press, 1981), 8.

17. Richard Striner, *Father Abraham: Lincoln's Relentless Struggle to End Slavery* (New York: Oxford University Press, 2006).

18. See Robert E. May, *The Southern Dream of a Caribbean Empire, 1854–1861* (Baton Rouge: Louisiana State University Press, 1973); and John Hope Franklin, *The Militant South, 1800–1861* (Cambridge: Harvard University Press, 1956).

19. Albert Gallatin Brown, in M.W. McCluskey, ed., *Speeches, Messages, and Other Writings of the Hon. Albert G. Brown, a Senator in Congress from the State of Mississippi* (Philadelphia: J. B. Smith, 1859), 588–99.

20. See Eugene D. Genovese, *The Political Economy of Slavery* (New York: Random House, 1965), 258.

21. Abraham Lincoln, "'A House Divided,' Speech at Springfield, Illinois," June 16, 1858, *Collected Works*, 2:467.

22. Alexander Stephens, quoted in Richard N. Current, *Lincoln and the First Shot* (New York: Harper and Row, 1963; reprinted, Long Grove, Ill.: Waveland, 1990), 131.

23. Abraham Lincoln, "Speech at Chicago," July 10, 1858, *Collected Works*, 2:500–501.

24. Stephen A. Douglas, "Mr. Douglas's Speech," in "First Debate with Stephen A. Douglas at Ottowa, Illinois," August 21, 1858, ibid., 3:9.

25. Stephen A. Douglas, "Senator Douglas's Reply," in "Sixth Debate with Stephen A. Douglas at Quincy, Illinois," October 13, 1858, ibid., 3:261.

26. Lincoln to Elihu B. Washburn, December 13, 1860, ibid., 4:151.

27. Lincoln to William Kellogg, December 11, 1860, ibid., 4:150.

28. Lincoln, "Message to Congress," March 6, 1862, ibid., 5:144–46.

29. Charles Sumner, "'Stand by the Administration,' Letter to _____," June 5, 1862, in *The Works of Charles Sumner*, 15 vols. (Boston: Lee and Shepard, 1870–83), 7:116–18.

30. Lincoln to Horace Greeley, August 22, 1862, *Collected Works*, 5:388–89.

31. Frederick Douglass, *Life and Times of Frederick Douglass, Written by Himself* (Hartford, Conn.: Park, 1881; facsimile ed., Secaucus, N.J.: Citadel, 1983), 359–60.

32. Lincoln to Nathaniel Banks, December 24, 1863, *Collected Works*, 7:90.

33. Lincoln quoted in Douglass, *Life and Times*, 363–64.

34. Harry V. Jaffa, *Crisis of the House Divided: An Interpretation of the Lincoln-Douglas Debates* (Chicago: University of Chicago Press, 1959), 395.

35. Roger L. Ransom, *The Confederate States of America: What Might Have Been* (New York: W.W. Norton, 2005).

36. Abraham Lincoln, "Annual Message to Congress," December 3, 1861, *Collected Works*, 5:53.

9

"As Good as It Can Be Made": Lincoln's Heroic Image in Nineteenth-Century Art

Harold Holzer

It is difficult to imagine the young Abraham Lincoln's log cabin boyhood homes decorated with pictures—not even the ubiquitous early prints of his hero, George Washington, that adorned so many rustic and remote American outposts by the early nineteenth century. Such images, inexpensive and surprisingly available even on the frontier, began appearing in such settings by the first decade of the new century, assuming pride of place alongside the religious icons of old—becoming what historian Robert Philippe has called the "heirs of the sacred picture."[1]

Yet somehow, even in the absence of visual tributes to the country's secular saints that other youngsters of the time encountered daily, Lincoln became familiar with George Washington's life and looks—enough to learn to revere him and identify the first president as his idol. As one of his early biographers put it, "Lincoln revered the memory of Washington, keeping his image before him as a pattern to be imitated in his own life and conduct."[2] In a patriotic speech marking George Washington's 110th birthday in 1842, Lincoln revealed an empathy approaching idolatry. "Washington is the mightiest name on earth," he declared. " . . . To add brightness to the sun, or glory to the name of Washington, is alike impossible. Let none attempt it."[3] Abraham Lincoln never did. No doubt it would have astonished and gratified him had he lived to see the many engravings and lithographs that appeared in 1865 linking the nation's savior to its founder (see figure 1).

In one of the most meaningful incidents of his early life, young Abe had borrowed from an Indiana neighbor a copy of Mason Locke Weems's *Life and Memorable Actions of George Washington*, the reverential biography that

introduced the fable that little George cut down a cherry tree. It remains
something of a historical irony that Lincoln, a boy who was frequently
scolded by his father for *not* cutting down *enough* trees, was so besotted
by a book that celebrated a hero who proved his virtue by cutting down a
tree by mistake and then confessing his sin to his father. Nonetheless, there
can be no doubt that the hagiographical book profoundly influenced him.
It not only introduced Washington to Lincoln but also led to an incident in
Lincoln's own boyhood that became nearly as legendary as the cherry-tree

Fig. 1. James F. Bodtker, after Gilbert Stuart (the Lansdowne portrait of
Washington) and Mathew B. Brady gallery (the February 9, 1864, photo-
graph of Lincoln), *The Father, and the Saviour of Our Country*. Lithograph,
Milwaukee, 1865. Courtesy of The Lincoln Museum, Fort Wayne, IN. Neg. no. 305.

fiction in Washington's. In those impoverished days, young Abraham slept in a loft tucked beneath the eaves of a log cabin roof, and when it rained, it poured—not only outside but inside as well. One such storm drenched the precious book he had on loan. To pay for it, "Honest Abe" toiled at its owner's farm "pulling Corn Blades at 25 cts a Day." To future biographers, he had proven his own Washington-like integrity by working off his debt—even if one acquaintance later insisted that it was the angry neighbor, not the shamed boy, who decided that the price of the book had to be redeemed in labor. The truly significant result was that the young man got to keep the volume for himself.[4]

He never forgot it. Nearly forty years later, speaking just days before taking office as president of the United States, Lincoln could still recall the "small book" from "away back in my Childhood," as he put it during an emotional visit to the scene of one of Washington's great triumphs, Trenton, New Jersey. There the president-elect confided to an audience of legislators who, like himself, had "all been boys" and knew that "these early impressions last longer than any others," that the Founders and their ideals might yet steel America for the approaching battle to save democracy. As he declared:

> I recollect thinking then, boy even though I was, that there must have been something more than common that those men struggled for. I am exceedingly anxious that that thing which they struggled for; that something even more than National Independence; that something that held out a great promise to all the people of the world to all time to come; I am exceedingly anxious that this Union, the Constitution, and the liberties of the people be perpetuated in accordance with the original idea for which that struggle was made, and I shall be most happy indeed if I shall be an humble instrument in the hands of the Almighty, and of this, his almost chosen people, for perpetuating the object of that great struggle.[5]

Such reverence for the blessings of God, the power of ideas, and the bravery of heroes evokes a sympathetic response from modern readers even without knowing about Lincoln's long and deeply personal attachment to Weems's book and its subject. Here was Lincoln identifying himself directly with the "original idea" and "great promise" of the American Revolution. Its perpetuation, he was declaring in advance of civil war, was already, in his view, a "great struggle" that implicitly called for leaders who were "more than common." Perhaps in true vindication of the American dream, we might say—looking backward with the knowledge of what came later—the crisis even required a new generation of common men who were more than common themselves.

That the collective biography of the heroic American past influenced Lincoln and his contemporaries is indisputable. Often forgotten, however, is the additional fact that portraits of heroes, too, were capable of eliciting feelings of love and communion from the American public. Many editions of Weems's Washington biography, it should be noted, boasted a simple woodcut frontispiece engraving of the father of his country. When Lincoln was still a young man, a Boston magazine marveled that "prints of Washington dark with smoke are pasted over the hearths of so many American homes that" surely, "in some of its innumerable representations," his famous face had "met every eye" in the nation."[6] Washington's visage was as much a part of national memory as his life story.

Lincoln saw—and knew—that face as well as he knew the story of his life. Early on, he understood that great men posed for great portraits. Lincoln himself sat for only one photograph before his election to Congress and would not be portrayed in portrait prints until 1860.[7] But from the day he set foot in Washington, D.C., to begin his one-term career in the House of Representatives, Lincoln was confronted there by powerful, larger-than-life images that reminded him of the eternal influence of the great American heroes who had preceded him to the nation's capital.

The U.S. Capitol Rotunda, for example—the republic's national town square—was encircled by large paintings depicting the heroes of the American Revolution: here were visual tributes to Washington and Jefferson, among other Founders, personal idols to the nation and to Lincoln himself. In this city, authentic heroes might walk among the living, too, only to pass on suddenly to join the immortals. During his time in Washington, Whig congressman Lincoln (and Democrat Stephen A. Douglas as well) represented their home state as "managers" of a bipartisan ball scheduled to celebrate George Washington's birthday, in the city named for him, on February 22, 1848. But when former president John Quincy Adams, an antislavery hero, collapsed on the House floor and died the day before—a tragedy Representative Lincoln personally witnessed—the celebration was postponed until March. That July, Lincoln attended the dedication ceremony for the grandest tribute yet planned for the city, the Washington Monument.[8]

A few years later, President Zachary Taylor's death inspired not only a stirring eulogy from Lincoln but also an outpouring of memorial portraiture, just as Taylor's nomination for the nation's highest office two years earlier had triggered a flood of campaign prints emphasizing "Old Rough and Ready's" frontier origins and unaffected manner. (Lincoln, as the Taylor example shows, was not the first log-cabin nominee hero so enshrined in popular prints.)[9] Thus, seeing both publicly situated art and privately collected reproductions, Lincoln learned to appreciate the power of the visual tribute.

In Washington, Lincoln also learned how wrongly conceived heroic portraiture could arouse controversy and ridicule. Every day of his term, Congressman Lincoln would have observed Horatio Greenough's much-mocked neoclassical statue of George Washington, looming atop its pedestal outside the east steps of the Capitol, past which Lincoln would have strolled from his boardinghouse, located nearby, on the spot where the Library of Congress now stands. The statue did not lack for ostentation: it was modeled after one of the Seven Wonders of the ancient world, Phidias's legendary sculpture of the Greek god Zeus at Olympia.[10] Here was a visualization of Washington as American deity: seated on a throne, half-naked, draped in a toga, and holding a scepter. Whether Lincoln thought it ridiculous, we do not know, but recalling his sense of humor, we can only imagine what he might have remarked about it.

Not surprisingly, George Washington never posed for any sculptor in quite this way. Instead, the imaginative Greenough modeled his statue's head on Jean Antoine Houdon's widely reproduced life mask and invented the rest, hiring European models to pose for Washington's torso. The resulting composite, awkwardly conjoining the artistic traditions of realism and symbolism, was likely designed to inspire every public servant who passed in its shadow—and perhaps, too, to quicken the pulse of any politician ambitious enough to see himself one day walking in Washington's shoes.

But in an era that came to celebrate the rough and ready above the grand and draped, Greenough's statue suffered an ignominious history. Intended to grace the Capitol Rotunda, it sat there only briefly, while engineers fretted that it was so heavy that it would break through the floor. Ultimately, adverse critical and public reaction, not its gargantuan weight, earned its banishment outdoors. One newspaper nicknamed the Greenough "Georgy-Porgy," while a visiting New Yorker wrote home to observe, "It looks like a great . . . Venus of the Bath . . . with a huge napkin lying across his lap and covering his lower extremities, and he preparing to perform his ablutions is in the act of consigning his sword to the care of the attendant until he shall come out of the bath." Eventually, political leaders thought it best to banish it outside to the park.[11]

Even there, the Greenough statue's reputation continued to sink. Visitors jokingly complained that it was disconcerting to see the half-naked Washington exposed to the freezing winter. Soiled by soot and pigeon droppings, it was finally lugged off to the Smithsonian, no longer considered a tribute but at best a curiosity, at worst a laughingstock. It should surprise no one familiar with American taste that by the time a heroic seated statue of Abraham Lincoln was unveiled in Washington in 1922, a few miles from the Capitol at a new Lincoln Memorial, its subject was carefully dressed in his familiar, everyday clothes. Even if he was enthroned like Greenough's bare-chested Washington, with his hands gripping classically inspired symbols of justice and authority—the Roman fasces—and even if the temple and its murals, if not its occupant, were neoclassical, viewers primarily confronted an informal, accessible Lincoln—gigantic, but approachable. Even so, it seemed no less heroic.[12] Its sculptor, Daniel Chester French, strove for what art historian Christopher H. Thomas summarized as "simplicity and universality."[13]

Four score years earlier, Greenough's George Washington statue represented the standard model of heroic portraiture that Lincoln first saw in the nation's capital. So did the plan, which Lincoln embraced, to build a huge classical obelisk to stand on a swampy knoll between the Capitol and the White House. That it rose only a third of the way and then remained an unsightly stump through the Civil War years and beyond may have reminded Lincoln that even the Father of his Country could suffer indignity at the hands of those pressing to celebrate his immortality with the best of intentions but the worst of financing plans. America's record of commissioning public art was, at best, mixed. Lincoln, who never lost his belief in private enterprise, would be content to let entrepreneurial artists assume primary control over his own image.[14]

It was in Washington, D.C., that Lincoln also discovered the existence of another kind of visual tribute, a genre that permitted more Americans than those concentrated in its capital to see its heroes for themselves. These were mass-produced images designed for display in private homes, like the endless engraved and lithographed adaptations of Gilbert Stuart's portraits of Washington, or the famous engravings of the Webster-Hayne debate on the floor of the U.S. Senate. We know that Lincoln understood the potential impact of these domestic icons, if only through one of his funny stories about the response evoked by one print portrait of George Washington. It seemed that an American living in England had grown weary of Englishmen deriding George Washington, so he hung a picture of the first president in his host's outhouse. No, it was not a sign of disrespect. As Lincoln pointed out, "it was very appropriate . . . for their [*sic*] is Nothing that Will Make an Englishman Shit So quick as the Sight of Genl Washington."[15] Not many years later, as fate would have it, Lincoln himself would become a familiar, often grotesquely lampooned, figure in political cartoons that took pictorial disrespect one step further.

Before he achieved national prominence of his own, however, Lincoln and his contemporaries generally saw their heroes posed in stiffly formal settings, gesturing meaningfully. Lincoln was no stranger to the tradition of the grand physical gesture as a symbol of authority, though he would seldom in the future affect such postures himself. Washington's upheld hand in the Greenough statue replicated and reinforced illustrations Lincoln had studied from his childhood copy of William Scott's *Lessons in Elocution*, the primer that introduced Lincoln to the art of public speaking—and gesturing. Scott recommended that orators learn not only how to form words but how to accompany them with proper movements of their arms and hands: "The right arm should be held out, with the palm open," advised the book, and then, when lowered, the "left hand raises itself, into exactly the same position as the right was before . . . and so on, from right to left, alternatively, till the speech is ended." Such gestures could help a speaker to "solicit . . . refuse . . . promise . . . threaten . . . dismiss . . . invite . . . entreat . . . express aversion, fear, doubting, denial, asking, affirmation, negation, joy, grief, confusion, penitence. . . ."[16] This was how heroes, and future heroes, declaimed.

Later, when Lincoln finally began to achieve national fame himself, he got a firsthand lesson in the aesthetic and traditional values of the human body in heroic art. Arriving to pose for his portrait at the studio of sculptor Leonard Wells Volk in Chicago in April 1860, Lincoln got the opportunity to study Volk's photographs of Greek and Roman statuary, surely among them classical nudes, while waiting to sit for his own bust. Then Volk told his subject he "desired to represent his breast and brawny shoulders as nature presented them." Obligingly—and apparently undissuaded by his recollection of the Greenough fiasco in so portraying George Washington—Lincoln, as Volk recalled, promptly "stripped off his coat, waistcoat, shirt, cravat, and collar, threw them on a chair, pulled his undershirt down a short distance, tying his sleeves behind him, and stood up without a murmur for an hour or so" to pose bare-chested.

He might well have been more embarrassed than he admitted. When the session was over, Lincoln dressed hurriedly and fled the studio. But then he returned only a few minutes later, sheepishly explaining to Volk: "I got down on the sidewalk and found I had forgotten to put on my undershirt, and thought it wouldn't do to go through the streets this way." Sure enough, the sculptor glanced behind Lincoln, and saw the sleeves of his undergarment dangling below his frock coat. This time Lincoln let Volk help him get his clothes back on properly.[17] Volk's original life mask (see figure 2), which sculptor George Grey Barnard later hailed as the best representation ever made of "the most wonderful face left to us,"[18] became the model for a dozen different mass-produced Volk sculptures—including both nude and draped neoclassical, heroic busts suitable for display in private homes (see figures 3 and 4), as well as for heroic full-length statues for the new state capitol in Springfield, Illinois, and atop an obelisk at the Soldiers' and Sailors' Monument in Rochester, New York.[19] All these adaptations, those made for private parlors or public places, bear perpetual witness to Lincoln's willingness to facilitate the kind of heroic art that had immortalized the peerless Washington. And they offered Americans their first opportunities to visualize Abraham Lincoln. But the outlines of that image would soon change. Like Washington before him, the prairie politician was not made for ornate or classically inspired portraiture.

During the presidential campaign of 1860, he was often visualized as a plainly dressed, plain-spoken, Zachary Taylor–like candidate whose greatest virtue was his rise from frontier obscurity. Lincoln became the subject of an extraordinary outburst of image-making that year, like the lithograph showing the Republicans' presidential and vice presidential nominees encircled by Lincolnian log rails emblematic of his days as a hardworking frontiersman (see figure 5). Such metaphors were key to the development of Lincoln's own enduring, and reputation-enhancing, *anti*heroic image—that of a rail-splitter who wore homespun clothes, carried a log rail, not a scepter, and told the kind of jokes he had privately spun on George Washington's image years before.

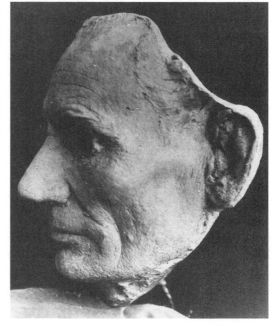

Fig. 2. Leonard Wells Volk, plaster cast of life mask of Abraham Lincoln, 1860.
Courtesy of The Lincoln Museum, Fort Wayne, IN. Neg. no. 998.

Fig. 3. Leonard Wells Volk, nude, or Hermes, bust of Lincoln, inscribed: *L. W. Volk/Sculptor/1860.* Courtesy of The Lincoln Museum, Fort Wayne, IN. Neg. no. 1553.

Fig. 4. Leonard Wells Volk, draped bust of Lincoln, inscribed: *Lincoln from life/L. W. Volk 1860.* Courtesy of The Lincoln Museum, Fort Wayne, IN. Neg. no. 3167.

Fig. 5. W. H. Rease, *The Union Must and Shall Be Preserved: Free Speech, Free Homes, Free Territory*. Lithograph, Philadelphia, 1860. Courtesy of The Lincoln Museum, Fort Wayne, IN. Neg. no. 3356.

It is worth noting that Lincoln hardly chose this image for himself, as some have implied. Historians have long commended Lincoln for "allowing" himself to be so portrayed in campaign biographies and portraiture alike.[20] Yet, in truth, there is no evidence that he was complicit in the creation of any of these images. In Lincoln's day, prints were conceived of, and distributed by, the publishers themselves, not the political campaigns. As noncommissioned commercial ventures that relied on public patronage to succeed, they reflected the public yearning for a new kind of presidential image, not the imposition of that image on the public.

Ultimately, however, Lincoln became a more active agent in his elevation into the American pantheon of heroes. How and why he did so may help explain how, eventually and uniquely, Lincoln evolved, at least in part through heroic portraiture of a special kind, into what David Herbert Donald has called an amalgam of "hero" and "demigod."[21]

After 1860, Lincoln began posing for photographers more often, as the fashion grew for visiting-card photos and leather albums to display them.

Most of these were studio poses, but in 1862 photographer Alexander Gardner was on the scene to provide perhaps the most newsworthy Lincoln photographs ever made. They captured him on the battlefield—at least near where a battle had raged at Sharpsburg, Maryland—during a tense visit to prod General George B. McClellan back into action. The results might justly be called the first true presidential photo opportunities; they are certainly the first photographs to show a commander-in-chief on a battlefield of war. With his signature top hat planted on his head, Lincoln towered over "Little Mac" and his staff in their group poses, standing taller than ever and, what was more, in a military setting (see figure 6). Even seated in the general's tent for a conference, an American flag serving as an emblematic tablecloth, Lincoln looked every bit the commander-in-chief, with McClellan receding into the shadows (see figure 7). But the real genius behind these pictures was not their timeliness alone—an immediacy that belies the four-to-ten seconds required to expose each plate[22]—but the clever posing, cropping, and retouching that Gardner employed. A close examination of the original plate reveals that McClellan's tent sat just in front of a handsome house that looks ample enough to have accommodated the presidential visit. But such a domestic setting would not have yielded the proper military atmosphere, so the two men convened outdoors, and the nearby civilian dwelling was deemphasized.[23]

The Gardner photographs created a new way of visualizing Abraham Lincoln—as an imposing, on-the-job, and thoroughly modern commander-in-chief. His height clearly rendered him the superior physical position in all the standing poses Gardner took that day: his immense height was such that the photographer needed no gestures or props to identify the president as the central figure in the pose. Just as Lincoln had introduced a new dialectic into American oratory, he was—perhaps unknowingly—introducing a new heroic attitude into American portraiture.

Yet by the time the New York artist Francis B. Carpenter arrived in Washington to paint Abraham Lincoln and his cabinet in 1864, Lincoln was in serious political trouble. The war had raged inconclusively, at great cost in human life and treasure, for two years more, with no end in sight. Lincoln had successfully fought off a challenge to his renomination but now faced General McClellan, whom he had dismissed from army command, as his formidable Democratic opponent for the White House. Lincoln's Emancipation Proclamation may have ended slavery, but it had also sufficiently threatened racist white America to generate huge Republican losses in the off-year elections of 1862 and a serious threat to a second term for the Emancipator.

Fig. 6. Alexander Gardner, photograph of Abraham Lincoln, George B. McClellan, and McClellan's staff on the battlefield of Antietam, near Sharpsburg, Maryland, October 3, 1862. Courtesy of The Lincoln Museum, Fort Wayne, IN. O-62.

Fig. 7. Alexander Gardner, photograph of the president and General McClellan on the battlefield of Antietam, near Sharpsburg, Maryland, October 3, 1862. Courtesy of The Lincoln Museum, Fort Wayne, IN. O-66.

Against this backdrop, it is interesting to note, Lincoln did nothing to encourage the reintroduction of his four-year-old political image as the self-made product of the Western frontier. Now, exercising more control than ever over the contours of his public image, he bravely chose to emphasize his authorship of the Emancipation Proclamation, apparently believing that it demanded appropriate heroic tributes in art. "If my name ever goes into history, it will be for this act," he remembered saying as he prepared to sign the final proclamation on January 1, 1863.[24] It is a story he told not to a journalist but to an artist. This may help explain why he now proved more willing than ever to sit for artists who suggested depicting him as an emancipator. Philadelphia artist Edward Dalton Marchant, for example, was granted unfettered access to the president in 1863 to paint him as the liberator of the race. However, Marchant's canvas—and the 1864 campaign engraving it inspired—hearkened back to classical iconology (see figure 8).[25] It showed the president, dressed in highly formal regalia (a white tie no less), posing before a statue of "Liberty" whose chains break apart symbolically as he takes pen in hand to sign the Emancipation Proclamation. The image is hardly known today, perhaps because of its attempts at formal symbolism.

Fig. 8. John Sartain, after Edward Dalton Marchant, *Abraham Lincoln, 16th President of the United States.* Engraving published by Bradley & Co., Philadelphia, 1864. Courtesy of The Lincoln Museum, Fort Wayne, IN. Neg. no. 3326.

To Francis B. Carpenter, who proposed painting the president's entire cabinet on the day it first met to hear him suggest freedom for the slaves, Lincoln similarly gave unlimited access to the White House, along with six months' time to work out his ideas and the honor of an exhibition in the East Room to display his finished canvas.[26] Carpenter's concept was radically different from Marchant's. The artist aspired to create a picture that did nothing less than "commemorate this new epoch in the history of Liberty." America's invigorating new history, he believed, was "no dream of fable, but a substantial fact—the immaculate conception of Constitutional Liberty." It "need borrow no interest from imaginary curtain or column, gorgeous furniture or allegorical statue," Carpenter insisted. It would be free of "the false glitter of tapestry hangings, velvet table-cloths, and marble columns." There would be no "accessories or adjuncts." Art, Carpenter declared, "cannot dwell always among classic forms, nor clothe its conceptions in the imagery of an old and worn-out world . . . and its ideals must be wrought out of the strife of a living humanity." As the painter put it, "I had no more right to depart from the facts, than has the historian in his record."[27] With a work free of "accessories or adjuncts," he would elevate the plain man of the people into a national icon.

This proved easier said than done. Life sittings alone did not provide the poses he felt best reflected his aspirations. As a remedy, Carpenter sought photographic models from which he could paint. Ever cooperating on the venture, Lincoln agreed to pose before the cameras at Mathew Brady's gallery on February 9, 1864. Brady himself was absent; he was at the front, photographing the Civil War. But it turned out to be the day the Lincoln image—and the primary technology for promulgating it—changed forever. We can safely assume that Carpenter himself arranged the poses, and no one ever did so more brilliantly. The results included the future models for the Lincoln penny (see figure 9), the old five-dollar bill (see figure 10), and the revised five-dollar bill of the twenty-first century, not to mention the quintessential intimate portrait of Abraham Lincoln: the famous photograph with his son Tad. All the poses went on to achieve popularity of their own as photographic keepsakes and further fame as models for engraved and lithographed portraits.

Carpenter was not trying to produce photographic icons that day, even though he did. Nor was he aware that the pictures Brady's photographer took that day would outstrip his painstakingly planned canvas in fame. The artist never even got the credit he deserved for posing them. What he was after at Brady's was merely the perfect pose for his Lincoln canvas. The poses

Fig. 9. Mathew Brady studio, photograph of Abraham Lincoln in profile, Washington, D.C., February 9, 1864. Courtesy of The Lincoln Museum, Fort Wayne, IN. O-89.

Fig. 10. Mathew Brady studio, photograph of Abraham Lincoln seated, Washington, D.C., February 9, 1864. Courtesy of The Lincoln Museum, Fort Wayne, IN. O-92.

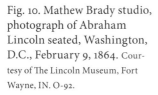

on which he lavished special attention were the close-ups of Lincoln's face and a majestic, full-figure pose, each a marvelous view of how the president looked just three days shy of his fifty-fifth birthday. But the question of how best to portray Lincoln declaring what the artist believed was a second Declaration of Independence—for a canvas he had every hope would some day hang in the Capitol Rotunda alongside Trumbull's national icon of the first Declaration of Independence—continued to vex Carpenter.

Still unsatisfied, the painter ushered Lincoln to Brady's for a second studio session, and then, a few weeks later, summoned one of the photographer's camera operators to the White House where, in the president's private office, all but obscured in its weak natural light, Lincoln posed again, both sitting and standing, at the very table where he had signed the proclamation on January 1, 1863. Whatever their unavoidable technical flaws, the poorly lighted results were breathtaking pictures, some of the first ever to show a president inside the White House, though the public did not get to see them for generations. At last, Carpenter had photographic models worth adapting. He quickly proceeded to work them into both seated and full-figure sketches, as his scrapbook shows.[28] Ultimately, the artist chose to paint Lincoln simply sitting in his chair at the head of the cabinet table, dominating the scene merely by listening, not speaking. The president does not even appear at the center of the canvas.[29]

The president proclaimed it "as good as it can be made."[30] The press agreed. Even acknowledging its "rawness, lack of finish, and commonplace-ness—such as might be expected of a young artist who has grappled with a subject so difficult and yet so interesting now and forever," correspondent Noah Brooks still pronounced the painting "a measurable success." Brooks presciently predicted that its "chief faults which are now noticeable will be remedied in the engraving." As a popular print, he believed, it would be "prized in every liberty-loving household as a work of art, a group of faithful likenesses of the President and cabinet, and as a perpetual remembrance of the noblest event in American history."[31] Such became precisely the case with the publication of Alexander Hay Ritchie's hugely popular engraved adaptation in 1866 (see figure 11).

In appreciation, an influential art journal declared, "The hour has arrived when the necessities of our country not only justify, but inexorably demand, the production of a series of national paintings." By 1866, Francis B. Carpenter would respond to this call for nation-affirming visual representations by advertising his Emancipation canvas as his own "Great National Picture."[32] The painting, its promoters emphasized, showed an unhesitating Lincoln

Fig. 11. Alexander Hay Ritchie, engraving, after a painting by Francis Bicknell Carpenter, *The First Reading of the Emancipation Proclamation before the Cabinet.* Published by Derby & Miller, New York, 1866. Courtesy of The Lincoln Museum, Fort Wayne, IN. Neg. no. 2825.

braving certain political denunciation to issue the order. Lincoln would have been overjoyed to read the *New York Tribune's* assessment that the picture proved "by all odds, next to Trumbull's Picture of the 'Declaration of Independence'—a picture worth all the rest in the Capitol put together—the best work of this class that has been painted in America."[33]

Lincoln had known those Rotunda paintings intimately in the 1840s. They had helped a young congressman—and, in engraved adaptations, a young nation—visualize national identity and memory. And now a painting of Lincoln himself was declared worthy to be included among them. But it was not to be. Carpenter was no Trumbull.

Yet Americans never entirely lost their taste for heroic art in public places. Francis B. Carpenter did eventually persuade Congress to buy his realistic Emancipation Proclamation canvas, but only after its engraved adaptation had become a huge bestseller. Not until Carpenter found a wealthy patron to buy and donate it did the huge painting earn its place in the Capitol—not in the Rotunda, as the artist always hoped, but on a wall too cramped for the canvas outside the Senate chamber, where today only visitors to its galleries can glimpse it. Somehow, a decade after it was painted, Carpenter's immense canvas seemed in a way too small for the hero it celebrated.

The Rotunda would instead welcome a traditional heroic sculpture carved in Italy by a young American woman named Vinnie Ream, who had also enjoyed life-sittings in the White House with Abraham Lincoln to create a portrait bust—the photographed results of which were so popular that even the president's family collected a copy for its own family album (see figure 12).[34] But except for the sad, homely face she portrayed realistically, her final statue, commissioned later by Congress, hearkened back to antiquity, portraying Lincoln extending his arm in the classical heroic posture, grasping the Emancipation Proclamation in a gesture meant to suggest the granting of liberty (see figure 13).[35] Public art still called for such conventions. Those who held such aspirations for Vinnie Ream's Lincoln statue, also cop-

ABRAHAM LINCOLN.
By Vinnie Ream.

Fig. 12. Alexander Gardner, photograph of Vinnie Ream's sculpture *Abraham Lincoln*, ca. 1865. From the Lincoln family album collection. Courtesy of The Lincoln Museum, Fort Wayne, IN. Neg. no. 4035.

ied in its day by photographers, must have been caught short by some of the violent criticism it aroused, with one newspaper condemning it as "a formless thing . . . lifeless and soulless" and suggesting she could hardly have completed it "without some man's help."[36]

Had it not been for a widely reported accident, the statue would likely have met the same fate as Greenough's banished statue of Washington. But when workers began carting the Ream statue from its place in the Rotunda, they accidentally damaged the Emancipation Proclamation scroll that "Lincoln" clutched in his hand. Vinnie Ream's sculpture remained where it was first unveiled, its scroll, if not its reputation, restored.[37]

"No monument can increase or prolong the fame of Lincoln," New Hampshire senator James Willis Patterson wisely observed on the day Vinnie Ream's statue was unveiled, adding grandly: "His secured greatness adds

Fig. 13. Bell & Bros., stereopticon photograph of Vinnie Ream's statue of Lincoln in the Capitol Rotunda. Published for the *Views of Washington* series, ca. 1870. Author's collection.

a luster to the marble which we this day dedicate to his memory, and will survive when this work of genius itself and this massive pile shall have crumbled and mingled with the indistinguishable earth." But Patterson had missed a crucial point. Tributes—"works of genius"—like those created by Ream and the artists who had preceded her in creating heroic images of this quintessentially simple man had indeed helped secure his greatness and did nothing less than elevate his image in permanent national memory.[38]

Lincoln's old friend Henry Clay Whitney—who watched his onetime legal colleague rise from prairie lawyer to martyred president—would have agreed. Predicting that Abraham Lincoln's countenance would be "reproduced *ad infinitum* in bronze, granite, and marble," he remained convinced that Lincoln had earned the grandest celebrations in art, quoting John Milton to summarize the hero's transfiguration:

> A pillar of state; deep on his front engraven,
> Deliberation sat, and public care;
> . . . his look
> Drew audience and attention still as night,
> Or summer's noontide air.[39]

Notes

1. Noble E. Cunningham Jr., *Popular Images of the Presidency: From Washington to Lincoln* (Columbia: University of Missouri Press, 1991), 19; Robert Philippe, *Political Graphics: Art as a Weapon* (New York: Abbeville, 1980), 172.

2. Francis Fisher Browne, *The Every-Day Life of Abraham Lincoln* (Hartford, Conn.: Park Publishing, 1886), 32–34. See also Edmond S. Meaney, *Lincoln Esteemed Washington* (Seattle, Wash.: Frank McCaffrey, 1933), 9–13.

3. Roy P. Basler, ed., *The Collected Works of Abraham Lincoln*, 9 vols., hereafter referred to as *Collected Works* (New Brunswick, N.J.: Rutgers University Press, 1953–55), 1:279.

4. A. H. Chapman, quoted in Douglas Wilson and Rodney O. Davis, eds., *Herndon's Informants: Letters, Interviews, and Statements about Abraham Lincoln* (Urbana: University of Illinois Press, 1998), 101.

5. *Collected Works*, 4:235–36.

6. *American Magazine of Useful and Entertaining* Knowledge, no. 2 (1836), quoted in Noble Cunningham, *Popular Images of the Presidency from Washington to Lincoln* (Columbia: University of Missouri Press, 1991), 19.

7. For Lincoln's only photograph of the 1840s, see Charles Hamilton and Lloyd Ostendorf, *Lincoln in Photographs: An Album of Every Known Pose* (Norman: University of Oklahoma Press, 1963), 4–5.

8. Earl Schenck Miers, ed., *Lincoln Day by Day: A Chronology, 1809–1865*, 3 vols. (Washington, D.C.: Lincoln Sesquicentennial Commission, 1960), 1:303–4, 314.

9. Lincoln's Taylor eulogy is in *Collected Works*, 2:83–90. For Taylor's campaign prints, see Bernard F. Reilly Jr., *American Political Prints, 1766–1876: A Catalog of the Collections in the Library of Congress* (Boston: G. K. Hall, 1991), 270–73. For a typical memorial image, see Cunningham, *Popular Images*, 76.

10. The author is indebted to the Civil War Institute, Gettysburg College, for inviting him to publish his first thoughts on these themes in *Standing Tall: The Heroic Image of Abraham Lincoln*, 43rd annual Fortenbaugh Memorial Lecture (Gettysburg, Pa.: Gettysburg College, 2004). The discussion of Washington as Lincoln's boyhood hero was first offered at the National Endowment for the Humanities' "Heroes of History" Lecture at Ford's Theatre, October 18, 2004, later published online by the NEH. For more on Greenough, see Wayne Craven, *Sculpture in America*, rev. ed. (Newark, N.J.: University of Delaware Press, 1984), 107–8; and Christopher A. Thomas, *The Lincoln Memorial and American Life* (Princeton, N.J.: Princeton University Press, 2002), 119–20.

11. For a nineteenth-century photograph of the statue *in situ* outdoors, see Dorothy Meserve Kunhardt and Philip B. Kunhardt Jr., *Twenty Days* (New York: Harper & Row, 1965), 116; and Craven, *Sculpture in America*, 108–9. The Metropolitan Museum owns a bare-shouldered, ca. 1832 marble bust of Washington by Greenough, which the sculptor thought so successful "in pleasing my countrymen that I think of getting up a statue of him." See Thayer Tolles, ed., *American Sculpture in the Metropolitan Museum of Art*, vol. 1, *A Catalogue of Works by Artists before 1865* (New York: Metropolitan Museum of Art, 1999).

12. For evidence that modern critics rued the memorial's traditional design, see Thomas, *Lincoln Memorial*, 140; for the symbolic meaning of the fasces, see James Hall, *Dictionary of Subjects and Symbols in Art*, rev. ed. (London: John Murray, 1984), 119.

13. Thomas, *Lincoln Memorial*, 123.

14. Miers, *Lincoln Day by Day*, 1:302, 314.

15. Abner Ellis's recollection, in Wilson and Davis, *Herndon's Informants*, 174.

16. William Scott, *Lessons in Elocution; or, A Selection of Pieces in Prose and Verse for the Improvement of Youth in Reading and Speaking . . . to Which Are Prefixed Elements of Gesture* (Boston: Isaiah Thomas, 1811), 33–36.

17. Leonard Wells Volk, "A Lincoln Life-Mask and How It Was Made," in Rufus Rockwell Wilson, ed., *Intimate Memories of Lincoln* (Elmira, N.Y.: Primavera, 1945), 243–44.

18. Quoted in Donald Charles Durman, *He Belongs to the Ages: The Statues of Abraham Lincoln* (Ann Arbor, Mich.: Edwards Brothers, 1951), 3.

19. For pictures of Volk's heroic Lincoln statues, see ibid., 13, 15.

20. In a recent example, presidential historian Michael Beschloss wrote of Lincoln: "He knew the voters wanted down-to-earth candidates like Jackson who could touch their hearts. Thus in 1860, Lincoln let himself be presented not as the well-to-do lawyer he had become, but instead as 'Honest Abe the Rail Splitter.'" Michael Beschloss, *Presidential Courage: Brave Leaders and How They Changed America* (New York: Simon & Schuster, 2007), 101.

21. David Donald, *Lincoln Reconsidered: Essays on the Civil War Era* (New York: Vantage Books, 1961), 162–63.

22. There is no consensus among period sources about the length of exposure time required to make wet-plate photographs; contemporary estimates vary between four and fifteen seconds. See, for example, T. Frederick Hardwich, *A Manual of Photographic Chemistry, Including the Practice of the Collodion Process*, 4th ed. (New York: H. H. Snelling, 1858), 140 (three seconds to six seconds in "bright spring and summer months," up to four times longer in "dull winter months" or "in the smoky atmosphere of large cities"); N. G. Burgess, *The Photograph and Ambrotype Manual: A Practical Treatise on the Art of Taking Pictures . . .* , 5th ed. (New York: Wiley & Halstead, 1858), 150 ("about ten or fifteen seconds, in ordinary temperatures"); A. S. Heath, *Photography: A New Treatise, Theoretical and Practical of Their Processes and Manipulations on Paper, Dried and Wet Glass, Collodion and Albumen* (New York: Heath & Brother, 1855), 54–55 ("from one to ten seconds for views, and from 30 to 40 seconds for a portrait in the shade").

23. The pose nonetheless achieved enduring fame. Gardner published it in his two-volume, $150 edition, *Gardner's Photographic Sketch Book of the Civil War* (1866, reprinted, New York: Dover, 1959).

24. Lincoln quoted by *Washington Chronicle* editor John Wein Forney, in Francis B. Carpenter, *Six Months at the White House with Abraham Lincoln: The Story of a Picture* (New York: Hurd & Houghton, 1866), 269.

25. For discussion of Edward D. Marchant's 1863 portrait of Lincoln, see Harold Holzer, Gabor S. Boritt, and Mark E. Neely Jr., *The Lincoln Image: Abraham Lincoln and the Popular Print* (New York: Charles Scribner's Sons, 1984), 102–10.

26. Carpenter arrived at the White House on February 5, 1864.

27. Carpenter, *Six Months at the White House*, 9, 11–12, 25.

28. For a glance at the Carpenter sketchbook, see Harold Holzer and Mark E. Neely Jr., *Mine Eyes Have Seen the Glory: The Civil War in Art* (New York: Orion, 1990), 74–75.

29. Carpenter, *Six Months at the White House*, 27. Carpenter did believe, he said, in "allegory," and he positioned the most liberal members of the cabinet to the left-hand side of the canvas, the conservatives to the right, with Lincoln mediating from the middle.

30. Ibid., 28.

31. P. J. Staudenraus, ed., *Mr. Lincoln's Washington: The Civil War Dispatches of Noah Brooks* (New York: Thomas Yoseloff, 1967), 361–63.

32. "American Painters: Their Errors as Regards Nationality," *Photographic and Fine Art Journal*, August 1857 (reprinted from *Cosmopolitan Art Journal*), 232; Carpenter, *Six Months at the White House,* 28; for advertisement, see addendum to Carpenter's book entitled *The Publications of Hurd and Houghton, New York*, 4.

33. "Carpenter's Great National Picture," promotional appendix to Henry J. Raymond, *The Life and Public Services of Abraham Lincoln . . .* (New York: Derby & Miller, 1865), n.p.

34. Mark E. Neely Jr. and Harold Holzer, *The Lincoln Family Album: Photographs from the Personal Collection of a Historic American Family* (1990; Carbondale: Southern Illinois University Press, 2006), 102.

35. Its dedication was reported in the *New York Times*, February 13, 1878; see also Harold Holzer, Gabor S. Boritt, and Mark E. Neely Jr., "Francis Bicknell Carpenter (1830–1900): Painter of Abraham Lincoln and His Circle," *American Art Journal* 16 (Spring 1984): 78.

36. *New York Daily Tribune*, January 31, 1871.

37. Glenn V. Sherwood, *Labor of Love: The Life and Art of Vinnie Ream* (Hygiene, Colo.: SunShine, 1997), 163, 175–76.

38. Ibid., 163.

39. Henry C. Whitney, *Life on the Circuit with Lincoln* (Boston: Estes & Lauriat, 1892), 599–601.

10

Lincoln and the Nature of "A More Perfect Union"

Herman Belz

Although much criticized in recent decades, it is doubtful that national sovereignty and identity will any time soon be abandoned as a form of political association. How peoples and nations come into existence, constituting themselves on the basis of distinctive values and purposes, will remain a central concern of political and historical analysis. Nowhere else does this question possess the peculiar significance it has in the United States, long considered the first new nation of modernity. In recent scholarship, doubt is expressed that the country was founded in a spirit of nationalism.[1] Skepticism is similarly directed toward the sense of nationality that appeared during the Civil War, on the ground of its disregard for the rights of minorities—either the states that attempted to secede or the slaves emancipated by the Union government.[2] From the postmodernist point of view, American national identity exhibits the least edifying features of the principal political ideology of modernity.

As a corrective to this view, I argue that the Union of the American people was founded on a distinctive and genuine sense of nationality. I contend further that the statesmanship of Abraham Lincoln affirmed this nationality by preserving, through augmentation and amelioration, the "more perfect Union" established by the Constitution. My analysis rests on the premise that the phenomenon of national sovereignty results from historical rather than natural forces. As a historical matter, however, nationalism can present itself as the outcome of an organic process, contingent events, or intentional human action based on reflection, deliberation, and practical reason.

The American Founders tended toward the third of these points of view. In the words of political philosopher Ralph Lerner, they were "thinking revolutionaries": deliberative, practical reasoners who, through the application of the improved "science of politics," acted in favor of private rights and public happiness for "the amelioration of popular systems of civil government."[3] In the framing of republican constitutions, James Madison observed, the Founders "accomplished a revolution which has no parallel in the annals of human society. They reared the fabrics of governments which have no model on the face of the globe. They formed the design of a great Confederacy, which it is incumbent on their successors to improve and perpetuate."[4]

In the line of constitutional succession from the founding, Abraham Lincoln was the statesman upon whom, in Madison's words, the principal burden of perpetuating the American republic fell. Lincoln correctly understood that the duty to preserve the Union required the making of a more perfect union. When, as president-elect, he determined that the secession movement must be resisted, he rightly understood the nature of the Union. Lincoln stated the essence of his reasoning in the First Inaugural Address. He affirmed the principle that "the Union of these States is perpetual," and he echoed Madison's idea of republican improvement. Recounting the nation's origin, he emphasized that a declared object for ordaining and establishing the Constitution was "*to form a more perfect union.*" He argued that if it was lawfully possible for a state, or a part of a state, to destroy the Union, then "the Union is less perfect than before the Constitution, having lost the vital element of perpetuity."[5] Lincoln recognized the moral meaning of the crisis: "I appeal to all loyal citizens to favor, facilitate and aid this effort to maintain the honor, the integrity, and the existence of our National Union, and the perpetuity of popular government; and to redress wrongs already long enough endured."[6]

Resolving a constitutional debate that began with the ratification of the Constitution, Lincoln's action in the secession crisis disclosed the nature of the Union with clarity, force, and finality. In order to secure their independent existence as a nation, it was necessary for the people of America to constitute themselves in the form of a more powerful and authoritative government. In the crisis of republican nationality provoked by proslavery states' secession in 1861, Lincoln rose to the challenge of making a more perfect union that was intrinsic to the founding of the United States as a free political society.

———

From 1787 to 1861, debate over the nature of the Union formed the central theme and sustaining motif of American politics. In the most obvious sense, it concerned the meaning of the federal principle with respect to the relative constitutional powers of the state and national governments. In a more subtle and elusive sense, the nature of the Union consisted in a manifold of social and cultural meanings, including civility, friendship, patriotic feeling, attachment to local traditions and institutions, religious beliefs, passions, interests, ambitions, and aspirations. Thought concerning constitutional and political matters was related to the conditions and modes of living signified in the cultural manifold of union. If debate over constitutional authority was inconclusive because of ambiguity inherent in a system of government that was described as "partly federal, partly national," the nature of the Union was even more ambiguous with respect to cultural attachment and moral aspiration.

In the view of political scientist Rogan Kersh, at the inception of the government the concept of *union* served to gloss over significant differences on a range of substantive matters. The appeal to union "lacked definite content, lodging a dangerous ambiguity near the heart of American political institutions."[7] This circumstance, however, provided reason and justification for ongoing debate over the constitutional nature of the Union as an intrinsic and practical feature of federal-system politics, without forcing the question to the point of final resolution. In other words, sustained debate over the respective powers and authority of the states and the national government was a way to avert more deep-seated and potentially violent conflict over moral values. Yet constitutional reasoning based on the constitutional text was not simply functional. Reflective of social realities, it had its own distinctive intelligibility, integrity, and authority grounded in practical reason.

The concept of a more perfect union was written into the Preamble to the Constitution. Although in a legal-hermeneutical sense the Preamble is not part of the Constitution, it provides a transition from the authority of the people as constituent power to the governing instrument of national union.[8] The Preamble identifies the ends, objects, and principles of the Constitution as fundamental political law. In separating from Great Britain, the people of America formed a political union to protect their external and internal security as a nation. The determination to make a more perfect union in 1787 required the affirmation and strengthening of institutions and activities through which communication and association of the people of all sections with each other would be extended and enhanced.

The idea of perfection employed in the preambulary context is ambiguous. In ordinary usage, *perfect* has the connotation of being flawless, without defect or blemish, referring to a state of excellence that is virtually an ideal condition. Considered in the context of eighteenth-century political thought, *perfect* has a classic metaphysical and teleological connotation. It refers to the bringing of a thing to fullness or completeness of being, such that it lacks nothing essential to its identity, enabling it to be the kind of thing it is meant to be according to the design and intent of its maker. To avow in the Preamble to the Constitution the intent to form "a more perfect Union" and "secure the Blessings of Liberty to ourselves and our Posterity" was to project into the future the attachment of the people to the principles of republican freedom stated in the Declaration of Independence, the nation's primary document of foundation. As a form of political association, union could be based on a variety of purposes and ends. The American union was created as a community of free and independent people. The more perfect Union of 1787 was intended to sustain, augment, and ameliorate the existing revolutionary union, in order to fulfill the end of republican freedom as the basis of American nationality.

In the view of the framers, the potentiality and plenitude of republican freedom implicit in the Preamble, and inherent in the Constitution as fundamental law, had always to be actualized. The principles were fixed and enduring; the duty of their application and construction would necessarily be undertaken in changing historical contexts. For Lincoln, as for the Founders, actualization posed a problem because it was not obvious what measures were required to give substantive content to the constitutional object and obligation of making a more perfect union.

The fundamental issue in American government and politics has always been the nature of the Union. In approaching this problem, a threshold question arises concerning the relation between theory and practice. In order to make a more perfect union, it is necessary to know what kind of political association the Founders intended to create. Considered from a constitutional and legal standpoint, rather than from a social and cultural perspective, what was the identity of the units or component parts that were joined into a united political whole? Was constituent sovereignty assumed to be located in the people of America as individual persons, or in the states of America in their severalty and independence? In short, did the Founders intend to create a union of people or a union of states?

A politically plausible answer was that the framers created a union that was both a national republic of persons and a confederation of republican states. That is to say, the Constitution combined two different forms of political association: a republican government based on the principle of the sovereignty of the people, and a confederation of independent political societies based on the principle of state sovereignty. In this view, the Constitution synthesized parallel and potentially conflicting tendencies toward republicanism and federalism as organizing principles of American politics. The Declaration of Independence, stating the necessity for the inhabitants of America as "one People" to declare the causes that impelled them to dissolve their political connection to the people of Britain, expressed the idea of republican unity in the people as a whole. In referring to "these United Colonies" as "Free and Independent States" absolved from allegiance to Great Britain, the Declaration suggested the alternative idea of a confederation of sovereign states. The Articles of Confederation defined America more as a union of states than as a republic of citizens. The document determined that "Each state retains its sovereignty, freedom, and independence, and every Power, Jurisdiction and right, which is not by this confederation expressly delegated to the United States in Congress assembled." At the same time, the states were bound by the Articles of Confederation and their "union" was declared to be "perpetual."

The Constitution altered the institutional structure of that union by forming an extended federal republic. It established a republican government for the country as a whole, combined with a confederation of state republican governments for the management of local affairs. The people of the United States of America, which is to say the people of America as a nation, were represented in the U.S. House of Representatives. The states of America were represented in the U.S. Senate. The Constitution was framed by delegates of the states and ratified and made operational by the people of the United States acting in popularly elected conventions in the states. In the language of the document, the Constitution was ordained and established by the authority of "We the People of the United States."

The American Union was neither a republic nor a confederation, simply. It was a compound of two dissimilar concepts of political association—the republican principle tending toward consolidation or centralization, the federal principle tending toward dispersal or decentralization of government power. Was it theoretically possible, however, for the constitution of a nation to consist in two different principles of political association? Must it not become one thing or the other, according to the principles of political science, including the concept of sovereignty that formed the intellectual horizon of modern government and the law of nations?

The theory of sovereignty held that supremacy in political government was a unitary thing that could not be divided. It was axiomatic that one government could not exist within another government. Precisely such an institutional arrangement, however, was what the Constitution appeared to establish: a government of the whole Union possessing sovereign powers to be exercised for national purposes, and state governments exercising sovereign powers for local purposes.

In the practice of federal republican politics, a basic rule of constitutional fidelity emerged to guide political action. This was a rule of practical reason—the practical reason of the Constitution, we may call it—holding that neither the national government nor any of the state governments could reduce the other to itself or otherwise destroy it. This was an unwritten rule that depended for its efficacy on attachment, commitment, and aspiration to the republican principle of consent as the basis of American nationality.[9]

Prudence, wisdom, and practical reason were needed to meet the challenge of preserving the constitutional Union. In a dynamic, diverse, and increasingly pluralistic society, there was danger that, for partisan or ideological ends, politicians would promote either consolidation of power in the national government or decentralization of power in the states. Claiming fidelity to the Constitution, they would eliminate the ambiguity inherent in the principle of divided sovereignty on which the Constitution was established.

From the beginning of the government in 1789, controversy over the nature of the Union was grist for the mill of partisan politics. Indeed, the Constitution was ratified in a manner that gave rise to the inference that the Union was not necessarily intended to exist in perpetuity.[10] Legal interpretive ambiguity notwithstanding, the design of the Constitution was integrative, not disintegrative. The practical reason of the Constitution, in other words, made control of the national government the paramount goal in federal-system politics. Assertion of decentralization in the name of states' rights was a default strategy adopted by the electoral minority. States devised means of protesting measures that they believed consolidated power unconstitutionally in the national government. By the same token, the national government enforced laws against the acts of state officers and citizens believed to violate the Constitution to the point of being insurrectionary.

Both constitutional constructions—"state interposition" against alleged national usurpation of state powers, and "national interposition" against alleged state obstruction of national law—could be viewed as aimed at maintaining the Constitution and the Union. Depending on the specific means employed, however, the construction of the powers of the national and state governments involved in these actions could be perceived as an abuse of constitutional authority and as disunionist, if not revolutionary, in nature.

The nature of the Union as a federal republic based on the concept of divided sovereignty is clearer in retrospect than it was at the time.[11] From 1820 to 1860, the nature of the Union was eminently debatable. No clear, convincing, and unequivocal answer could be agreed upon as a matter of constitutional interpretation. Was this a salutary or a threatening circumstance? It was not undesirable insofar as the dialectic of constitutional debate, though superficially divisive, at a deeper level had the effect of binding opposing sides to each other through adherence to the Constitution. Continuing debate over the nature of the Union, tied to policy disagreement and occasionally punctuated by compromise in the spirit of mutual accommodation, could be accepted as the price of union. Whether or not a spirit of compromise could be sustained, however, depended on what the people and their political leaders on opposing sides of constitutional and policy debates were willing to agree to disagree about.

Controversy over the nature of the Union with respect to the federal principle mainly concerned the relative powers of the national and state governments. Controversy over the nature of the Union with respect to the republican principle concerned the compatibility of the institution of slavery with republican society. In the deepest sense, the slavery question posed a moral choice over the social organization of American nationality.[12] The Constitution recognized the existence of slavery in several states. Whether this fact meant that slavery was a national institution, permanently protected under the norms of republican government regardless of future social development in the country as a whole, was debatable. The political and moral obligation to form a more perfect union that was intrinsic to the establishment of the Constitution implicated this question from the outset. From 1820 to 1860, as social and cultural distinctions between the sections assumed more definite form, slavery became the central issue in American politics. Among the controversies it provoked, the one that lent itself most plausibly and rationally to political and constitutional debate was over the nature of the Union in both its federal and republican aspects.

Determination of new or revised constitutional meaning about the nature of the Union, it is clear in retrospect, was bound to occur because of the historical development of the country. Whatever form it might take, the substantive issues at stake were the relative powers of the state and national governments and the future of slavery in republican society. Professing fidelity to the Constitution, both North and South claimed to be the true bearer of American nationality. Appealing to founding principles, each side accused the other of revolutionary intent to subvert its social institutions.

The nature of the conflict was such that, in a peculiarly American way, the cause of constitutionalism invoked by the sectional rivals, and the nature of the Union itself, implicated the revolutionary principles on which the nation was founded.

It was axiomatic in American politics that the nation was founded on the natural rights of life, liberty, and the pursuit of happiness. By inference and express enumeration, the natural rights reasoning of the Declaration of Independence comprised the distinct yet related ideas of government by consent of the governed and the right to revolt against that government. In Lockean political theory, both ideas were intended to limit the exercise of powers entrusted to government by the people as constituent power. In traditional political thought, the right of revolution was a dangerous notion that presented itself as the lawless destruction of government authority, rather than its limitation. Properly understood in the terms of liberal political theory, however, the right of resistance and revolution was not a license willfully to place oneself outside or above the law. Grounded in reason and guided by prudence, it was the moral right to appeal to the first principles of justice and right under "the Laws of Nature and of Nature's God."

The most formidable challenge posed by the achievement of national independence was to prevent a tradition of revolutionary politics from developing in the United States. For the sake of the more perfect union established by the Constitution, it was necessary to institutionalize the right to overturn the government in peaceful forms, lest it become a wanton instrument of political rebellion. This object was secured through the design and establishment of constitutional means by which the people could alter or abolish an unjust and abusive government and institute a new government to secure their safety and happiness. In *The Federalist* no. 40, for example, James Madison justified the departure of the Federal Convention from strict adherence to the forms of the Articles of Confederation by citing the authority of the Declaration of Independence and the acts of "patriotic and respectable citizens" who wrote it.[13] From the framers' point of view, the Declaration not only justified revolution "with a theory of legitimate and rightful governance" but also provided "a statement of basic principles for the guidance of an established society."[14]

Nevertheless, given the contingency of political life, the relationship between revolution and constitution in liberal political thought was a source of tension and ambiguity in American politics from the outset. As noted, the division of sovereignty gave rise to reciprocal threats of "interposition" by the states and by the national government in situations where each accused the other of constitutional violation. This practice can be viewed as a constitutional construction aimed at transforming the right of revolution into nonviolent political practices. On the one hand, theories of state interpretation, nullification, and secession were advanced as constitutional strategies for defending the rights and liberties of states and their citizens against unjust and abusive consolidation of power in the national government. On the other hand, the theory of national supremacy held that the government of the United States, in relation to all objects in which it was competent under the supremacy clause of the Constitution, could "legitimately control all individuals or governments within the American territory."[15]

From the standpoint of traditional political theory, it was counterintuitive to suppose that political stability could be maintained by treating alleged constitutional violations as occasions for invoking the right of revolution. Such an approach appeared to be a vicious form of circular reasoning that made preservation of the Constitution depend on revolutionary rectification. Constitutionalism could in this way be conceived of as nothing other than successful revolution institutionalized.[16] Against this political fantasy, it was necessary to be mindful of the sober reality that exercise of the right of revolution was a risky undertaking. Situations might arise in which unorganized individuals in states, or the people of a state as an organized body claiming to exercise their sovereignty, might determine the necessity of defending their rights through force and violence. According to the Declaration of Independence, however, the right to revolt was to be exercised only with justification; it was not a right of rebellion to be exercised at will. Prudence was therefore required in appealing to the right of revolution to correct constitutional error, lest reformist action be mistaken for lawless rebellion.

Constitutional politics was the horizon in which the debate over the nature of the Union was conducted from 1820 to 1860. Territorial expansion was the occasion, and construction of the federal and republican principles in relation to slavery the substantive issues requiring resolution. The Louisiana Purchase, the admission of Missouri as a slave state, the annexation of Texas, the Mexican War leading to the acquisition of Utah and New Mexico territories, the organization of a state government in California and its admission to the Union in the Compromise of 1850—all brought into view specific value conflicts that divided an increasingly pluralistic society. Each political episode presented its own particular constitutional questions that, considered from legal and institutional perspectives, related mainly to the federal principle of union. Taken altogether, the constitutional issues implicated the moral, philosophical, and social meanings of the republican principle.

The tolerable degree of complementarity between federal and republican concerns that prevailed in the founding era eroded. Controversy emerged over whether the principle of divided government sovereignty on the one hand, or republican freedom on the other hand, was the central idea in American public sentiment. Proslavery and antislavery opinions lined up in opposition on this question, the former tending toward federalism, the latter toward republicanism as the ground of American nationality. Not everyone agreed, however, that it was necessary or wise in a pluralistic society to identify a central idea in public opinion. Considered from the perspective of ideologically neutral politicians, such as Democrat senator Stephen A. Douglas and Whig senator Henry Clay, a claim could be made that value pluralism itself was the central idea in American public life. The ambiguity of value pluralism was a virtue that complemented the pragmatic indeterminacy of divided sovereignty, affording maximum flexibility in negotiating the tortuous path of the nation's continental expansion. In this view, the moral consensus reflected in the compromises of the Constitution was sufficient to preserve the more perfect Union of the Founders.

In relative historical terms, Lincoln came late to the debate over the nature of the Union. The basic structure of the controversy in relation to the federal principle was defined in the debate over ratification of the Constitution, the Kentucky and Virginia Resolutions of 1798, the Hartford Convention in 1815, and the Nullification Crisis in 1832. In these disputations, the functional ambiguity of the principle of divided sovereignty enabled advocates of both state and national powers plausibly to claim the purpose of preserving the Union. It was uncertainty over the meaning of the republican principle, analytically distinguishable yet practically inseparable from the question of federalism, that threatened to divide the country when Lincoln, in the Peoria speech in October 1854, joined the debate over the nature of the Union by attacking the Kansas-Nebraska Act.

Lincoln's approach to politics was premised on a holistic view of the American people as a political society organized on the principle of a federal-republican union. In language suggestive of the concept of *subsidiarity*,[17] he asserted that the legitimate object of government was to do for "a community of people" what they needed to have done but could not do for themselves "in their separate and individual capacities." Included in this class were roads, bridges, and other internal improvements; common schools; care of the helpless and afflicted; and estates of the deceased. A second class of common objectives of government, springing "from the injustice of men," comprised military defense in time of war and protection against deprivation of life, liberty, and property by force, fraud, and noncompliance with contracts (*Collected Works*, 2:221–22).

Lincoln's constitutional outlook was that of an orthodox Whig politician whose understanding of the federal principle generally emphasized the role and authority of the national government. With respect to the republican principle, Lincoln accepted the Founders' view of the need for moderation in the practice of popular self-government. On this count, his construction of the nature of the Union led him to oppose various forms of popular sovereignty advanced by the Democratic Party from 1846 to 1860. During this period, Lincoln was chiefly concerned with the conflict between slavery and republican freedom, an issue that had implications for the national commitment to a more perfect union. The several strands of constitutional meaning involved in the debate over the nature of the Union were foreshadowed in Lincoln's Springfield Lyceum Address in 1838, titled "The Perpetuation of Our Political Institutions."

Lincoln indicated the main themes of constitutional construction that would define his achievement as a federal-republican statesman. He reflected on the duty to protect the safety and happiness of "the American people," under the government of a system of political institutions for liberty and equal rights, against the disintegrative and antirepublican consequences of democratic licentiousness. Mob rule pervaded the country, vitiating political authority and breaking down "the attachment of the People," the "strongest bulwark any Government and particularly of those constituted like ours." Believing the danger to the country lay in internal rather than external sources, he exclaimed, "As a nation of freemen, we must live through all time, or die by suicide." The specific danger was that the breakdown of law would provide opportunity for ambitious men, in their desire to gratify their ruling passion, to pull down the country's institutions, "whether at the expense of emancipating slaves, or enslaving free men." To preserve the nation, Lincoln urged, the people should be "united with each other" in "*reverence for the constitution and the laws.*" Let regard for the Constitution become "the *political religion* of the nation" (*Collected Works*, 1:108, 112–15).

The idea that fidelity to the Constitution was analogous to religious faith might be considered problematic in an expanding, pluralistic society, especially one in which the principle of divided government sovereignty created a disposition for value conflicts to assume a sectional form. Not only was moral controversy latent in the slavery question from the beginning of the

Union, but federal-system politics also encouraged distinctions between individuals, groups, localities, and sections of the country with respect to questions of justice and morality. In the formative period of Lincoln's political career, the matter of internal improvement policy posed this issue as a problem of constitutional interpretation.

In a speech on national internal improvement policy in the House of Representatives in 1848, Lincoln advanced the Whig argument for cooperative and integrative federalism between the states and the national government. He defined the federal principle, as a constitutional standard regulating the relative powers of the national and state governments, to be a rule of generality and locality.[18] Significantly, Lincoln approached the federal division of authority from a prudential and discretionary point of view, in contrast to Democratic opposition to national internal improvements based on doctrinaire, categorical thinking.

Lincoln contended that no object of government patronage was so exclusively general as not to be of some local advantage, and none so local as not to be of some general advantage. To illustrate, he pointed out that the object of the navy, namely, to be ready for war and to protect commerce on the high seas, was the same as that of a national system of internal improvements. "The driving a pirate from the track of commerce on the broad ocean, and the removing a snag from its more narrow path in the Mississippi river," he reasoned, "can not . . . be distinguished in principle. Each is done to save life and property, and for nothing else." Democrats objected to a national policy of internal improvements on the ground that while the burden of cost would be general, the benefit would be local and partial, "involving an obnoxious inequality." Lincoln argued, however, that "the converse is also true. Nothing is so *local* as not to be of some *general* benefit." The Illinois and Michigan canal, for example, lying entirely within the state of Illinois, was beneficial to people in Louisiana and New York (*Collected Works*, 1:483).

The mutual involvements intrinsic to federalism as a principle of union supplied a range of incentives. Lincoln said that a state, objecting to the inequality of local and partial benefits resulting from a national policy of improvements, might refuse to undertake local improvements lest they produce a degree of general benefit. "A state may well say to the nation 'If you will do nothing for me, I will do nothing for you.'" Thus if the argument of inequality was sufficient anywhere, Lincoln pointed out, "it is sufficient every where; and puts an end to improvements altogether." Properly understood, however, the rule of generality and locality was an incentive for a better, or more perfect, union. Lincoln believed that "if both the nation and the states would, in good faith, in their respective spheres, do what they could in the way of improvements, what of inequality might be produced in one place, might be compensated in another, and that the sum of the whole might not be very unequal" (*Collected Works*, 1:483–84).

If in federal-system politics the issue of unjust inequality was raised in the context of commercial interests, the question of slavery posed it in a far more threatening way. Referring to internal improvements, Lincoln reflected: "But suppose, after all, there should be some degree of inequality. Inequality is certainly never to be embraced for its own sake; but is every good thing to be discarded, which may be inseparably connected with some degree of it? If so, we must discard all government." Practical reason and sound judgment were required. Lincoln advised that in deciding whether to embrace or reject a thing, "the true rule" was not whether there was any evil in it, but whether it had more of evil than of good. He summarized: "There are few things *wholly* evil, or *wholly* good. Almost everything, especially of governmental policy, is an inseparable compound of the two; so that our best judgment of the preponderance between them is continuously demanded" (*Collected Works*, 1:484).

Slavery tested the rule of prudential judgment that, throughout his career, Lincoln regarded as the practical reason of the Constitution. From being a matter that Americans could agree to disagree about, slavery by the mid-nineteenth century was the kind of polarizing issue that excluded a rational middle ground in which the spirit of compromise might be invoked. The structure of divided sovereignty as a principle of union, at least in a theoretical sense, provided institutional opportunity, if not motive, for compromise. The disposition of the republican principle, however, in its insistence on natural rights of individual liberty and equality, was otherwise. In spirit and sensibility, the republican idea as a principle of association was holistic and integrative. As the sectional controversy over slavery grew more intense, the republican principle of union militated against the federal principle.

In the spirit of constitutional fidelity under the federal principle, Lincoln was prepared to recognize a sphere of state dominion over individual human liberty in relation to slavery in states where it existed. After the annexation of Texas in 1845, he wrote to an Illinois abolitionist: "I hold it to be a paramount duty of us in the free states, due to the Union of the states, and perhaps to liberty itself (paradox though it may seem) to let the slavery of the other states alone." It was equally clear, however, in Lincoln's view that "we should never knowingly lend ourselves directly or indirectly, to prevent that slavery from dying a natural death—to find new places for it to live in, when it can no longer exist in the old." Beyond the controversy that was shaping up over slavery in national territories, Lincoln pointed to a more deeply problematic issue in concluding: "Of course I am not now considering what would be our duty, in cases of insurrection among the slaves" (*Collected Works*, 1:347–48).

As opinion in free and slave states grew increasingly polarized over the place of slavery in republican society, each side sought control of national authority in order to establish its conception of moral and social order in the country as a whole. In this sense, nationalization of the slavery question strengthened the integrative and centralizing tendency that the republican principle encouraged in national politics. This political motive was not obvious, however, with respect to the establishment of slavery in territories outside state jurisdiction, where the authority of national, state, and prospective territorial governments was constitutionally unclear.

The issue of governmental legislative authority over slavery, congressional or otherwise, was a question to which the Constitution gave no express answer.[19] Determination of constitutional meaning on this issue depended on one's construction of the Constitution. Any such construction would, in turn, have a feedback effect on the larger controversy over the nature of the Union as a federal republic. Lincoln's opposition to the Kansas-Nebraska Act, expounded in the Peoria speech in October 1854, brought together these strands of disputed constitutional meaning. In a practical sense, the speech laid the premises for Lincoln's construction of the nature of the Union in the secession crisis.

Popular sovereignty formed the constitutional premise of the Kansas-Nebraska Act of 1854. Senator Douglas's conception of popular sovereignty differed from that of the Founders. In their view, the Constitution was based on the constituent power of the people of the United States, evident in direct popular election of the House of Representatives and ratification of the Constitution in popular state conventions. These institutional arrangements recognized the idea of popular sovereignty as a constitutive element of federal republican union.

Lincoln followed the Founders' thinking. He defined popular sovereignty in general as the sovereignty of the people of every nation and community to govern themselves. In a speech in 1858, he said popular sovereignty was an old idea that "was floating about the world" long before Douglas was born. Popular sovereignty, he asserted, first "took tangible form" in the words of the Declaration of Independence: "'We hold these truths to be self-evident: that all men are created equal; that they are endowed by their Creator with certain inalienable rights; that among these are life, liberty, and the pursuit of happiness; that to secure these rights, governments are instituted among men, *deriving their just powers from the consent of the governed.*'" In the Declaration lay "the origin of Popular Sovereignty as applied to the American people," Lincoln concluded. "If that is not Popular Sovereignty, then I have no conception of the meaning of words" (*Collected Works*, 3:94).

Three definitions of popular sovereignty were advanced in the dispute over territorial slavery and, by extension, in the debate over the federal and republican character of the Union. The first was Douglas's conception, according to which the people of a territory had authority to decide the slavery question for themselves. The second conception was proslavery popular sovereignty, reserving all questions concerning slavery exclusively to decision by the sovereign people of the slave states. Lincoln and the Republican Party adopted a third view of popular sovereignty, as embodied in the republican government provisions of the Constitution. Advocates of each version of popular sovereignty claimed for it constitutional sanction. What distinguished Lincoln's view was his outspoken conviction that popular sovereignty, expressing the idea of republican nationality, should be understood in the light of principles of reason and justice embodied in the Declaration of Independence.

The territorial slavery problem implicated the nature of the Union on both federal and republican coordinates of national identity. From the standpoint of federalism, the question concerned the locus of legislative power over or in national territory, with respect to the establishment of slavery. In Douglas's view, the power resided in the people of the territory as a delegation of authority from Congress. Although not constitutionally competent itself, Congress could nevertheless confer on territorial inhabitants the power to legislate on slavery. The proslavery interpretation of popular sovereignty held that the people of a territory could decide the slavery question, provided that property and liberty rights of citizens of the United States, in their dual capacity as state and national citizens, were recognized. In this way, the notion of popular sovereignty was brigaded with the principle of state sovereignty as a constitutional support for the defense of slavery.

In Lincoln's opinion, the constitutional division of sovereignty, expressed practically in the rule of generality and locality, applied within the United States. It did not apply, however, in territories acquired under the sovereign authority of the United States. In the Peoria speech, Lincoln recognized the constitutional rule, original to the creation of the Union, by which each state was authorized to regulate its domestic concerns in its own way. This rule admittedly had reference to slavery as an existing institution in several states. Lincoln argued it had no bearing, however, on "the carrying of slavery into NEW COUNTRIES," as the prohibition of slavery in the Northwest Ordinance of 1787 made clear (*Collected Works*, 2:267).

Under the federal principle of generality and locality, the government of the Union had authority over the question of slavery in Nebraska Territory. In Lincoln's view, Congress, representing the people of the whole country, had the power to make law in new communities on the public domain. "[I]s not Nebraska, while a territory, a part of us?" he asked. " Do we not own the country? And if we surrender the control of it, do we not surrender the right of self-government?" Nebraska Territory "is part of ourselves"—that is to say, the people of the United States—and hence was subject to the legislative authority of Congress. Lincoln considered the objection that the national government ought not to control the territory. "If you say we shall not control it because it is ONLY part, the same is true of every other part; and when all the parts are gone, what has become of the whole? What then is left of us? What use for the general government, when there is nothing left for it [to] govern?" (*Collected Works*, 2:267).

Lincoln saw in Douglas's doctrine of popular sovereignty a motive toward disintegration of the Union. Beyond its denial of national authority, popular sovereignty threatened to reduce policy making to the level of individual choice. Defenders of the Kansas-Nebraska Act argued that because the people of Nebraska had a particular interest in the question, "you must leave it to each individual to say for himself whether he will have slaves." By what standard, however, did the citizens of Nebraska Territory have a "better moral right" than the people of the thirty-one states to say whether slavery should go into the thirty-second state at all? Furthermore, if the people of Nebraska had a sacred right to take and hold slaves there, by the same logic, it was "equally their sacred right to buy them where they can buy them cheapest; and that undoubtedly will be on the coast of Africa." In Lincoln's view, this conception of popular sovereignty would lead to the repeal of the national prohibition of the slave trade as an unconstitutional restriction on the sacred right of self-government (*Collected Works*, 2:267–68).

In a political sense, popular sovereignty was intended as a compromise between Southern proslavery and Northern Democrat opinion. In a constitutional sense, it split the difference between national and state power by treating the controversy over slavery as a matter of choice for autonomous individuals in the territories. In the discourse of twenty-first-century rights jurisprudence, popular sovereignty functioned as a kind of "right of privacy" intended to immunize moral choice against intervention by outside authority with respect to the most public and politically controversial matters.[20]

The authority-dissolving logic of popular sovereignty threatened the integrating force of republican freedom as a principle of national union. Lincoln's apprehension of this threat is seen in his focus in the Peoria speech on the moral confusion introduced into republican society by the Kansas-Nebraska Act. By repealing the Missouri Compromise, Douglas's measure would give slavery a new lease on life. More important than the locus of constitutional power over slavery was the question that Lincoln now raised: whether the repeal, "with its avowed principle [of popular sovereignty], is intrinsically right" (*Collected Works*, 2:261).

It was past the time when aversion to moral reflection on slavery in national politics formed the better part of constitutional virtue. The South claimed, on the principle of equal justice, the right to take slave property into the territories as the equivalent of the North's taking its property. Lincoln said, "This is perfectly logical, if there is no difference between hogs and Negroes." Lincoln insisted there was a difference, and that Southerners themselves, in their customs, practices, and public acts, such as prohibition of the international slave trade, recognized "the humanity of the negro." Why, moreover, would some white owners of slaves, "at vast pecuniary sacrifices," "liberate them"? Lincoln attributed emancipation to a "sense of justice, and human sympathy, continually telling you, that the poor negro has some natural right to himself—that those who deny it, and make mere merchandize of him, deserve kickings, contempt and death" (*Collected Works*, 2:265).

Douglas's aggressive promotion of popular sovereignty in relation to the slavery question provided opportunity for Lincoln to clarify the issue of moral integrity in the nature of the Union as a republican community. Douglas claimed the moral high ground in the American political tradition by equating popular sovereignty with "the sacred right of self-government." Lincoln in the Peoria speech stipulated essential premises in the construction of a *more perfect union* that would overcome the heresy of Democratic popular sovereignty, not only in the form it took in the territorial slavery controversy, but also in the exercise of proslavery Southern state sovereignty in the secession crisis.

Lincoln affirmed the right of self-government as the theoretical basis of the nature of the Union. "My faith in the proposition that each man should do precisely as he pleases with all which is exclusively his own, lies at the foundation of the sense of justice there is in me. I extend the principles to communities of men, as well as to individuals." The "doctrine of self-government is right—absolutely and eternally right," Lincoln insisted, "but it has no just application, as here attempted." He added, "Or perhaps I should rather say that whether it has such just application depends upon whether a negro is *not* or *is* a man. If he is *not* a man, why in that case, he who *is* a man may, as a matter of self-government, do just as he pleases with him." If, however, he *is* a man, then it is "a total destruction of self-government, to say that he too shall not govern *himself*." Lincoln summarized: "If the negro is a *man*, why then my ancient faith teaches me that 'all men are created equal,' and that there can be no moral right in connection with one man's making a slave of another. . . . [N]o man is good enough to govern another man, *without that other's consent*. I say this is the leading principle—the sheet anchor of American republicanism" (*Collected Works*, 2:265–66).

Constitutional conviction in the cause of a more perfect union entailed rededication to the republican principle. In retrospect, it is obvious that the country's black inhabitants were the most obvious beneficiaries of perfected republican unionism. Republican aspiration and improvement also had significant implications for white Americans, however, not only in the material sense of free-soil territorial settlement but also in the moral sense of parity in constitutional relations between slave and free states.

In Lincoln's view, existing constitutional arrangements were "degrading" to the free states. First was the legal obligation free persons had toward slave owners "to catch and return their runaway slaves to them—a sort of dirty, disagreeable job," which the slaveholders were generally unwilling to perform for one another. Of more immediate practical significance was the three-fifths clause for the apportionment of representatives, giving the South a great advantage "in the control of the government—the management of the partnership affairs." Lincoln argued statistically that "each white man in South Carolina is more than double of any man in Maine." It was "an absolute truth, without an exception, that there is no voter in any slave State, but who has more legal power in the government, than any voter in any free State. There is no instance of exact equality." While manifestly unfair, this system of representation was in the Constitution and had to be accepted. "But when I am told that I must leave it altogether to OTHER PEOPLE to say whether new partners are to be bred up and brought into the firm, on the same degrading terms against me," Lincoln objected, "I insist, that whether I shall be a whole man, or only, the half of one, in comparison with others, is a question . . . which no other man can have a sacred right of deciding for me" (*Collected Works*, 2:268–69).

In the Peoria speech, Lincoln gave notice to proponents of popular sovereignty that in opening national territory to slavery they were igniting controversy on a long-accepted constitutional rule of representation that, in the view of a growing body of Northern opinion, had a corrupting effect on the nature of the Union as a republican political community. As in 1850, when debate over the admission of California as a free state provoked threats of Southern secession, speculation about disunion revived in the wake of the Kansas-Nebraska Act. Implied in Lincoln's animadversions against, and assessment of, the consequences of popular sovereignty for American society was the prospect of disunion.

"Let no one be deceived," he warned. "The spirit of seventy-six and the spirit of Nebraska, are utter antagonisms." There was danger that "in our greedy chase to make profit of the negro," the "white man's charter of freedom" would be cancelled and torn to pieces. Lincoln declaimed: "Our republican robe is soiled, and trailed in the dust. Let us repurify it. Let us turn and wash it white, in the spirit, if not the blood, of the Revolution." It was necessary "to turn slavery from its claims of 'moral right,' back upon its existing legal rights" and the argument of necessity. Lincoln proposed to "re-adopt the Declaration of Independence" for application in practices and policies supported by all Americans and by "lovers of liberty everywhere." A sense of aspiration in fulfillment of national purpose appeared in Lincoln's exhortation: "If we do this, we shall not only have saved the Union; but we shall have so saved it, as to make, and to keep it, forever worthy of the saving. We shall have so saved it, that the succeeding millions of free happy people, the world over, shall rise up, and call us blessed, to the latest generations" (*Collected Works*, 2:275–76).

———

There is in Lincoln's expression of unionist sentiment a note of contingency that is at odds with the mythic aura of perpetual national existence suffusing his reputation in American memory. The suggestion of conditionality in the Peoria speech reflects the instability of American politics in the mid-1850s, after the formation of the Republican Party. Each section professed loyalty to the Constitution and recriminated the other as disunionist in nature. Lincoln, although following rhetorical convention in describing federal-state relations in the language of *confederacy, confederation, compact, business partnership,* and *family,* assumed the ground of national sovereignty in defending the Republican Party against the charge of disunionism. In doing so, he clarified essential elements of constitutional orthodoxy concerning the nature of the Union that had been established in the historical practice of federal-system politics (*Collected Works*, 3:483, 495, 4:18, 275).

Although there was no express reference to it in the text of the Constitution, the perpetuity of the Union was implicitly assumed in the duty of constitutional maintenance and preservation. Nevertheless, as a practical matter and depending on circumstances, disunion in the form of constitutional failure or inadequacy was a contingency that might present itself. In the formation of the Republican Party as a sectional organization, Democrats and other observers perceived a threat to national unity.

In the mid-1850s, Lincoln dwelt at length on the charge of disunionism, deeming it "the most difficult objection we have to meet" (*Collected Works*, 2:350). In a speech at Galena, Illinois, in July 1856, he denied the Democratic argument that the Republican proposal to exclude slavery from national territories would cause the dissolution of the Union. To pass such legislation would require "a decided majority," Lincoln noted. "We, the majority, being able constitutionally to do all that we purpose, would have no desire to dissolve the Union." Even if the Supreme Court, as was rumored, should attempt to decide the question of territorial slavery, Lincoln said, Republicans would submit to the decision, whatever it might be. He challenged Democrats to do the same. If they would not, then "who are the disunionists, you or we?" Lincoln asked. "We, the majority, would not strive to dissolve the Union; and if any attempt is made it must be by you, who so loudly stigmatize us as disunionists" (*Collected Works*, 2:355).

Lincoln proceeded to explain the practical reason of the Constitution that defined the nature of the Union: "But the Union, in any event, won't be dissolved. We don't want to dissolve it, and if you attempt it, *we won't let you*. With the purse and the sword, the army and navy and treasury in our hands and at our command, you *couldn't do it*." A Republican administration would use constitutionally delegated powers to preserve the Union. "This Government would be very weak, indeed, if a majority, with a disciplined army and navy, and a well-filled treasury, could not preserve itself, when attacked by an unarmed, undisciplined, unorganized minority." Lincoln declared: "All this talk about the dissolution of the Union is humbug—nothing but folly. *We* WON'T dissolve the Union, and *you* SHAN'T" (*Collected Works*, 2:354–55). Lincoln's terse admonition underscored the nature of the Union as a sovereign political society competent to defend its existence against revolutionary subversion in whatever form it might present itself.

The character of disunionist action and the circumstances in which it actually occurred were significantly different from those contemplated by

Lincoln in 1856. The noninterventionist strategy of popular sovereignty had a debilitating effect on Northern Democrats, including President James Buchanan, who came increasingly under Southern influence. Lincoln's election in 1860 signified the failure of Southern efforts, in the *Dred Scott* case and the fight over the Lecompton constitution in Kansas, to secure national protection for slavery. Within days of the election, disunion began in earnest. Acting in the name of absolute state sovereignty and with the advice of United States senators, the secession movement assumed the posture of an organized, armed minority. By authority of popular conventions in seven slave states, secessionists organized the Confederate States of America, in the process violating national laws and seizing federal property in acts of lawless rebellion.

The secession movement forced the country to consider questions of constitutional construction analogous to those arising in the formation of the Union. Preeminent and fundamental was the nature of the Union. To meet the crisis, Lincoln drew upon the deposit of authority grounded in the conduct of federal-system politics from the beginning of the government. Theoretical debate and partisan conflict validated certain basic propositions. Far from the indeterminate, voluntary compact of state-nations posited in secessionist theory, the Union was a national polity constituted on the principles of republican consent and divided government sovereignty. No political party regarded the Union, in relation to either individual citizens or states, as a political association that depended on a self-legislated, subjective standard of law enforcement. Although political minorities occasionally threatened disunion to secure their ends, such threats were not proof of the existence of a constitutional right of secession.

It is well known that Lincoln paid closest attention to the Nullification Crisis, marking the outer limit of previous state protests against national law. In his proclamation to the people of South Carolina in 1832, President Andrew Jackson treated the claim of a right of secession from the Union— the logical extension of the claimed right to nullify laws of the Union—as a constitutional absurdity. Much as theorists of state sovereignty might speculate otherwise, practical experience established the proposition that secession, if actually undertaken, would require violation of national law and present itself as rebellion. It was on this basis that Lincoln, in December 1860, reassured political associates that "the right of a state to secede is not an open or debatable question. It was fully discussed in Jackson's time, and denied not only by him but also by a vote of . . . Congress."[21]

The passions and interests aroused in the slavery controversy provoked Southern leaders to claim constitutional immunity in the exercise of the right of secession.[22] Facing an existential challenge to national authority, Lincoln, through his speeches and actions in the secession crisis, showed Southern disunion to be lawless and unjustified rebellion. To destroy the common good of the Union for the sake of protecting slavery was constitutional heresy and moral dereliction. Lincoln was convinced it must be resisted to preserve and advance the cause of a more perfect union.

Secession forced Lincoln to discuss the constitutional nature of the Union in concrete and specific terms. In a speech in Indianapolis, February 11, 1861, en route to his inauguration, Lincoln for the first time since the election spoke directly to the constitutional issues in dispute. Venturing into the legal and semantic thicket surrounding the question of states' rights, he inquired into the meaning of *coercion* and *invasion* of states.

The South insisted that the federal government had no authority to compel states to remain in the Union. Lincoln asked: "What, then, is coercion? What is invasion?" He conceded that marching a federal army into South Carolina without the consent of her people would be invasion and coercion, if the people did not give their consent and were forced to submit. It would not be coercion, however, for the federal government to hold or retake forts belonging to it, or to enforce the laws of the United States for the collection of duties on foreign imports. If professed "lovers of the Union" would resist such measures as invasion and coercion, then the means of preserving the Union, "in their own estimation, is of a very thin and airy character." Lincoln said that, in the view of those who would regard enforcement of national law as coercion, the nature of the Union, considered as a family relation, was "not like a regular marriage at all, but only as a sort of free-love arrangement—to be maintained on what the sect calls passionate attraction" (*Collected Works*, 4:195).

Lincoln's biting and irreverent analysis of states' rights continued in a more sober tone. Referring to a long-standing Democratic rhetorical trope, he inquired, "What is the particular sacredness of a State?" It was not the power and authority of a state as recognized in the Constitution, which "all of us agree to" and "abide by." Rather, it was the assumption "that a State can carry with it out of the Union that which it holds in sacredness by virtue of its connection with the Union." The "sacredness" of states' rights referred to "that assumed right of a State, as a primary principle, that the Constitution should rule all that is less than itself, and ruin all that is bigger than itself." So to conceive the nature of the Union was absurd. If a state and a county were equal in extent of territory and population, Lincoln reasoned, "wherein is that State any better than the county? Can a change of name change the right? By what principle of original right is it that one-fiftieth or one-ninetieth of a great nation, by calling themselves a State, have the right to break up and ruin that nation as a matter of original principle . . . to play tyrant over all its own citizens, and deny the authority of everything greater than itself?" (*Collected Works*, 4:195–96).

Lincoln's analogy of a state to a county, defining a state as "a certain district of country with inhabitants," scandalized advocates of states' rights.[23] That the federal-state relationship should be considered in this light reflected the extent to which secession drove the debate over the nature of the Union to the level of fundamental principles. In fact, Lincoln's analogy recalled the thinking of national-minded delegates at the Federal Convention of 1787 who, in contrast to those who regarded the states "as so many political societies," viewed them "as districts of people composing one political Society."[24] The question of the nature of the Union, involving propositions that under normal political circumstances were not viewed as mutually exclusive, and which already in 1787 were perceived as arguments in a "controversy [that] must be endless," now presented itself as requiring conclusive resolution in the most practical sense.[25]

In the secession crisis, Lincoln clarified and confirmed the nature of the Union as a federal republican government, founded on the constituent sovereignty of the people of the United States. His determination of constitutional meaning established that the federal government was competent to defend the existence of the nation. Lincoln's construction confirmed the traditional nationalist understanding of the federal principle in circumstances that threatened its extinction by the forces of state sovereignty.

The teleology of the Constitution—that is to say, its intentionality and purposes according to the design of its Founders—was paramount. The leading object of the Constitution was to strengthen the ties between the states to promote the unity of the country as a whole. To achieve this end did not mean eliminating differences of opinion on politics and policy between the people of the United States and their representatives in the government of the Union. Forming a more perfect Union meant fulfilling the reason for its existence, making it the better and more fully realized federal republic that the American people intended it to be. The principles of American nationality possessed objective, rational, and substantive meaning. They were not mere symbolic forms to be given whatever subjective content might emanate from an appeal to the passions and interests of popular sovereignty. The application of moral and political principles in specific situations was of course controversial, all the more so in the democratizing, pluralistic society of nineteenth-century

America. As Lincoln understood, however, such disagreement did not mean that no right judgment could be made concerning the moral significance and political status of slavery in the American republic.

Not without reason is Lincoln's defense of the nation in the First Inaugural Address identified in public memory with a conviction of the historical inevitability of perpetual union. In a more historically realistic and empirical sense, however, his achievement is intelligible as a construction of the Constitution based on the doctrine of national majority-rule orthodoxy. With prudential wisdom and moral integrity, Lincoln in the First Inaugural justified national majority-rule orthodoxy as a matter of constitutional practical reason. His exercise of federal republican authority in the secession crisis moved the country decisively toward a resolution of the debate over the nature of the Union.

Lincoln's task in the First Inaugural was to explain why secession was wrong and preservation of national union right. Recurrence to history, political science, and jurisprudence, while relevant, was not in itself sufficient. It was necessary to establish, as a matter of fundamental political law, the reason and justice of federal republican union as the theoretical and practical alternative to anarchical minority rule.

Lincoln declared: "I hold, that in the contemplation of universal law, and the Constitution, the Union of these States is perpetual." The permanence of the Union as a national government was necessarily implied in the course of its historical development, which Lincoln summarized in briefest outline. The colonies' resistance to British rule marked the origin of the Union. It was "matured and continued" in the Declaration of Independence, and its perpetuity pledged by the states in the Articles of Confederation. The main object of the Constitution "was *'to form a more perfect union.'*" Abstractly considered, perfecting the Union meant fulfilling the ends of republican liberty, equality, and consent for which the nation was founded. In the immediate circumstances, the obligation to form a more perfect Union required the determination that "destruction of the Union, by one, or by a part only, of the States," was not "lawfully possible." The nature of the Union was such, Lincoln said, "that no State, upon its own mere motion, can lawfully get out of the Union." State ordinances of secession were therefore legally void, and acts of violence in states against the authority of the United States, if undertaken, would be judged insurrectionary or revolutionary, according to circumstances (*Collected Works*, 4:264–65).

Lincoln's position was not simply that sound political science did not authorize willful and arbitrary disintegration of government, and that the obligation to obey law in a political community cannot coexist with a right to disobey that same law. The fundamental premise of Lincoln's policy was that the practical reason of republican government precluded recognition of secession as a right of the minority.

With statesmanlike forbearance and intellectual precision, Lincoln reflected on the nature of constitutional politics in the federal Union. No organic law, he observed, could be framed "with a provision specifically applicable to every question which may occur in practical administration." Questions had arisen concerning the return of fugitive slaves and the prohibition of slavery in the territories for which the Constitution provided no clear answer. In deciding them, the country necessarily divided into majority and minority factions. As a practical matter, "If the minority will not acquiesce, the majority must, or the government must cease. There is no other alternative; for continuing the government is acquiescence on one side or the other." Decision by the majority was recognized in principle and in practice as constitutionally legitimate in republican America. Lincoln summarized the principle of republican constitutionalism: "Plainly, the central idea of secession, is the essence of anarchy. A majority held in restraint by constitutional checks and limitations, and always changing easily, with deliberate changes of popular opinions and sentiments, is the only true sovereign of a free people." In political life, the rule of unanimity was impossible, and the rule of a minority "as a permanent arrangement . . . wholly inadmissible. . . . Whoever rejects [the majority principle], does, of necessity, fly to anarchy or to despotism" (*Collected Works*, 4:268).

The First Inaugural defined the constitutional nature of the Union as a national republic organized on the principles of federal government and republican freedom. As chief executive, Lincoln established this construction in his management of the Fort Sumter crisis, his response to armed secession, and his conduct of the Civil War. Justification of the federal republican nature of the Union required demonstration that secession, far from a rightful claim, was yet another attempt—if the most dangerous and violent—to institute minority rule based on the pretension to absolute state sovereignty. In actuality, it was unjustified rebellion against orthodox national majority-rule federal republican constitutionalism.

———

Lincoln demonstrated the practice of constitutional politics for the sake of a more perfect union. An institutional articulation of federalism and republicanism as interrelated principles of association, the Union in its historical development from colonial origins had an inbuilt intentionality of purpose and end. The basic principles and values of the whole and the parts were the same. Application of the principles, in the form of specific policy measures and institutional practices, was subject to variation and difference of opinion reflecting pluralistic tendencies in republican society. The federal principle, operationalized in the rule of generality and locality, recognized the element of distinction and variety in American life that was expressed in the emergence of sectional character and identity.

North and South were similar in many basic respects and different in one critical respect. As Lincoln observed in the First Inaugural, "One section of our country believes slavery is *right*, and ought to be extended, while the other believes it is *wrong* and not to be extended. This is the only substantial dispute" (*Collected Works*, 4:268–69). The controversy Lincoln noted could to some extent be accommodated under the federal rule of generality and locality. Slavery was a domestic, municipal institution and, as such, subject to exclusive state regulation. At the same time, from the beginning of the government there was a sense in which slavery was, or had the potential to become, a national issue. When in due course potentiality became actuality, it was the vulnerability of slavery to moral criticism from the standpoint of republican freedom that proved decisive.

In the late antebellum period, the South defended slavery as a "positive good," rather than as the necessary evil it was previously considered to be. This change in rhetorical strategy was in part a response to growing Northern opinion that slavery had a corrupting effect on republican government and a demoralizing influence on free society. Recovery of moral virtue and integrity in republican government was the Republican Party's reason for being and for its opposition to the spread of slavery. The party's victory in the election of 1860 gave rise to the expectation of constitutional reform and policy change concerning slavery to the end of making a more perfect union.

Although defense of national authority was paramount, in the First Inaugural Lincoln was mindful of the requirements of the republican principle in the preservation of the Union. For example, in discussing legislation to reassure the South of Republican willingness to enforce the fugitive slave clause of the Constitution, Lincoln recommended measures to protect the civil rights of blacks. In any law on this subject, he advised, "ought not all the safeguards of liberty known in civilized and humane jurisprudence to be introduced, so that a free man be not, in any case, surrendered as a slave?" He further suggested that provision be made "by law for the enforcement of that clause in the Constitution which guararranties [*sic*] that 'The citizens of each State shall be entitled to all previleges [*sic*] and immunities of citizens in the several States'" (*Collected Works*, 4:264). Lincoln's appeal to the privileges and immunities clause directly challenged Chief Justice Taney's opinion in the *Dred Scott* case defining the constitutional status of "the negro race as a separate class of persons" who were "not regarded as a portion of the people or citizens of the Government then formed."[26]

In the deepest sense, Americans went to war in 1861 to resolve constitutional controversy over the nature of the Union and the moral and legal status of slavery in republican society. What was dimly apparent in earlier sectional disputes now became forebodingly clear. Black Americans' citizenship and civil rights were implicated in the meaning of republican self-government and intrinsically related to the nature of the Union and the identity of the people of the United States. Reluctantly and inexorably, these several issues, theoretically distinct yet practically inseparable, were contested in the form of federal republican politics under the doctrine of national majority-rule orthodoxy.

From his turning-point experience in 1854, Lincoln grasped the gravity and depth of the crisis of national integrity signified by the slavery controversy. His executive management of the secession crisis, at once prudent and audacious, honored and upheld the Founders' intent to create a permanent national union of authority and obligation. The situation recalled Lincoln's warning in the Springfield Lyceum Address that the danger to American institutions was internal, that "As a nation of freemen, we must live through all time, or die by suicide." Secession, later aptly described by Republican Reconstruction planners as "state suicide," was destruction from within. Had the South held its fire at Fort Sumter, there is no telling what would have happened. When the secessionists decided to resolve the debate over the nature of the Union by armed force, however, Lincoln was prepared for the coming of war.

Treating secession as unjustified rebellion, Lincoln began the process of "reinaugurating" the authority of the Union on a more truly republican basis.[27] His action took the form of the Proclamation Calling Militia and Convening Congress, April 15, 1861, in which he provided a concise statement of the constitutional nature and purpose of the war. Under the Militia Act of 1795, Lincoln called 75,000 state militia, including militia from Southern states, into national service in order to execute the laws of the United States in seven seceded states, against combinations too powerful to be suppressed by the ordinary course of judicial proceedings or by the powers vested in the marshals by the law. Lincoln commanded persons composing the unlawful combinations to disperse and retire peaceably within twenty days. In support of the measure and as a statement of justification, he declared: "I appeal to all loyal citizens to favor, facilitate and aid this effort to maintain the honor, the integrity, and the existence of our National Union, and the perpetuity of popular government; and to redress wrongs already long enough endured" (*Collected Works*, 4:331–32).

The proclamation exceeded the formal requirements of enforcement of existing national law. Pointing to substantive matters of political and constitutional reform, Lincoln identified the integrity and perpetuity of national union and republican government as the ends for which military power was to be exercised. The proclamation presented the essence of Lincoln's construction of the nature of the Union. National union under the federal principle and popular government under the republican principle were theoretically and practically related. What threatened the existence of the Union had a subversive effect on the character of republican freedom. The integrity of the Union could not be reduced to the exercise of sovereign authority over national territory; it was intrinsically related to the moral excellence of republican government and society.

Lincoln's principal aim throughout the antebellum period was to heighten public awareness of the injustice and corruption of republican freedom caused by the existence, and the constitutional recognition, of slavery. The moral wrong lay not simply in slavery's denial of the natural right of human liberty to black persons. Equally consequential was the vitiation of republican equality and consent required in the three-fifths clause of the Constitution, conferring a privileged position in the operation of the federal government on owners of slave property and citizens in the slave states.

Lincoln was never reluctant to attack the aristocratic privilege constitutionally extended to the slave power. When the South decided on armed rebellion to secure what it had loudly declared to be the right of "peaceable secession," he accepted the opportunity presented to reconstruct the Union on a more fully realized republican basis. Reversing the course of national disintegration resulting from popular sovereignty, both in its Northern Democrat and Southern secessionist forms, Lincoln exercised the war power of the government to fulfill the constitutional obligation to form a more perfect Union.

Notes

1. See John Murrin, "A Roof without Walls: The Dilemma of American National Identity," in Richard Beeman et al., eds., *Beyond Confederation: Origins*

of the *Constitution and American National Identity* (Chapel Hill: University of North Carolina Press, 1987), 333–48.

2. See Jeffrey Rogers Hummel, *Emancipating Slaves, Enslaving Free Men: A History of the American Civil War* (Chicago: Open Court, 1996); and Lerone Bennett Jr., *Forced into Glory: Abraham Lincoln's White Dream* (Chicago: Johnson, 2000).

3. Ralph Lerner, *The Thinking Revolutionary: Principle and Practice in the New Republic* (Ithaca: Cornell University Press, 1987); *The Federalist Papers*, No. 9, ed. Clinton Rossiter (New York: New American Library, 1961), 73–74.

4. *The Federalist Papers*, no. 14, 104–5.

5. *The Collected Works of Abraham Lincoln*, ed. Roy P. Basler et al., 9 vols., hereafter cited in text and notes as *Collected Works* (New Brunswick, N.J.: Rutgers University Press, 1953–55), 4:265.

6. Proclamation Calling Militia and Convening Congress, April 15, 1861, ibid., 4:332.

7. Rogan Kersh, *Dreams of a More Perfect Union* (Ithaca: Cornell University Press, 2001), 59.

8. George Anastaplo, *The Constitution of 1787: A Commentary* (Baltimore: Johns Hopkins University Press, 1989), 14.

9. From 1820 to 1850, the rule assumed the constitutional form of the practice of admitting slave and free states in pairs, in effect giving each section veto power in the Senate to limit the exercise of national power. Barry R. Weingast, "Political Stability and Civil War: Institutions, Commitment, and American Democracy," in Robert H. Bates et al., *Analytic Narratives* (Princeton: Princeton University Press, 1998), 148–90.

10. The key fact was ratification by the people of the United States, assembled in state conventions. In *McCulloch v. Maryland* (1819), Chief Justice John Marshall said the people acted thus because it was "the only manner in which they can act safely and effectively, and wisely," on the matter at issue. "No political dreamer was ever wild enough," Marshall observed, "to think of breaking down the lines which separate the States, and of compounding the American people into one common mass. Of consequence, when they act, they act in their States. But the measures they adopt do not, on that account cease to be the measures of the people themselves, or become the measures of the state governments." The opposite opinion about the nature of the Union, however, could be drawn from the ratification process. As Marshall noted, the state of Maryland viewed the Constitution "not as emanating from the people, but as the act of sovereign and independent States." In this view, the powers of the national government "are delegated by the States, who alone are truly sovereign . . . and possess supreme dominion." Henry Steele Commager, ed., *Documents of American History*, 7th ed., vol. 1 (New York: Appleton-Century-Crofts, 1963), 214.

11. Lack of clarity in the concept of *union* is reflected in the variety of rhetorical formulations employed to characterize the nature of the Union, including "partly federal, partly national," "compound republic," "extended republic,"

"federal republic," "confederate republic," "confederacy," "nation of states," and "states-union."

12. Daniel J. Elazar states that the conditions of moral choice in social organization involve the determination of transcendent political principles that are reflected in central political institutions and decisions. "Whether they knew it or not, Americans in the middle of the nineteenth century were face-to-face with the fundamental questions that make civil societies of all but the most primitive political communities." *Building toward Civil War: Generational Rhythms in American Politics* (Lanham, Md.: Madison Books, 1992), 14.

13. *The Federalist*, no. 40, 252–53.

14. Michael Zuckert, Review of *American Scripture: Making the Declaration of Independence*, by Pauline Maier, *Review of Politics* 60 (Spring 1998): 357, 359.

15. Chief Justice John Marshall, opinion of the Supreme Court in *Cohens v. Virginia* (1821), quoted in Commager, *Documents of American History*, 231.

16. See Harvey Wheeler, "Constitutionalism," in Fred I. Greenstein and Nelson W. Polsby, eds., *Handbook of Political Science*, vol. 5, *Governmental Institutions and Processes* (Reading, Mass.: Addison-Wesley, 1975).

17. *Subsidiarity* refers to the mode of compound political association, based on consensual relationships, that extends from smaller, particular forms of community self-government to larger, more general forms of self-government. Daniel J. Elazar, "Althusius' Grand Design for a Federal Commonwealth," in Johannes Althusius, *Politica* (abridged translation of *Politics Methodically Set Forth and Illustrated with Sacred and Profane Examples*), ed., trans., and introd. Frederick S. Carney (Indianapolis: Liberty Fund, 1995), xxxv–xlii.

18. In the July 4, 1861, special message to Congress, Lincoln would define the federal principle in the same way: "This relative matter of National power, and State rights, as a principle, is no other than the principle of *generality*, and *locality*. Whatever concerns the whole, should be confided to the whole—to the general government; while, whatever concerns *only* the State, should be left exclusively to the State. This is all there is of original principle about it." Application of the principle was a related practical matter of defining the boundaries between the national and state governments. This the Constitution did. Lincoln observed: "Whether the National Constitution . . . has applied the principle with exact accuracy, is not to be questioned. We are all bound by that defining, without question." Ibid., 4:435.

19. In the First Inaugural Address, explaining the origin of the crisis of the Union, Lincoln said: "*May* Congress prohibit slavery in the territories? The Constitution does not expressly say. *Must* Congress protect slavery in the territories? The Constitution does not expressly say" (4:267).

20. David F. Ericson, *The Shaping of American Liberalism: The Debates over Ratification, Nullification, and Slavery* (Chicago: University of Chicago Press, 1993), 125–26. "Douglas's injunction against states interfering with each others' institutions is derived from a much broader intuition which understands the principle of noninterference quite literally and which, therefore, enjoins citizens

from interfering with each others' affairs independent of state boundaries." Ericson notes Lincoln's agreement with the constitutional principle that prohibits states from overt interference against the institutions of other states. He observes: "Douglas, however, understands the principle of noninterference in a much more radical sense so that it means the citizens of one state can barely discuss the institutions of other states. Lincoln naturally resists this extension of the principle."

21. December 13, 1860, memo of John G. Nicolay, quoted in Michael Burlingame, "'I Will Suffer Death before I Will Consent to Any Concession or Compromise': President-elect in Springfield, 1860–61" (Unpublished manuscript, 2004), 1–2.

22. Exemplary of Southern theory was the speech of Jefferson Davis in the U.S. Senate, January 10, 1861, justifying peaceable secession in the nature of a right of revolution that imposed on others a duty of noninterference. Davis said:

> Men speak of revolution; and when they say revolution, they mean blood. Our Fathers meant nothing of the sort. When they spoke of revolution, they spoke of an inalienable right. . . . [T]hey did not mean that they were to sustain that by brute force. They meant that it was a right; and force could only be invoked when that right was wrongfully denied. . . . Are we, in this age of civilization and progress, when political philosophy has advanced to the point which seemed to render it possible that the millennium should now be seen by prophetic eyes; are we now to roll back the whole current of human thought, and again return to the mere brute force which prevails between beasts of prey, as the only method of settling questions between men?

Quoted in Jon L. Wakelyn, ed., *Southern Pamphlets on Secession: November 1860–April 1861* (Chapel Hill: University of North Carolina Press, 1996), 129.

23. Albert Taylor Bledsoe, *Is Davis a Traitor; or, Was Secession a Constitutional Right Previous to the War of 1861?* (1865; reprinted, Richmond, Va.: Hermitage, 1907), 104–6.

24. Remarks of Samuel Johnson, in *Notes of Debates in the Federal Convention of 1787 Reported by James Madison*, introd. Adrienne Koch (New York: Norton, 1965), 211.

25. Ibid.

26. Referring to the privileges and immunities clause, Taney said that if a black person were recognized as a state citizen within the meaning of the Constitution, then "whenever he goes into another State, the Constitution clothes him, as to the rights of person, with all the privileges and immunities which belong to citizens of the State. And if persons of the African race are citizens of a State, and of the United States, they would be entitled to all of these privileges and immunities in every State, and the State could not restrict them; for they would hold these privileges and immunities, under the paramount authority of

the Federal Government, and its courts would be bound to maintain and enforce them, the Constitution and laws of the State to the contrary notwithstanding." Quoted in Commager, *Documents of American History*, 1:342–43.

27. In his last public address, April 11, 1865, Lincoln referred to Reconstruction as "the re-inauguration of the national authority." *Collected Works*, 8:400.

Appendix: Chronology of Lincoln's America

Note: Boldface type indicates events directly related to Lincoln's life.

1809

- **February 12: Abraham Lincoln is born in Hardin County, Kentucky.**
- March 4: James Madison is inaugurated the fourth U.S. president.
- Washington Irving, under a pseudonym, publishes *A History of New York*.
- Thomas Paine dies.

1816

- **Lincoln family moves to Indiana.**
- Indiana is admitted to the Union as the nineteenth state.
- James Monroe is elected the fifth president.
- The American Colonization Society is founded.

1818

- **October 5: Abraham's mother, Nancy Hanks Lincoln, dies.**
- Illinois is admitted to the Union as the twenty-first state.
- Abigail Adams and George Rogers Clark die.

1819

- **December 2: Abraham's father, Thomas Lincoln, marries Sarah Johnston.**
- The U.S. Supreme Court renders its decision in *McCulloch v. Maryland*.

1831

- **March: Abraham Lincoln builds a flatboat and rides it down the Mississippi to New Orleans.**
- **April: He makes a second flatboat trip to New Orleans.**
- **July: He arrives in New Salem, Illinois.**
- January 1: William Lloyd Garrison publishes the first issue of the *Liberator*.
- November 11: Nat Turner leads a slave revolt.
- December 5: John Quincy Adams, a future leader of the antislavery movement, takes his seat in Congress.
- Edgar Allan Poe publishes *Poems*.
- John Greenleaf Whittier publishes *Legends of New England*.

1832

- Lincoln is defeated as candidate for the Illinois state legislature.
- April–July: He serves in the Black Hawk War.
- Chief Black Hawk is defeated.
- Andrew Jackson, the seventh president, is reelected, with Martin Van Buren as vice president.

1833

- May 7: Lincoln is appointed postmaster at New Salem.

1834

- January: Lincoln begins work as a surveyor.
- August: He is elected to the Illinois state legislature.
- He begins to study law.
- Cyrus McCormick patents a grain reaper.

1835

- August 25: Lincoln's close friend Ann Rutledge dies.
- December 12: He introduces a debtor relief bill in the state legislature.
- Part 1 of Alexis de Tocqueville's *Democracy in America* is published.

1836

- Lincoln is reelected to the Illinois state legislature.
- He is licensed to practice law.
- The Alamo falls.
- The first McGuffey Reader is published.
- Ralph Waldo Emerson publishes *Nature*.
- Roger B. Taney is named chief justice of the U.S. Supreme Court.

1837

- April 15: Lincoln moves to Springfield, Illinois.
- He becomes the law partner of John T. Stuart.
- March 4: Martin Van Buren is inaugurated the eighth president.
- Nathaniel Hawthorne publishes *Twice Told Tales*.
- Procter & Gamble and Tiffany & Company are founded.

1838

- January 27: Lincoln addresses the Young Men's Lyceum in Springfield.
- He is reelected to the Illinois state legislature.

- Frederick Douglass escapes from slavery.
- James Fenimore Cooper publishes *The American Democrat*.

1840

- **Lincoln is reelected to the Illinois state legislature.**
- William Henry Harrison ("Tippecanoe and Tyler Too") is elected the ninth president.
- *Two Years before the Mast* (Richard Henry Dana), *The Pathfinder* (Cooper), and *The Village Blacksmith* (Henry Wadsworth Longfellow) are published.
- Part 2 of Tocqueville's *Democracy in America* is published.

1842

- **November 4: Lincoln marries Mary Todd.**
- Phineas T. Barnum takes over the American Museum in New York City.

1844

- **Lincoln forms a law partnership with William Herndon.**
- **He campaigns as elector for Henry Clay.**
- Stephen Collins Foster publishes first song, "Open Thy Lattice, Love."
- May 24: Samuel F. B. Morse transmits first telegraph message between cities: "What hath God wrought."
- Poe publishes *The Purloined Letter.*
- Charles Goodyear receives a patent for vulcanizing rubber.
- James K. Polk is elected the eleventh president.
- Mathew Brady opens a photography studio in New York City.

1846

- **Lincoln is elected to Congress.**
- Elias Howe patents a sewing machine.
- Daniel Emmett writes "Blue Tail Fly."
- Herman Melville, Whittier, Poe, Hawthorne, and Cooper publish new works.
- The Smithsonian Institution is founded.

1849

- **Lincoln tries (unsuccessfully) to introduce a bill abolishing slavery in the District of Columbia.**
- **He secures a patent, becoming the first (and only) person elected president to hold a patent.**
- Gold is discovered in California.

- Henry David Thoreau is jailed for refusing to pay a poll tax.
- Francis Parkman, Whittier, Thoreau, and Longfellow publish new works.

1852

- **July 6: Lincoln delivers the eulogy for Henry Clay.**
- Harriet Beecher Stowe publishes *Uncle Tom's Cabin.*

1854

- **October 16: Lincoln gives a speech in Peoria, Illinois, responding to one given earlier by Stephen A. Douglas.**
- The Kansas-Nebraska Act is passed.
- Thoreau publishes *Walden.*
- Foster writes "Jeanie with the Light Brown Hair."

1855

- **Lincoln wins lawsuit for the Illinois Central Railroad.**
- **He begins work on the McCormick reaper case.**
- Walt Whitman publishes the first edition of *Leaves of Grass.*

1857

- **June 26: Lincoln speaks in Springfield and criticizes Taney and *Dred Scott* decision.**

1858

- **June 16: Lincoln gives his "House divided against itself" speech in Springfield.**
- **He holds seven debates with Stephen A. Douglas but fails to win his seat in U.S. Senate.**
- The Mason jar is patented.
- Longfellow publishes *The Courtship of Miles Standish.*
- The Ladies Christian Association (later to become the YWCA) is founded.

1859

- **Lincoln appears before the Illinois Supreme Court in six suits concerning the Illinois Central Railroad.**
- **March 26: He writes to William A. Ross regarding publication of his 1858 debates with Douglas.**
- April 16: Alexis de Tocqueville dies.

1860

- **February 27: Lincoln gives a speech at Cooper Union in New York City.**

- **May 9: He is nominated for president by the Republican National Convention in Chicago.**
- **November 6: He is elected president.**
- James Whistler finishes painting *Blue Wave.*
- Longfellow writes "Paul Revere's Ride."
- The U.S. population reaches 31 million.
- December 20: South Carolina secedes from the Union.

1861

- **February 11: Lincoln leaves Springfield for Washington, D.C.**
- **March 4: He is inaugurated the sixteenth president of the United States.**
- **April 15: He calls for 75,000 volunteers to respond to the Confederates' bombardment and capture of Fort Sumter.**
- The Civil War begins..
- Dorothea Dix is named Superintendent of Nurses.
- Yale awards the first Ph.D. degree in the United States.

1862

- **July 2: Lincoln signs the Morrill Land Grant College Act.**
- **In early September, he writes "Meditation on the Divine Will."**
- **September 22: He issues the preliminary Emancipation Proclamation.**
- Julia Ward Howe writes "Battle Hymn of the Republic."
- Henry David Thoreau dies.

1863

- **January 1: Lincoln signs the Emancipation Proclamation.**
- **October 3: He proclaims the last Thursday in November a Day of Thanksgiving.**
- **November 19: He dedicates the battlefield at Gettysburg, Pennsylvania.**
- John D. Rockefeller establishes a petroleum refinery in Ohio.
- Edward Everett Hale publishes *Man without a Country.*
- Clement C. Moore, author of *A Visit from St. Nicholas*, dies.

1864

- **Lincoln wins reelection.**
- **He vetoes the Wade-Davis bill, which called for radical reconstruction of the South.**
- April 8: The Senate approves the Thirteenth Amendment.

- Nathaniel Hawthorne and Stephen Collins Foster die.
- "In God We Trust" appears on U.S. coins for the first time.
- J. P. Morgan & Company is founded.

1865

- **March 4: Lincoln delivers his Second Inaugural Address.**
- **April 14: He is mortally wounded by John Wilkes Booth.**
- **April 15: He is declared dead at 7:22 A.M.**
- **May 4: He is buried in Springfield.**
- John D. Rockefeller founds the Rockefeller & Andrews firm.
- The Union Stock Yards open in Chicago.
- December 18: The Thirteenth Amendment is ratified.

Bibliography

"Abraham Lincoln Chronology." *Lincoln Lore*, no. 11 (June 24, 1929).

Basler, Roy P., ed. *The Collected Works of Abraham Lincoln*, 9 vols. New Brunswick, N.J.: Rutgers University Press, 1953–55.

Furnas, J. C. *The Americans: A Social History of the United States, 1587–1914.* New York: G. P. Putnam's Sons, 1969.

Johnson, Paul. *A History of the American People.* New York: HarperCollins, 1997.

Miers, Earl Schenck, ed. *Lincoln Day by Day: A Chronology, 1809–1865.* Dayton: Morningside House, 1991.

Morison, Samuel Eliot, Henry Steele Commager, and William E. Leuchtenburg. *A Concise History of the American Republic.* New York: Oxford University Press, 1977.

Morris, Richard B., ed. *Encyclopedia of American History.* New York: Harper & Row, 1976.

Contributors

Herman Belz
Professor of history at the University of Maryland. Author of *A New Birth of Freedom: The Republican Party and Freedmen's Rights, 1861–1866*; *Abraham Lincoln, Constitutionalism and Equal Rights in the Civil War Era*; and *A Living Constitution or Fundamental Law? American Constitutionalism in Historical Perspective.*

Joseph R. Fornieri
Associate professor of political science at Rochester Institute of Technology. Author of *Abraham Lincoln's Political Faith* and editor of *The Language of Liberty: The Political Speeches and Writings of Abraham Lincoln.*

Sara Vaughn Gabbard
Former vice president and director of development at the Lincoln Museum, Fort Wayne, Indiana, and editor of *Lincoln Lore*, the museum's bulletin, which was recognized in 2005, 2006, and 2007 by the *Chicago Tribune* as one of the nation's fifty best magazines. Coeditor (with Harold Holzer) of *Lincoln and Freedom: Slavery, Emancipation, and the Thirteenth Amendment.*

Allen C. Guelzo
The Henry R. Luce Professor of the Civil War Era and professor of history at Gettysburg College. Author of *Abraham Lincoln: Redeemer President* and *Lincoln's Emancipation Proclamation: The End of Slavery in America*, both of which won the Lincoln Prize, and most recently *Lincoln and Douglas: The Debates That Defined America* (2008).

Harold Holzer
Cochairman of the U.S. Lincoln Bicentennial Commission and senior vice president for external affairs at the Metropolitan Museum of Art. Author or coauthor of thirty books on Lincoln and the Civil War, including *The Lincoln Image*; *The Lincoln-Douglas Debates*; *Lincoln Seen and Heard*; *Lincoln as I Knew Him*; and *Lincoln at Cooper Union: The Speech That Made Abraham Lincoln President*, winner of a 2005 Lincoln Prize.

Myron Marty
History professor emeritus, Drake University. Coauthor (with Shirley Marty) of *Frank Lloyd Wright's Taliesen Fellowship* and coauthor (with David Kyvig) of *Nearby History: Exploring the Past around You.*

Mark Noll
Francis A. McAnaney Professor of History at the University of Notre Dame. Author of *The Civil War as a Theological Crisis* and *America's God: From Jonathan Edwards to Abraham Lincoln.*

James Oakes
Graduate School Humanities Professor and Distinguished Professor of history at the Graduate Center of the City University of New York. Author of *The Ruling Race: A History of American Slaveholders*; *Slavery and Freedom: An Interpretation of the Old South*; and *The Radical and the Republican: Frederick Douglass, Abraham Lincoln, and the Triumph of Antislavery Politics* (2008 winner of the Lincoln Prize).

Richard Striner
Professor of history at Washington College and a senior writer with the Dwight D. Eisenhower Memorial Commission. Author of *Father Abraham: Lincoln's Relentless Struggle to End Slavery.*

Frank J. Williams
Chief Justice of the Rhode Island Supreme Court, cofounder and chairman of the Lincoln Forum, and member of the U.S. Abraham Lincoln Bicentennial Commission. Author of *Judging Lincoln* and coauthor (with Harold Holzer and Edna Greene Medford) of *The Emancipation Proclamation: Three Views.*

Kenneth J. Winkle
Sorensen Professor of American History at the University of Nebraska–Lincoln. Author of *The Young Eagle: The Rise of Abraham Lincoln* and coauthor of *The Oxford Atlas of the Civil War.*

Index

Italicized page numbers indicate illustrations.